In Defense of Populism

In Defense of Populism

Protest and American Democracy

Donald T. Critchlow

PENN

University of Pennsylvania Press

Philadelphia

Published by
University of Pennsylvania Press
Philadelphia, Pennsylvania 19104-4112
www.upenn.edu/pennpress

Printed in the United States of America on acid-free paper
10 9 8 7 6 5 4 3 2 1

Library of Congress Cataloging-in-Publication Data

Name: Critchlow, Donald T., author.
Title: In defense of populism : protest and American democracy /
Donald T. Critchlow.
Description: 1st edition | Philadelphia : University of Pennsylvania Press, [2020] |
Includes bibliographical references and index. |
Identifiers: LCCN 2020006499 | ISBN 978-0-8122-5276-7 (hardcover)
Subjects: LCSH: Populism—United States—History. | Social movements—
United States—History. | Democracy—United States—History. |
United States—Politics and government—History.
Classification: LCC E183 .C877 2020 | DDC 320.56/620973
LC record available at https://lccn.loc.gov/2020006499

To my grandsons,
Alexander, Andrew, and Joshua, Critchlows all

Contents

Introduction
Social Protest and Democracy

I protest. This book does not offer a defense of demagoguery, xenophobia, racism, or illiberalism—the dark side often associated with populism in the American political tradition.

In Defense of Populism challenges didactic accounts of populism as either simply expressions of the oppressed demanding that the democratic dream be realized or anxiety-ridden, anti-intellectual, paranoid, anti-democratic reactions to a changing order.

Instead, this book submits that grassroots activist movements—populist movements, if you will—are essential to American democracy. At decisive points in American politics, social protest movements—whether on the left or the right—force established parties and leaders to bow to reform. In this way, anti-elitist social protest becomes absorbed by established powers. At the same time, the demands for democratic reform become institutionalized in the modern American state, ironically creating an enlarged bureaucratic government that is further removed from the people. This progression from protest to political absorption to institutionalization is evidenced in critical episodes in the American reform tradition. Indeed, American history is replete with these cycles of political disequilibrium followed by stabilization.

In arguing for the necessary importance of populism to political reform, this book explores specific episodes in modern American history that reveal the interplay of populist social action and party reform: agrarian populism in the late nineteenth century, anti-corporatism in the Progressive Era, class protest during the New Deal, the struggle for black equality in the early Cold War era, second-wave feminism in the 1970s, and anti-statist New Right protest in the late twentieth century. The creation of the modern regulatory and welfare administrative state, managed and overseen by seemingly distant bureaucrats, accelerated anti-elitist, populist reactions on the ideological right and left, which have become more pronounced in the last decades of the twentieth century and today.

A sizable cottage industry has attempted to define populism, but even critics find the term difficult to define precisely. For the purposes of this book, populism is presented as grassroots activism expressed in social movements against established elites and a call for citizens to be given a larger voice in politics. In offering this rather narrow definition, this book provides less a taxonomy of populist grassroots movements than an argument for the importance of grassroots activism, as disquieting as it is to its critics, *as essential to democratic reform in the American political tradition.* By relying on a simple definition that views populist social movements as expressions of anti-establishment and anti-elitism, we gain the opportunity to examine the role mass social protest plays in the larger American political tradition. In this way, populism need not be defined as an elaborate ideology or comprehensive political program but as a manifestation of mass hostility toward sociopolitical elites who are seen as unfairly benefiting from the status quo.[1]

Popular demand for political and economic reform can gestate for long periods, often reaching an intensity around, but not totally dependent on, a national crisis. The power of these grassroots movements through mobilization forces established parties to respond by accommodation, concession, preemption, and absorption of reform demands. The period in which social mobilization occurs is characterized by protest, political turmoil, and often violence. Protest, social disruption, and violence often coincide with these mass social mobilizations. In response to disruption, ultimately the general public loses sympathy for the agitators and demands the restoration of social order. Marked discord and turmoil characterize the period of disequilibrium before political parties and leaders turn to reform as a means of stabilizing society. Before political equilibrium is restored, however, a sense of profound disquiet prevails in society. Social and political discord is intensified.

Those living in these periods of disquiet experience profound anxiety that the world is being turned upside down and is coming apart. In such tumultuous times, the nation itself appears in free fall. Grassroots activism—populist protest against established political and economic elites—brings class resentment, social conflict, protest, and violence. Such times allow a platform for cranks as well as religious and social visionaries with schemes to make the world perfect. In this environment, conspiracy theorists of various sorts attract audiences who in the past would have ignored them. Cranks, visionaries, and activist followers unite around the rhetoric of anti-elitism and taking back power in the name of the people. Anti-party sentiment, denunciations of political corruption, and economic cabals manifest themselves in grassroots activism. Strong tendencies toward third-party formation find expression, as seen in the People's Party, the Progressive Party, and the Socialist Party, and later postwar parties including the Reform Party, the Libertarian Party, and the Green Party.

Grassroots social movements present odd mixtures of conservative and progressive tendencies but share anti-party sentiment in their origins. A consideration of the ways anti-party activism and the tendency toward third-party formation lead to establishment party revival invites fuller exploration. In the process, political discord expressed by grassroots activism emerges as political accord as an established party responds to voter discontent. Essential to this process of discord and reform are politicians who take up activist causes to force changes within their parties. These politicians can be motivated by both genuine concern and political calculation.

Any era of reform produces uneasy coalitions. For example, the Progressive Era, from 1901 to 1917, brought together middle- and upper-class good-government people, prohibitionists, labor, Single Taxers, socialists, agricultural and urban interests, pacifists, and imperialists. Inevitably, many grassroots leaders, especially visionary types, felt that the reforms did not go far enough and concluded that they had been betrayed by opportunistic political leaders and sellouts in their own movements. Nonetheless, these grassroots movements proved essential to reform.

When viewed in a broader perspective, though, successful grassroots American reform restores, at least momentarily, public confidence in the American party system. The importance of grassroots activism to party renewal cannot be understated. Yet, in the late nineteenth and early twentieth centuries, party reform and political reform meant the creation of an enlarged welfare and regulatory state charged with addressing the ills of industrial capitalism. Administered by nonelected experts—the new managerial class—and staffed by low-level clerks, this new creation—the modern state—appeared even more distant and often less responsive to average Americans.

In response to the modern welfare-regulatory state, an emergent conservative movement captured the reaction to "big government" in the post–World War II period. This movement brought together anti-collectivist intellectuals, corporate and small business associations opposed to government interference in the marketplace, and anti-communists. In the late 1960s, opposition to abortion and feminism led to grassroots movements organized around these and other cultural issues. Evangelical Christians added momentum to the movement. The grassroots right transformed the Republican Party into a voice of conservatism, and it helped fuel increasing polarization within the electorate. This political transformation should be placed within a larger context of early social protest movements that had reformed the political system. Yet seemingly there was deep discontent among large numbers of Americans that government was not working for them but against them.

The distrust of government spilled over to the activist left as well. The Federal Bureau of Investigation spying on the civil rights and antiwar movements, revelations of Central Intelligence Agency operations abroad, and moneyed influence in Washington fed left-wing suspicion of government. This distrust of government, shared by both the right and the left, occurred in an environment of increased political polarization within the electorate. In recent times, this polarization has been reflected in governance itself, as legislative reform became bogged down in partisan infighting. Principle and power prevailed in the nation's capital, with neither party appearing to give an inch to the other side. In this political climate, anger toward political and economic elites, special interests in Washington, Beltway insiders, globalists, and "the deep state" has erupted on the right and the left, creating a new age of populism. Donald Trump—and Bernie Sanders on the left—reflected this anger within the electorate. Both were reflections—and conduits, if you will—for expressing profound voter discontent; yet neither created this new age of populism. Unless political reform—or at least the appearance of reform acceptable to the voters—occurs, ours will be a period of immense turmoil with profound unintended consequences.

With the election of Donald Trump to the White House and the rise of nationalist parties in Europe, populism became for Trump's critics a bad word, connoting the irrationality of the masses and the dark side of democracy. Princeton University political scientist Jan-Werner Müller typified this approach in *What Is Populism?* in which he described populism at its core as anti-liberal and anti-democratic.[2] Populism has often been denounced by its opponents as an expression of the worst passions of the people. In this manner, populism is contrasted with enlightened, considered opinion—usually educated and elite opinion. A twist on the criticism of populism is that there is a kind of authentic populism truly expressing the legitimate interests of the people that can be contrasted with a version in which the masses are manipulated by self-interested elites. Thus, in this argument, there is in effect "good" populism and "bad" populism. Often the bad or manipulated populism is associated with more recent conservative grassroots movements, such as the anti-communism in the 1950s, the New Right in the 1970s, and the Tea Party today. Within these critiques of populism, the specter of fascism always seems to lurk.

American populism can be distinguished from populism in Europe and other regions in the world. American populism is distinctive in its demand for more direct democracy and greater ambivalence toward a strong leader to save the nation. Furthermore, within the American tradition, at least since the founding of the nation, populist rhetoric has been a constant refrain. Aspiring candidates and incumbents alike rail against the establishment, the need to clean up government, and the demand to throw the rascals out. Campaign rhetoric, however, should be separated from populism as seen in grassroots social movements. Here rhetoric is turned into genuine protest on a massive scale, sharply critical, especially in its inception, toward established political parties and prevailing powers. Populist grassroots activism tends toward great suspicion of and pronounced hostility toward the established major parties. Grassroots activism in its early formation is given to third-party alternatives. Only as grassroots social movements gain strength and are confronted by the vicissitudes of electoral victory and legislative achievement does the pragmatic reality of actual politics become apparent. Forming alliances with established politicians or political parties creates inevitable tensions between principled activists already distrustful of the system and those who understand that compromise is necessary to achieve reform. Here, weighing the balance between principle and opportunity presents a social movement and its leaders with an inevitable dilemma.

Grassroots activism becomes entwined with partisan politics, a natural result in a democratic polity. Grassroots reformers and politicians create uneasy alliances. Grassroots visionaries, often given to moral absolutes, and partisan politicians, anxious to win election for themselves and their parties, are not natural allies. Principles and partisanship are not exclusive, of course, but the purity of intention and practical achievement are not easily reconciled.

Discerning the exact impact of a single grassroots cause or movement, or a confluence of movements at a punctuated moment when established political leaders respond to popular demand, presents a difficult task for the historian. Simply concluding that grassroots activism creates an environment for reform does not say much for the simple reason that demands for reform can develop over long periods. Furthermore, to make a causal link at a specific point in time between grassroots activism and political reform creates an opportunity for specious history. Just because something happens at one moment in history while something else occurs at the same moment does not mean that one caused the other. For one thing, political reform can be simply a response to an economic or political crisis—external events, if you will—in which long-festering popular demand for reforms have no direct relationship. Obviously, an economic or political crisis creates an environment for reform or changes in political leadership and policy and legislative agendas, but the fact remains that grassroots activism in itself might not have a prominent role in influencing this change.

The transition from grassroots activism to party reform, when it occurs, is not linear. The gestation of grassroots reform that begins with visionary leaders often spans years and even decades before resulting in a political response. Party response to grassroots agitation depends on specific historical conditions. Political parties are generally resistant to radical change. As a consequence, arriving at an accurate general principle or a quantifiable measure predicting party response to grassroots agitation is impossible. Grassroots reform, however, remains essential to the social fabric of American democracy.

At any point in history, grassroots activism presents a cacophony of voices calling for reform of various sorts without programmatic coherence. Politicians responding to powerful reform sentiment, if it has gained traction within the larger public, seize upon such sentiment for partisan advantage. Calls for reform within a party are often led by outsiders seeking to challenge established and intransigent leadership. The eruption of reform within the political system often appears suddenly, but behind this volcanic explosion undercurrents of molten activity have been bubbling.

In developing the theme that grassroots movements are necessary to party reform, this book explores key episodes in grassroots activism from the progressive period to today. *In Defense of Populism* is not intended as an encyclopedic account of every grassroots reform movement in American history, even in the book's focus on the late nineteenth century to the present. Instead, the book focuses on prominent and influential visionaries who spawned grassroots movements, political entrepreneurs who responded to these movements, and professional politicians who directed angry sentiment toward legislative resolution. One goal is to invite further exploration by others. Examination of this reform process occurs through a narrative both thematic and chronological. Particular emphasis is given to key actors in grassroots activism, those who transit from grassroots activism to party politics, and political leaders who implement reforms, even while often disappointing grassroots activists by not going far enough with those reforms. Inevitably, many important grassroots leaders and movements are left out of the story, leaving some readers in all probability with opinions about the choices made in this book. Indeed, the myriad social movements that might have been discussed are suggested in a table compiled by a sociologist in 2005. In exploring grassroots activism and popular protest, this book focuses on selected social movements that had the most direct influence on the party system and that were most important to the American political tradition.

In Defense of Populism links social reform movements and party politics. Historians and sociologists have given great attention to social reform movements, while political scientists have focused largely on party politics, voter behavior, and the legislative-policy process. Historians have provided specific case studies of a variety of social movements, often relying on narrative to explore the historical context that gave rise to these theories. Sociologists have offered a rich literature on the dynamics of social protest movements. A number of political scientists have treated these movements as incipient interest groups or political parties.[3] Larger theoretical questions, such as the dynamics of social movements and political parties—realignments, legislative processes, political and policy agenda setting—are discussed in this book only in passing in order to focus on the larger theme of this book about the integral relationship of protest to democratic reform, and subsequent voter alienation. At the same time, some readers will take exception to the conflation of grassroots activism and populism.

Explaining social protests solely in terms of economic hardship or temporary hardship associated with social strain offers a simplistic notion as to how a grassroots movement gains popular support that translates into effective political change.[4] Conditions for social protest remain constant within any society because economic hardship, inequities, and conflict between the powerful and the downtrodden remain persistent. Critical to successful mobilization within a grassroots movement that translates into a larger populist expression depends on internal group resources, organization, and successful strategies for collective action. These are internal factors determining a successful grassroots organization or social movement. More important, however, is the particular cultural, societal, and political environment in which protest movements operate. This is especially the case within American democracy, in which culture, social structure, and a two-party system tend to negate the potential for class conflict, social violence, and the emergence of populist outbursts challenging the established economic and political order.

Social movements should not be seen as static. Activists come to a movement or cause with definite expectations and in the struggle itself can develop

Table 1. Top twenty-five U.S. social movement organizations in the twentieth century, by mention in articles in peak year, in the *New York Times* and *Washington Post*

Organization (Peak Year)	New York Times Articles	New York Times Front Page	Washington Post Articles
American Federation of Labor (1937)	1,050	205	476
Black Panthers (1970)	1,028	111	617
Congress of Industrial Organizations (1937)	786	186	325
National Association for the Advancement of Colored People (1963)	762	128	446
Ku Klux Klan (1924)	672	180	339
Anti-Saloon League (1930)	409	99	91
Townsend Plan (1936)	402	68	118
Students for a Democratic Society (1969)	381	90	174
Congress of Racial Equality (1963)	369	32	86
America First Committee (1941)	280	24	121
American Legion (1937)	263	70	200
John Birch Society (1964)	255	32	128
League of Women Voters (1937)	246	4	117
American Civil Liberties Union (1977)	231	24	102
Moral Majority (1981)	221	10	268
Southern Christian Leadership Conference (1968)	215	36	142
German American Bund (1939)	200	32	71
Student Nonviolent Coordinating Committee (1966)	195	47	76
Veterans of Foreign Wars (1950)	180	22	104
American Liberty League (1936)	174	53	136
Christian Coalition (1996)	170	52	253
Association Against the Prohibition Amendment (1930)	168	56	37
Weathermen (1970)	159	22	92
Symbionese Liberation Army (1974)	157	23	97
Jewish Defense League (1971)	145	31	91

Source: Edwin Amenta et al., "Age for Leisure? Political Mediation and the Impact of the Pension Movement on U.S. Old-Age Policy," *American Sociological Review* 70:3 (2005): 518–538, especially 518.

new strategies and alignments as a result of confronting the established political and social order.[5] Alliances with other grassroots movements present an
opportunity for schism, while not forming alliances can lead to sectarianism.
If struggle creates opportunities for political education, elites too learn during
prolonged struggle, pursuing a course of repression, accommodation, or as-
similation of grassroots opposition. Critical to understanding social movements and reactions by elites is whether citizens pursue selective incentives or
the collective good. As movements gain momentum, definitions of the "collective good" become increasingly diffuse. This becomes fully evident when
grassroots activism develops into a mass populist political movement. Fusion
with established parties further confuses the meaning of the "collective good"
as activists, movement entrepreneurs, and emerging or established politicians
accommodate to the populist cause.[6] The entrance of professional politicians
into a mass movement increases the likelihood of oligarchic control. The anti-
partisan impetus of grassroots activism thus is transformed into controlled
party leadership and administration. As politicians—emergent or past—take
control of an ascendant movement, the tendency of some followers will be to
fall away from the movement and feel a sense of betrayal. The focus of *In Defense of Populism,* however, is not understanding the dynamics per se of social
movements or resolving the sociological debate of individual motivations but
positing that populist movements are necessary for democratic renewal.

The narrative of this book allows, nonetheless, for lessons to be learned
about the whys and hows of successful grassroots activism. The successes
(and failures) of previous reform movements do not rest fully on the specifics
of their agendas. More important for this study is an examination of the dynamics of the reform process from visionary beginnings to popular mobilization, politicization, and consequences in restoring a sense of national purpose
and political order. *In Defense of Populism* posits a few of the essential factors
for a successful movement:

- new ideas and a realistic agenda;
- the enlistment of organizations initially outside the established political parties;
- division within the political, social, and cultural elites;
- the use of a shared language that makes an appeal to a larger audience
  beyond activist circles; and
- the mobilization of the larger electorate and recruitment of critical
  party leaders that force political and legislative change.[7]

These are not the only factors for ensuring the success of a reform movement. Historical circumstances, leadership, tenacity of the opposition, and an array of other elements can defeat a reform movement. Not all reform movements examined here succeeded, and even those that did had limited success if judged through the aspirations of reform leaders. Reform crusaders did not accomplish all of their goals, but they achieved much even in their own terms. More important, these reform movements—as episodes in American history—restored American confidence in the nation. These moments of reform offer lessons for today, not in resurrecting the specifics of any reform movement or proposing an agenda. Rather, by exploring past reform movements, *In Defense of Populism* warns that without pressure brought by mass mobilization, necessary political reform will fail, resulting in greater voter alienation, partisan polarization, and social conflict.

We have entered into one of those periods of political disequilibrium found often in American history. *In Defense of Populism* does not presume to offer a prescription as to what good reform means. This is a political decision, made by voters, party leaders, policy wonks, and pundits. Instead, this book explores some of the necessary ingredients for successful mass movements in times of political and cultural disequilibrium. By examining the success and limitations of previous reform movements, this book offers a general assessment as to whether America can be reformed today. The verdict is still out on this question because the factors necessary for successful reform are mostly missing. New ideas and a shared language appear absent in today's reform movements, whether it be the Tea Party, Black Lives Matter, or other activist reform groups. A sense of discontent prevails in American society today. Political opinion has become polarized; partisanship has prevented necessary enactment of reform legislation to address problems concerning national defense, the financial health of society, income inequality, a deteriorating infrastructure, and social ills, from crime to drug addiction, children in poverty, and immigration.

Still, in our winter of discontent, new ideas for reform, leadership, and a shared language are called for by those seeking a restoration of national purpose.

1 Populism
Prelude to "Big Government"

Populism emerged in the last decade of the nineteenth century like a tornado sweeping up through Texas into the South and spilling over into the Midwest, across the Mountain and Pacific Coast states. Gaining force from long agitation, complaint, and calls for reform by farmers and industrial workers throughout the late nineteenth century, the Populist movement gave rise to a new third party, the People's Party (commonly referred to as the Populist Party, although that was not its official name). This party, dissipated by its own internal frictions and contradictory alliances, was ultimately broken asunder by a huge electoral wall erected by Republicans in the presidential election of 1896.

Populism in the 1890s marked the culmination of storms of protest after 1865 over income inequality, railroad monopoly, unfair and oppressive labor practices, and political corruption on the local, state, and national levels. These protest movements were reflected in grassroots agitation expressed in currency reform (Greenbackism and Free Silver), anti-monopoly third parties, the Single Tax movement (Henry George), utopian socialism (Edward Bellamy), and labor protests and strikes. The formation of the People's Party brought these reform movements together, attempting to ally farmers with urban industrial workers. Already by the presidential election of 1892 and clearly by the midterm elections of 1894, the People's Party demonstrated its unviability as a third party challenging the two established parties. The obvious political solution for People's Party leaders was to fuse with the Democratic Party under the leadership of William Jennings Bryan, who successfully pushed forward his crusade for free silver in winning the Democratic Party presidential nomination in 1896. Bryan was a populist in sentiment, but he was a confirmed Democrat. His "Cross of Gold" speech at the Democratic Party national convention fired up the delegates and he won the party's nomination. When Bryan lost the presidential election to Republican William McKinley in 1896, the People's Party was all but dead. Bryan, though, remained a force in the Democratic Party for years to come. The Populist agenda lived on to find expression and implementation in the Progressive Era, from 1900 to 1917.

The political consequences of the Populist movement forced both major parties to undertake reform to varying degrees. Already by 1896, both the Democratic and Republican Party platforms incorporated calls for railroad regulation and the end of federal injunctions against organized labor. The most direct effect of Populism among Democrats was found in the Bryan wing of the party, which continued to play a major role well into the 1930s, as expressed in anti-imperialist and isolationist foreign policy positions and anti-monopoly and anti-corporate sentiment. The southern wing of the Democratic Party, largely agrarian, remained the bulwark of the party. Tragically, the Populist reform agenda was subverted in the Democratic South by the complete transformation of the party into a militant defender of white supremacy, often led by former Populists turned Democrats. In North Carolina, former Populist Furnifold M. Simmons joined Populist newspaper editor Josephus Daniels in making the state Democratic Party into a "white man's" party. In 1900, Democrats recaptured the North Carolina governorship and secured the enactment of a state constitutional amendment that effectively disenfranchised most black voters, who had been able to elect a few black candidates to minor offices in the eastern part of the state through a Populist-Republican alliance.[1] The Tarheel Democratic redemption was nearly as ruthless as white "redemption" during the post–Civil War Reconstruction era and occurred throughout the Democratic South.

Republicans on both the national and state levels stood most firmly against Populism, although in a few southern states, such as North Carolina and Tennessee, the GOP fused with Populist-oriented Republicans to oppose the Democratic Party control. Agrarian radicalism expressed itself among a few Midwest governors and U.S. senators, such as Robert La Follette in Wisconsin, George Norris in Nebraska, and William Borah in Idaho.

The 1893 economic depression and the formation of the People's Party forced the major parties to seek reform. Populist-Progressive reforms did not fully resolve many of the problems that still confronted labor, farmers, African Americans, the cities, and the economic order. It took a major economic depression in 1929 and the New Deal to enact further reform, encouraged again by grassroots activism in the 1920s, but the poignancy of progressive reform in the early twentieth century can only be fully understood within the context of grassroots activism in the post–Civil War years. Scholarly debate over the continuity between Populism and Progressivism, and between grassroots agitation in the late nineteenth century and in the first decades of the twentieth century, can be misleading. Direct organizational continuity is often absent. For example, the Greenback movement in the 1870s was not continuous with municipal reform at the turn of the century. However, some continuity among leaders of Henry George's Single Tax movement is found in administrative appointments made during the Woodrow Wilson presidency. Similarly, in the post–Civil War period, women continued the struggle for voting rights, which eventually culminated in the Nineteenth Amendment in 1920. Post–Civil War grassroots agitation took many forms in the late nineteenth century. Leaders and activists came and went in these movements, as did organizations and third-party formations. What is important, though, is that calls for reform, grassroots mobilization, and challenges to established political and social leadership built over time, with increasing crescendo, setting the stage for party renewal when forced by the depression of the 1890s and popular demand for change.

The Gilded Age

In the late nineteenth century, the United States became the most powerful and prosperous nation in the world. American economic growth was unprecedented. Driven by a combination of productivity growth and a rapid increase in population, including mass immigration, the American economy was a wonder to behold. At the end of the Civil War, the United States trailed the United Kingdom, France, and Germany in manufacturing. By 1894, the nation's value of manufacturing nearly equaled the value of manufacturing of these three countries combined. Huge fortunes were made in manufacturing and finance by taking advantage of new technological developments, improved transportation and communications systems, and organizational enterprise. Andrew Carnegie in steel, J. D. Rockefeller in oil, and J. P. Morgan in finance symbolized the robber barons of the age. The growing concentration of industry and finance—an inevitable result of corporate capitalism and the force of economies of scale—displaced the old mercantile economy centered on local and regional markets. Economic concentration and often unscrupulous business practices drove out merchants and owners of smaller enterprises in this new corporate order.

The new economy brought prosperity to many. A new middle class of white-collar employees was created. Homeownership increased. The corporation created new occupations for middle managers, accountants, service employees, and office workers. In 1870, less than 2 percent of the workforce was employed in clerical positions; by 1900, more than 35 percent was white collar. At the same time, however, social tensions intensified between labor and capital as workers sought unionization, shorter working hours, the end of child labor, and safer working conditions. Unemployment plagued industrial workers throughout the late nineteenth century, affecting nearly every family. Though real wages increased for skilled workers (74 percent) and unskilled workers (31 percent), in this economic transformation many semiskilled workers were displaced. As the agricultural economy expanded to the Midwest and Plains regions, farmers confronted a cycle of rising and falling farm prices and increased international competition. Faced with debt and often foreclosure, farmers called for inflationary measures to help alleviate their problems.

While industrial workers and farmers faced problems, older eastern cities and newer midwestern cities were transformed, simply overwhelmed by overflowing populations both foreign and native. In the decades between 1888 and 1920, more than 23 million immigrants came to America, 80 percent from eastern and southern Europe. By 1890, adult immigrants outnumbered native adults in eighteen of the twenty largest cities. This rapid urbanization created insurmountable problems in transportation, housing, sanitation, crime, and poverty.

In this environment, social tensions proved inevitable, as capital clashed with labor, and farmers with railroads, moneylenders, and agricultural corporations. Social tensions expressed themselves in protest against the wealthy, concentrated capital, and politicians who served their interests. "Down with Monopoly!" became a rallying cry for grassroots agitation throughout the late nineteenth century. Railroads were potent symbols of the monopoly problem, and many Americans disapproved of this concentration of wealth and power. By 1896, railroads accounted for more of the gross national product than did federal, state, and local government combined.[2] As the century drew to a close, more than 150,000 miles of railroad line had been laid. Fortunes were made in railroad construction and ownership. The result was mass overbuilding, laying more track than needed, and inevitable bankruptcy.

A similar pattern of consolidation emerged in the telegraph, steel, oil, and other industries. Financial pools and cartels gave rise to trusts aimed at squelching competition, regulating prices, excluding new competition, controlling labor, and exerting political influence of local, state, and national legislators, regulators, and political parties. Railroads exerted control over many state legislatures and were seen as another example of political corruption. Actual income or wealth disparity was difficult to measure then or later by historians studying inequality in the nineteenth century because of poor data.[3] Whether farmers were being exploited by moneylenders proves equally difficult to measure. Historians looking closely at mortgage rates and loans concluded that rates for farmers were not higher for midwestern agriculture than for eastern merchants.[4] Nonetheless, given that the period from the 1870s to the 1890s was one of price deflation punctuated by major and minor panics, it appeared to many that life was not getting better for the majority of Americans. Whatever the hard facts, a common perception among many Americans in this time was that the new wealth of the nation was not being shared fairly. "The rich are getting richer, and the poor poorer" was a constant refrain throughout the late nineteenth century by farmers, workers, and opponents of monopoly.

In 1885, in the midst of a decline in prices that had begun three years earlier, a financial panic hit Wall Street. The effects of the panic were severe. An estimated 5 percent of businesses failed, another 5 percent were forced to close at some point during the year, and an estimated one million workers were unemployed. Labor launched a campaign for an eight-hour workday. On May 1, 1886, a general strike involving 350,000 workers across the country created a national work stoppage. In Chicago, the movement turned violent three days later when a bomb went off in the ranks of 180 policemen who had gathered to disperse a labor rally held at Haymarket Square in the center of the city. The late-night rally had been called by radical anarchists to protest the recent shooting of a striker at the McCormick Reaper works. After the bomb went off, gunfire erupted on both sides, leaving at least eight people dead. In the aftermath of the riot, anti-radical hysteria swept the city. Dozens of radicals were rounded up by the police, and eight anarchists were arrested and placed on trial. At the trial, the prosecution was unable to tie any defendant directly to the throwing of the bomb. The prosecution brought forward witnesses and presented considerable circumstantial evidence that the anarchists had been involved in bomb making and were planning terrorist attacks. The defendants were not well served by a politicized defense counsel inexperienced in criminal law. All were found guilty, with seven defendants sentenced to death and the eighth given a prison sentence.[5]

Henry Demarest Lloyd, a lawyer and a radical journalist for the *Chicago Tribune,* denounced the trial as a travesty of justice. He was joined by prominent reformers and labor leaders who launched a national campaign to have the governor of Illinois, Richard J. Oglesby, grant clemency to the defendants. Lloyd met personally with the governor. In the end, Oglesby, faced with an Illinois Supreme Court and U.S. Supreme Court decision upholding the verdict, commuted the sentences of two of the defendants to life. Four of the defendants originally sentenced to death were executed on November 11, 1887; two others had their sentences commuted; and the final defendant committed suicide in jail. Lloyd concluded, "The American Republic has already ceased to exist. It is rotten before it is ripe."[6]

The Haymarket riot proved to be just the beginning of class violence. Full-scale class warfare erupted with the 1893 depression, which occurred just a month after reform Democrat Grover Cleveland came into the White House. The Depression of 1893, probably the most devastating economic downturn in American history to that time, unleashed labor protest and heightened farmer agitation.[7] By the end of 1893, 600 banks and 15,000 businesses had failed, and one-fourth of the railway capital of the country was placed in receivership. Business liabilities increased almost tenfold. Developers who had overextended their markets in the Mississippi Valley by building railroads into freightless territory and expanding farm acreage went belly-up. An estimated one to three million workers were laid off, with the unemployment rate reaching an estimated 40 percent. In this environment, decades of anti-monopoly agitation and farmer discontent erupted with full force.

When the small, struggling industrial union of American Railway Workers, under the leadership of Eugene Debs, went out on strike in support of the Pullman Car Workers in 1893, class war reached a fever pitch. Railroad owners, organized into the Managers Association, refused mediation and instead imported strikebreakers from Canada. They then convinced President Grover Cleveland's U.S. attorney general Richard Olney to bring 3,400 sworn deputies to Chicago to break the strike. Strikers responded with a full-scale riot, ripping up train tracks in Chicago. President Cleveland ordered four companies of federal troops to Chicago to restore order. The *Chicago Tribune* declared, "Strike Is Not War." Debs was arrested on the charge of conspiracy to obstruct federal mails. He was released only to be rearrested for contempt of court and sentenced to six months in prison. The strike was crushed, and so was Debs's union.

Social movements require leaders with ideas. Ideas provide the foundation for a successful social movement. Leaders can offer grand visions for social transformation, or they can promote ideas little more than blurred reflections of the past mirrored in the present. In the late nineteenth century, Henry George and Edward Bellamy stood out as inspiring proponents of social change. Both men set the intellectual stage for the populist revolt that erupted in the 1890s.

Henry George, by trade a printer, presented in his book *Poverty and Progress* (1880) a panacea for eliminating capitalism's ills through a "single tax" on undeveloped land. Edward Bellamy, an eccentric New Englander, offered in his best-selling novel *Looking Backward* (1887) a utopia built around a military-like society. Both men inspired social movements. At first, George welcomed the emergence of the People's Party, but then quickly repudiated it when the party refused to endorse his "single tax" scheme. Nonetheless, Single Taxers, as his followers were called, played important roles in the Populist movement. Following the success of *Looking Backward*, Bellamy found himself the unlikely leader of a movement to form Nationalist Clubs across the country to fulfill the utopia outlined in his novel. When the People's Party emerged a few years later, Bellamy quickly aligned himself with the Populist cause. The once shy, hermit-like Bellamy threw himself enthusiastically, indeed fanatically, into work on behalf of the People's Party. The importance of these two men lay not in their individual activities but in the social movements their ideas inspired. Their individual ideas and movements presented a prelude to the populist revolt.

Each became an icon in American reform circles as they excoriated the inequities accompanying industrial capitalism. Idolized by their followers, they emerged as articulate speakers on the behalf of those demanding restraint of capital, better working conditions for labor, and greater democracy. They spoke on the behalf of reform, but their eccentric personalities and their different ideas about how best to reform society reveal the richness of the American reform tradition following the Civil War.

Henry George and the Single Tax Movement

Henry George, now largely forgotten except by a few historians, emerged in the late nineteenth century as one of America's most prominent and influential radicals next to labor leader and socialist Eugene Debs.

In 1879, witnessing the growing concentration of wealth and class conflict, and experiencing abject poverty himself, George, a printer's devil, struggling journalist, and occasional political operative, presented a simple, albeit radical, solution to the ills of the nation caused by monopolies: a single, high tax on undeveloped property. Such a tax, he argued, would drive out real estate and land speculators, force the development of housing and office buildings, and raise revenues for public services. Not since Alexander Hamilton had a popular writer seen taxation as an instrument for social change. His idea of a single tax, expressed in a popular economic and literary masterpiece, *Progress and Poverty* (1879), influenced an entire generation. George's influence spread to Canada, Ireland, New Zealand, Australia, and many other countries, but his greatest impact was in the United States. In the late nineteenth century, the concept of a single tax was more influential in American reform circles than was Marxism, which was mostly confined to recent German immigrants.

Single Taxers were found in organized labor, especially in the Illinois Federation of Labor, and were an important force in the election and administration of Democratic governor John P. Altgeld, in agrarian reform movements, in municipal and state reform, and among intellectuals, including Lincoln Steffens, a muckraking journalist, who considered himself a Single Taxer before he became a socialist. A similar path was followed by Henry Demarest Lloyd, another pioneer muckraking journalist. The most famous attorney of his day, Clarence Darrow, also proclaimed himself a Single Taxer. Speaking from Logan, Ohio, after George's death, former Democratic presidential candidate William Jennings Bryan declared George one of the "world's foremost thinkers."[8] Altgeld, a German immigrant, captured the impact of single tax ideas in his eulogy of Henry George in 1897, when he declared that "he made almost as great an impression on economic thought on the age as Darwin did on the world of science."[9]

In Oregon, William Simon U'Ren, who fell under the influence of George, won election in 1896 to the state House of Representatives running as a Populist. Later, as head of the Direct Legislation League, he pushed through an initiative and referendum amendment to the state constitution in 1898, ratified by the legislature and voters the same year. In Toledo, Ohio, Samuel Jones, a businessman turned Single Taxer, won election as mayor in 1897, a position he served for four terms and during which he instituted free kindergartens, playgrounds for children, free public baths, an eight-hour workday for city workers, and city government reform. Tom Johnson, an industrialist who became a reformer after reading *Progress and Poverty*, won election as mayor of Cleveland, Ohio, in 1901 and served until 1909. His lieutenants, Frederic Howe and Newton D. Baker, later joined the Woodrow Wilson administration, as did another Single Taxer, George Creel. These

Single Taxers shared with Henry George the view that monopolies—land, railroad, and corporate—were subverting American liberty.

Whatever his flaws as an economic theorist, George presented his case for a single tax with brilliant literary skill, incisive statistics, cogent argument, and a remarkable understanding of previous economic theory, especially given that his formal education ended at the age of fourteen. The self-taught George easily held his own on the debate stage with formally trained economics professors.

Raised in a lower middle-class Philadelphia family, George left home at the age of fourteen, drifting from job to job—a seaman, a gold prospector, and a laborer.[10] In 1858, eighteen-year-old George arrived in San Francisco. Three years later he met his wife, with whom he had four children. He worked as a journalist at various newspapers, but he often found himself unemployed and his family on the verge of starvation. For a brief period, he became the manager of a Democratic anti-monopoly newspaper, *The Reporter*. His anti-monopoly views derived from his experiences in California, a state characterized by land and business monopolies and vast wealth differences. Fortunes had been made in gold mining, railroads, shipping, and real estate. Californians, such as Leland Stanford, Collis Huntington, Mark Hopkins, and Charles Crocker, became fabulously wealthy building the first transcontinental railroad, the Central Pacific. For many, though, California was a state of class warfare, frontier violence, racism, and poverty.

George became involved in Democratic politics, which in the Bay Area was pro-labor, anti-monopoly, and anti-Chinese. His attacks on railroad monopolies were forceful, gaining him a reputation in labor circles. He became associated with Denis Kearney's Workingmen's Party in San Francisco. Although George broke with Kearney's party because he concluded that nativism distracted from economic reform, George wrote in the *New York Tribune* that Chinese migrants to San Francisco were "long-tailed barbarians," "making princes of our capitalists" who were "crushing workers into dust."[11]

In 1871, George attacked the land monopoly in a small pamphlet, *Our Land and Land Policy*, as an obstacle to opportunity for small independent farmers.[12] This booklet became the basis for his lengthy book *Progress and Poverty*. Published in 1879 under the full title *Progress and Poverty: An Inquiry into the Cause of Depressions and of Increased Want with Increase of Wealth—The Remedy,* the book was not what might be described in the twenty-first century as reader friendly.[13] George made clear his intended audience in his dedication: "To Those Seeing the Vice and Misery That Spring from the Unequal Distribution of Wealth and Privilege." In five hundred pages, George took his readers through a largely inductive argument that misery and wealth was produced by land speculation. George presented an elaborate argument based on "common observation and common knowledge" that labor is the basis of all wealth, and therefore there was a "fundamental and irreconcilable difference between property in things which are products of labor and property at large." "Exclusive property in land," he wrote, "is necessarily a denial of property in labor." Speculation in land, he continued, is "the true cause of industrial depression."[14] Therefore, he concluded that the way to prevent unproductive speculation, avoid depression, rectify the problem of poverty, and remedy class conflict was to impose a high tax on undeveloped property. Such a tax would redirect investment to industry, housing, local businesses, and productive land ownership. Real estate speculation drove up interest rates that diverted capital from productive investment. Through a single tax on undeveloped land, he maintained, no other taxes were necessary, including taxes on imports through tariffs or an income tax. (Later some of his followers supported a constitutional amendment for an income tax, but they saw this as only the first step to the real solution to the ills of monopoly and corporate capitalism: the single tax.) His remedy, as he said, was both simple and radical.[15]

George sought a middle way between laissez-faire capitalism and socialism. In the last section of the book in which he focused on remedies, he offered four: greater economy in government, cooperation of labor and capital, greater governmental direction and intervention in the economy, and greater distribution of land. He denounced the greed of capitalism and spoke of labor as wage slavery. His rhetoric in *Progress and Poverty* was radical as was his remedy, the single tax. He was not a revolutionary, nor was he a socialist.[16] He was a radical, however, within the American political tradition. His followers played prominent roles in labor unions and within the People's Party, often diverging over socialist demands for public ownership of railroads, the telegraph, and the telephone.

George moved to New York City to help promote his book, which eventually sold an estimated one million copies. When George accepted an offer by the New York editor of the *Irish World* to travel to Ireland to write about the land question in 1881, Ireland was in complete turmoil caused by a tragically stalled economy with famine sweeping across many parts of the island. Land League agitation and protests led authorities to crack down. English authorities began pressuring the pope in Rome to have the Land League condemned.

When George arrived, he was warmly greeted by Irish radicals and reformers calling for land reform and self-rule. Police authorities began tracking his movements. When George was arrested in the small town of Loughrea for carrying pro–Irish Land League literature, he drew international attention.

When he returned to New York in 1881, George was welcomed by local labor unions, which were dominated by Irish Catholics. He attracted the attention of Francis G. Shaw, a wealthy prewar abolitionist, who offered to have a thousand copies of *Progress and Poverty* printed to distribute to libraries throughout the country. Further momentum came when Louis Post, editor of the widely circulated penny paper, the *Truth,* with its working-class readership, serialized the book and began reporting on George's public talks throughout the city. Terence Powderly—leader of the Knights of Labor; mayor of Scranton, Pennsylvania; and an important national voice—issued a circular in 1893 urging members to read George's book. George, who had joined the Knights just shortly before (one did not need to be a union member to join), found a growing audience for his book.[17] In 1886, after a series of strikes the previous year, membership in the Knights soared to 700,000 members. Although Knight membership fell following the Chicago Haymarket riot in 1886, George became a leading voice of reform, one of the most widely read reform authors since Harriet Beecher Stowe had written *Uncle Tom's Cabin* three decades earlier.

In 1886, George became directly involved in politics when he accepted the nomination of the United Labor Party to run for mayor of New York.[18] George declared himself a Lincoln Republican before the Civil War, but his politics were really closer to those of a Jacksonian Democrat. His father had been a strong Jackson supporter drawn by hatred of the U.S. Bank. In California, George had drifted back to the Democratic Party, but his political allegiance was to the single-tax cause. Behind the United Labor Party stood the New York Central Labor Union with its strong ties to the Knights of Labor and American supporters of the Irish Land League. The Central Labor Union formed the United Labor Party following violent strike by city transit workers the previous year.

Launched in September 1886, George's campaign proved spectacular and for a moment looked like it was going to put him into the mayor's office in a three-way race against Tammany Hall–backed Democrat Abram Hewitt and Republican candidate Theodore Roosevelt. George presented himself as the candidate standing against monopolies and political corruption through a platform resting on the land tax and ballot reform. He gave more than a hundred speeches during the campaign, and one evening delivered eleven speeches, racing from place to place. George was a powerful, spontaneous speaker who relied on a few handwritten notes. His denunciations of capitalists, monopolies, and class privilege drew enthusiastic crowds from the laboring classes. Joining him on the stump stood another charismatic figure, a well-educated Catholic priest, Father Edward McGlynn, who served as pastor in the heavily Irish immigrant parish of St. Joseph Church on Sixth Avenue. McGlynn, who had earned a doctorate in theology in Rome, became a Single Taxer after having read *Progress and Poverty* when it first appeared. McGlynn's support for George drew opposition from the Catholic hierarchy, which finally ordered McGlynn not to speak in support of George. The McGlynn controversy drew press attention and fired up George's supporters.

As the campaign became increasingly heated, Democrats attacked George as campaigning for "free land," "free lunch," "free cigars," "free rides," "no police," and "no boss." He was charged with seeking "to substitute the ideas of anarchists, nihilists, communists, socialists, and mere theorists for the democratic principle of individual liberty."[19] In an atmosphere of hysteria following the great railroad strikes of the previous year and the Chicago Haymarket terrorist bombing earlier in May, such attacks on George proved deadly. On Election Day, Hewitt beat George and Roosevelt decidedly. George supporters claimed election fraud, but Hewitt won by nearly 22,000 votes (90,000 total) to George's vote (68,000), which called into question their accusation.

By the late 1880s, George had become a national figure. His quixotic campaign in 1887 for the secretary of state in New York under the United Labor Party, in which he came in a distant third, revealed more about the weakness of the party than it did about the attraction of George. The concept of a single tax to cure the nation's ills attracted quite a few people, but the larger appeal of George was his anti-monopoly views. In this regard, George was similar to other leading reform figures of the day.

Edward Bellamy and the Nationalist Movement

Horrified by growing class warfare and violence, Edward Bellamy, an eccentric, obscure New England journalist and novelist, undertook to project the possibilities of a new social order in a utopian anti-capitalist novel, *Looking Backward,* published in 1888. Neither he nor his publishers had any idea that the novel would become a national best seller, second only at that time to Harriet Beecher Stowe's *Uncle Tom's Cabin.* The book sold 60,000 copies the first year, only to soar to 100,000 copies the next. Like Stowe's novel, *Looking Backward* aroused public opinion and grassroots activism. Demands for bulk orders came from the West Coast, and in the Midwest farm belt a fifty-cent edition became a best seller.[20] Inspired by Bellamy's call for a new society based on a national industrial army, Nationalist Clubs sprang up around the country. These Nationalists, as they were called, played an important role in the emerging agrarian Populist movement, especially in California and to a lesser extent Illinois.

Bellamy made for a rather quirky political prophet. Raised in Chicopee Falls, Massachusetts, in a middle-class home, the son of a Baptist minister, he lived with his parents until he was married at age thirty-two. After attending Union College, where he studied for two semesters, Bellamy traveled to Europe for a year. He briefly studied law after returning home and then turned to journalism, first at the *New York Post,* then at the *Springfield Union.* After he contacted tuberculosis, he left journalism for a year to convalesce in Hawaii and then returned to Chicopee Falls. Thereafter he turned to freelance journalism and a literary career, publishing three novels before undertaking *Looking Backward.*[21]

Until the success of *Looking Backward,* those who knew him considered Bellamy an odd personality. Although not unfriendly, he was a self-contained man, often retreating to his room in his parents' house to spend hours reading. He was a loner. Even after his marriage, Bellamy spent inordinate hours in his room, often not talking to anyone for days. He loved his two daughters and would play with them and take them on picnics and outings, but he was inordinately self-centered.

Bellamy intended *Looking Backward* as a kind of fairy tale challenging the ostentatious materialism of his age. As a native of a small New England town, he was horrified by the breakdown of community in the age of industrial capitalism, and he abhorred the class violence he read about in the newspapers. Although repulsed by monopolistic capitalism, he projected a new society built around state ownership of industry and an ethos in which individualism was replaced by cooperation. The novel tells of Julian West, who awakes in the year 2000, after having fallen into a hypnotic state in 1887 as the world is being torn apart by social conflict. He discovers that society has been transformed into a world of structured cooperation, abundance, and purpose. Monopolists and organized labor, seeing the failure of competitive capitalism, have agreed to form a cooperative society organized around an industrial army. One large trust has replaced competing trusts. Young people are directed through universal education to discover their talents and then enlist into an industrial army in which selfishness was replaced by a serene selflessness. Food and goods are freely distributed, eliminating the need for money. In this harmonious world, there is no need for a military, or departments of state or the treasury, or the legislative branch of government. Instead, industrial and administrative functions have been combined into a structure of foremen (ranked as captains) and superintendents (colonels), overseen by commanders (major generals) who represent ten great departments comprising all allied trades and guilds. An executive counsel selects the commander in chief. Other nations are brought together in a larger world council, while each nation remains sovereign.

The novel's plot is rather mechanical and its characters one-dimensional. Dialogue, much like that in Ayn Rand's novels a half-century later, is didactic and stilted, but Bellamy's novel was no worse and a good deal better than many popular novels of the period. The novel's strength rests in its blueprint for a better, more harmonious society. Bellamy was imaginative: in the novel, a kind of credit card system replaces money; the city is a garden city with neighborhoods full of clubhouses and dining halls; and citizens are surrounded by beautiful architecture, art, and landscape gardens. Bellamy cleverly replaced the term *socialist* with *nationalist*.

Bellamy's novel captured the anxiety of his age, a sense shared by many that the nation was coming apart and the future grim. This was the age in which some thought capitalist greed and corporate concentration had replaced economic opportunity, political corruption had subverted democracy, and empty rhetoric had substituted for substantive individual freedom. Like a lightning bolt in dark skies, *Looking Backward* brought light.

Over the next two years, Nationalist Clubs formed in twenty-seven states across the country.[22] California had the largest number of clubs with sixty-four, New York followed with twenty-one, and Massachusetts was third with eleven. In early 1891, Rhode Island put forward a Nationalist ticket in the state election, and in California and Michigan, candidates were nominated for Congress, the state legislature, and local offices. Though Nationalism never became a mass movement, its greatest influence came in the formation of the People's Party. Eight members of the Nationalist Committee attended the founding conference of the new party in Cincinnati in May 1891, while five Nationalists served on the party's committee of resolutions. In California, Nationalists played an especially important role in shifting many farmers in the state Farmers' Alliance toward the formation of the People's Party. By 1890, the Farmers' Alliance had become the state's largest farmer organization, but by the time of the People's Party's first state convention in 1891, the farmers' movement had been transformed into a third-party movement. In this dramatic shift, Nationalists played a critical role by bringing urban radicals into an uneasy alliance with farmers.[23]

Witnessing the rise of the Nationalist movement, Bellamy himself became politically inspired. The once reclusive writer became a political activist. He found himself in agreement with millions of American farmers who called for a third party. Beginning in 1890, for the next two years, Bellamy poured his energies into the Populist cause. He began to see farmers, who were the majority of the population at that time, as the trustees of his Nationalist program. He established a newspaper, *New Nation*, to promote the Nationalist and Populist cause. And after the Cincinnati Convention in 1891, he declared, "The *New Nation* welcomes the Peoples' Party [*sic*] into the field of national politics."[24] He contacted Henry Demarest Lloyd, another bourgeois radical and a recent recruit to Populism. Bellamy and Lloyd became frequent correspondents, sharing their hopes for the new third-party movement. Lloyd believed privately that Bellamy's plan to reorganize society around an industrial army was downright despotic, but he shared Bellamy's commitment to reform. Lloyd believed that farmers had at long last "seen the light," but his faith in radical political change rested in the working class. While on a trip to England, he had become a convert to Fabian Socialism, a movement inspired by such intellectuals as Sidney and Beatrice Webb, playwright Bernard Shaw, and science fiction writer H. G. Wells. In 1889, Lloyd contributed to a collection of essays, *Fabian Essays in Socialism*. Lloyd appears not to have known that the Fabians were already faction ridden, less by ideological differences than by personal differences. Lloyd saw in the People's Party the beginnings of a labor party, bringing together organized labor, militant farmers, and middle-class radicals into a third party.[25]

George and Bellamy, along with other radicals of the day such as Lloyd, stood against monopolistic capitalism. They denounced what they saw as class privilege and political corruption, which they believed came with concentrated wealth. They called for the voice of the people to be heard, and both George and Bellamy believed that a new day in America was about to dawn.

First Signs of Farmer Agitation

The year 1890 appeared to be a propitious time for the formation of the new party. Agricultural prices had dropped, farmers were in debt, and Republicans seemed in disarray. The reaction against the passage of the high protection tariff, known as the McKinley Tariff, produced a backlash in the 1890 midterms.[26] The Midwest became a slaughterhouse for Republican candidates. Republicans lost five congressional seats in Kansas, seven in Illinois, six in Missouri, six in Michigan, and three in Nebraska. The bloodbath extended to Pennsylvania, where Republicans lost three seats, and to Maine, where they lost five seats. William McKinley, the author of the tariff and a representative at the time, lost his own Ohio seat. Aroused agrarians captured nearly two congressional seats for every one incumbent Republican seat that was won.

This unrest was not new. Farmer discontent and fledgling farmer organization following the Civil War had expressed itself in various movements and parties, including the formation of the National Grange of the Order of Patrons of Husbandry and the Greenback Party in the 1870s.[27] The Grange pushed for pricing regulation of railroads through state commissions. In Illinois, Grangers ran anti-monopoly candidates in 1873, winning fifty-three seats, and for a brief period became the dominant party in the state. The model was followed in other states, setting the stage for the formation of the National Labor Party and the Greenback Party.[28] The latter enjoyed some success when candidates campaigned on free silver (currency based on a silver standard), opposition to monopolies, and expansion of federal homestead land. When prosperity returned in the early 1880s, Grange and Greenback Party membership began to decline.[29] In 1880, Greenback presidential candidate General James Weaver, who later ran as the People's Party presidential candidate, won only 3 percent of the popular vote. The Greenback Party disappeared, but the Grange continued to exist by sponsoring county and state agricultural fairs, endorsing political candidates, and hosting informational meetings on agricultural issues.

Farmer agitation revived in full force, however, with the fall in agricultural prices in the late 1880s. At the same time the price of silver fell from $1.32 an ounce to $0.63 in 1894. Farmers had begun to organize into what became known as the Alliance Movement. Thousands of farmers throughout the South and Midwest formed cooperative societies to control costs through centralized purchasing and grain storage, preventing price gouging.

Debt ridden and further burdened with falling prices for their crops, farmers sought monetary remedies. Charles Macune, a Texas Alliance leader, proposed in 1889 a captivating scheme to provide capital for farmers through a subtreasury plan. The scheme was relatively simple: the federal government would establish warehouses and grain elevators in every county and allow farmers cheap loans based on the amount stored. In short, Macune's subtreasury plan proposed the federal government enter directly into storage of crops, pricing, and the agrarian loan market. In 1887, Macune, who had become president of the Southern Alliance, moved to Washington, D.C., to lobby for his plan. The subtreasury plan elicited wide enthusiasm among farmers, although not without dissent. Henry George denounced the plan as collectivist.[30]

Alliance membership expanded rapidly. Within a three-year period, from 1886 to 1889, the Texas Alliance alone grew from 38,000 to 225,000 members.[31] The Alliance promoted the subtreasury plan, government regulation of railroads, and economic cooperation among farmers. State Alliance groups pressed for other measures, including education reform. The Alliance called for school textbooks to be distributed free of charge to students. The Colored Alliance, the counterpart to the whites-only Farmers Alliance, focused even more on education, calling for more funding to be given to segregated schools in the South.[32] The Colored Alliance emerged as an important force among black farmers and found common cause with some white Alliance leaders.

Nonetheless, many impediments stood in the way of unifying the Southern, Northern, and Midwestern Alliances. The South remained a Democratic stronghold, while the Midwest was dominated by the Republican Party. Behind these differences stood the issue of race. Many Midwestern Alliance leaders refused to align themselves with the South for ideological and political reasons having to do with the deliberate exclusion of black voters, often through physical terror and legal barriers. For many Northern Populist leaders, especially those in midwestern states, the Civil War had been fought to free black slaves. Northern Republicans had supported constitutional amendments guaranteeing citizenship and voting rights to blacks. Moreover, Republicans in the North and South saw the black vote as critical in breaking the Democratic lock on the South. They saw the Southern Alliance supporting new racial segregation laws, which came to be known as Jim Crow. These new laws focused largely on urban segregation of streetcars, theaters, and public parks, but rural whites within the Southern Alliance demanded segregation of textile mills and processing plants in rural districts.[33] Merger talks between the Northern and Southern Alliance hit a snag when Milton George, representing the North, refused to accept Charles Macune's insistence on a "whites only" alliance. Long after the two regional alliances were merged, the national president of the Farmers' Alliance, Leonidas Polk of Tennessee, continued to hold that federal protection of black voting rights was "the greatest crime of modern times."[34]

The racism expressed by Alliance leaders and followers also expressed itself in calls for Chinese immigration exclusion and limits on foreign immigration generally. Populist farmers demanded that "Congress take prompt action to devise some plan to obtain all lands now owned by alien and foreign syndicates."[35] At the same time, Alliance leader J. H. Powers, president of the Farmers' Alliance in 1892, asked whether the "ignorant and vicious population" of recently arrived immigrants should be allowed to vote "while intelligent women all over the land" are denied the right to vote. Then he continued, "Why the foreigner, ignorant of our language, and perhaps opposed to all restraint of law and order, should be permitted to vote after a resident of but a few months on payment of a paltry sum for his papers, which perhaps is furnished by some scheming politician?"[36]

In the end, the regional Alliances were merged, but the tensions within the organization continued to find expression in the formation of the People's Party, which had begun to take shape parallel to the merger of the regional Alliance groups.

Forming the People's Party

The Populist movement reflected deep discontent among farmers in the South and the Midwest. Populists also gained support in the West and among urban radicals and segments of labor, especially among miners. The inability of state parties to respond to farmers' complaints opened the door for a third-party movement.[37] The Republican Party dominated in most midwestern states, but in its pursuit of economic growth, the party became aligned, if not controlled, by business interests, especially railroads. As a consequence, midwestern Republicans resisted change, and once confronted by grassroots Populist agitation, the GOP responded too late to prevent third-party mobilization. In most midwestern states, Democrats were a minority party, so they were open to forming alliances with the emerging Populist movement. Democrats in the South maintained power by playing on racial fears of poor white voters. In states where two-party competition was higher, the Populists tended to do less well.

Although many Populist speakers and leaders spoke of Thomas Jefferson's vision of an agrarian republic, the People's Party was forward looking in its call for government regulation of industry and in its support for direct election of U.S. senators, secret ballots, women's suffrage, and an income tax.[38] The party supported the formation of agricultural cooperatives to bring business efficiency to farmers. Although the People's Party platform in 1892 and 1896 included a plank calling for government ownership of railroads and communications systems, this plank was contentious from the outset. The People's Party was not a socialist party.

The three principal goals of the Populist movement were regulation of industry, federal aid to farmers, and monetary reform. Monetary reform included demands to replace the gold standard with government paper money and new silver coins.[39] The idea was to expand the money supply. The reform press circulated books and pamphlets, such as Sarah Emery's *Seven Financial Conspiracies* (1887), Seymour Norton's *Ten Men of Money Island* (1887), and William Harvey's extremely popular pamphlet *Coin's Financial School* (1894). These books called for expanding currency and cheap credit to close the gap between the rich and the poor and to counter the "money conspiracy" of London and New York bankers who were accused of controlling the world's gold supply. The Populist vision was to employ statist methods as a means of restoring small competitive capitalism.

Ideologically, many Populist leaders (who were not alone in this regard) embodied the anti-Semitism and racism of the day. Some historians describe these prejudices within the Populist ranks and leadership as no worse than those found in contemporary American political rhetoric. This perspective dismisses perhaps too easily the viciousness of bigoted rhetoric coming from Populist leaders, such as Ignatius Donnelly and Mary Lease, in their open talk of a Jewish financial conspiracy.[40] Progressive views, though, can be confounded with reactionary views. For example, such female Populist leaders as Bettie Gay and Mary Lease linked women's social progress to biological evolution.[41] Gay employed evolutionary theory to encourage brainier and more cultivated women to have more children to produce "a mentally great race."[42]

Politically, the Populist movement presented an amalgam of various political and ideological alliances, always fragile and never fully cemented. Regionally, it was an alliance of farmers in the South and Midwest, with some Mountain states thrown into the mix. While expressing common complaints about railroads, monopolies, and money lenders, farmers did not suffer equally. Furthermore, farmers did not always vote only for their economic interests. Midwestern farmers voted along traditional ethnic and religious lines, as well as economic lines.[43] Meanwhile, Northeastern farmers benefited from local urban markets and showed little interest in Populism.

These awkward alignments within the People's Party were not easily cemented. For example, an alliance with "labor" sounded good in theory, but in reality "labor" itself was divided among socialists, anarchists, conservative trade unionists, and more militant unions.[44] The Illinois Populists divided on a plank (known as Plank 10) pushed by the Socialist Labor Party calling for "the collective ownership by the people of all means of production and distribution."[45] Downstate Single Taxers led the opposition against Plank 10.

Many of the political leaders that emerged within the party brought long experience in third-party efforts, going back to the Greenback Party. Ignatius Donnelly from Minnesota typified those Populist leaders who were experienced in politics.[46] Before moving to Minnesota as a real estate developer, Donnelly entered politics in his hometown of Philadelphia first as a Democrat, and then declared himself a Republican in 1857 on his arrival in Minnesota. He won election twice as state lieutenant governor before being elected to Congress in 1862 for three terms. Defeated for reelection in 1868, he became a lobbyist in Washington for Jay Cook, a Philadelphia banker and railroad magnate, before declaring he was disgusted with money in politics. He returned to Minnesota where he was elected to the state senate under the Anti-Monopolist Party ticket, which was soon amalgamated with the new Greenback Party. He sought to reenter Congress on a fused Democrat-Greenback ticket in 1878. He lost narrowly, but his involvement in politics remained obsessive. He joined the newly formed Minnesota Farmers' Alliance in 1885, ran for the House again with a coalition of Democrats, Liberal Republicans, and Farmers' Alliance voters, only to lose by 1,000 votes of 32,000 cast. While running for office, he campaigned for Democrat Grover Cleveland in hopes of getting a position in the administration, only to fail to get an appointment. His attraction to the People's Party came naturally. Donnelly was a genuine radical with a strong opportunistic streak.

The movement for a new party, the People's Party, got off to a fiery start. In June 1890, Kansas farmers took the first step by organizing a third party. The newly formed People's Party in Kansas swept into office in a wave election that year, taking the majority of the legislature with ninety-two seats and electing newspaper editor William A. Peffer to the U.S. Senate. Jeremiah "Sockless Jerry" Simpson won election to Congress after mocking his opponents' fancy socks.[47] As one critic observed, "It was a fanaticism like the Crusades, a season of shibboleths and fetishes and slogans. Reason slept."[48]

As Populism made fast headway in the Midwest, calls for a new third party took on a fierce momentum, drawing in old activists and new enthusiasts. On May 19, 1891, activists calling for a new party came together in Cincinnati to inaugurate a National People's Party. This was followed by a conference in St. Louis held in late February 1892, which resulted in the call for a national convention to nominate a presidential candidate for the new party.[49]

First Strides: The 1892 Election

The convention was held in Omaha on Independence Day in 1892, and James Weaver, an 1872 presidential candidate for the Greenback Party, received the nomination. Weaver had been a general in the Union Army during the Civil War, which hurt him with voters in the South. A former Iowa Republican who had lost the Republican nomination for governor in 1875 because of opposition from anti-prohibitionists and business interests, Weaver turned to the recently formed Greenback Party. He won election to Congress in 1875 on a Greenback ticket. Weaver captured almost 9 percent of the popular vote among more than 11 million votes cast. The result was a significant showing for a third-party candidate.

In 1892, faith in the Populist cause remained firm, even though a close analysis of the election showed signs of trouble ahead. Weaver carried four states--Kansas, New York, Montana, and Washington--for a total of twenty-two electoral votes. He failed to penetrate the South, however, unable to get above 25 percent of the vote in any state except Alabama. He lost the cities, and he fared poorly in the Far West except in mining areas. In midwestern states east of the Mississippi, he failed to get more than 5 percent of the vote. Among state-level elections, the results were mixed. Populists won the governorships of Kansas, Washington, and North Dakota and swept the election in Colorado. Nonetheless, Populist state leaders such as Tom Watson in Georgia lost his congressional seat, while Ignatius Donnelly came in third for the governorship of Minnesota. Donnelly marked the occasion when he wrote in his diary, "Beaten! Whipped! Smashed! Our followers scattered like dew before the rising sun."[50]

As true believers saw it, however, Weaver had won a million votes in a poorly financed and poorly organized campaign. The Populist third-party faithful remained certain that there was a mass of discounted voters just waiting to break ranks, if only they could hear the truth and be given a real alternative at the polls. They emphasized especially the gains being made in such states as Kansas, where in addition to winning the governor's mansion by electing Lorenzo Lewelling, a former Republican, they won the majority in the state legislature.

A closer look at Kansas, though, might have revealed the problems faced by Populist legislators once in office. Driven more by passion than the art of politics, they proved inept in translating their agenda into concrete legislation. This became evident in the first days of the opening legislative session, which turned into a fiasco.[51] Matters quickly deteriorated when People's Party representatives announced they were challenging the election of eighteen Republicans to be seated. Republicans elected their own House speaker. Rumors circulated that both sides were arming themselves, prompting the local sheriff to swear in fifty deputies to prevent armed conflict. As things got even more heated, state militia members were rushed in from Wichita. Democrats in the state House stepped into the breach by forcing Populists to accept the Democratic candidate for the U.S. Senate in return for giving Populists the lucrative contract for state printer.

Although Kansas Republicans pushed a legislative agenda including many Populist proposals, political division in the House prevented bills from reaching the governor's desk, including the proposed public election of the state railroad commission. Populists refused to compromise, so their agenda failed to be enacted other than some minor pieces of legislation. These legislative dead ends were experienced in other state legislatures as well. In the meantime, Governor Lewelling made a further miscalculation by trying to remove Populist firebrand Mary Lease from the board of state charities after she claimed the administration was taking bribes from Kansas City gamblers and railroad companies. Lease took the matter to the courts, where she won, leaving Lewelling with another black eye. When Lewelling came up for reelection, he lost. So did most of the People's Party candidates in the lower house as well as many within the Kansas People's Party congressional delegation. Those who remained in Congress found themselves overtaken by freesilver Democrats. Populists in Kansas and elsewhere found the art of politics difficult to reconcile with their purity of principle.[52]

The Demise of the People's Party

As the presidential election of 1896 approached, Populist spirits remained high, although many leaders in the party saw that the movement had reached a dead end politically unless it merged with the Democratic Party. The depression of 1893, the collapse of President Grover Cleveland's administration, silver fever, and rising labor protest fueled Populist hopes for 1896. Democrat Cleveland had won election to the White House in 1892 on a reform pledge.

A month after stepping into the White House, the economy crashed. As economic conditions worsened, Cleveland alienated both farmers and labor. Confronted by the flight of gold from the national treasury, Cleveland insisted on repeal of the Sherman Silver Purchase Act by a Republican Congress, the so-called Billion Dollar Congress, in 1890. The act required the Treasury Department to purchase 4.5 million ounces of silver money and to issue legal tender ("silver certificates") based on silver. Believing that this measure contributed to the flight of gold, Cleveland strong-armed Congress to repeal the measure. He hoped to smother the silver fire. Instead, the repeal of the Silver Purchase Act fueled calls for government to buy silver to back government currency. Silver sentiment swept the South and the West, with the conflagration spreading even to New England and New York. Silver literature proliferated in pamphlet after pamphlet, article after article. William H. Harvey's *Coin's Financial School*, published in 1894, was selling 5,000 copies a day within the year. Silver organizations distributed tens of thousands of copies.[53]

Further troubles came for the Cleveland administration when Eugene Debs's American Railway Union went on strike in July, paralyzing the nation as factories shut down and fruit, grain, and livestock were unable to reach the market. Cleveland's decision to send federal troops to Chicago, Los Angeles, and Sacramento alienated working-class voters aligned with the Democrats. Labor was further alienated when the administration ordered the arrest of about four hundred unemployed protesters marching under the quixotic banner of Coxey's Army, who had descended on the nation's capital in the spring of 1894.[54]

Voters in the midterm elections repudiated the Cleveland administration. Advantage went to the Republicans, however, not to the Populists. Republicans gained control of the House, with 245 seats compared with 104 Democrats, and of the Senate, with 44 Republicans compared with 39 Democrats and 6 Alliance senators. In twenty-four states, no Democrat won national office. During this Democratic decimation, however, Populists made few gains. People's Party faithful tended to overlook these setbacks by focusing on modest successes. In California, for example, an alliance of Populists, Single Taxers, and Nationalists won a striking victory when millionaire Adolph Sutro won the San Francisco mayor's election in 1894, running on a platform of municipal ownership of the Southern Pacific streetcars and professional administration of city government.[55] Elsewhere, though, Populists were in deep trouble.

In the South, Democrats won election through outright fraud and intimidation. Populists tried to counter by forming fusion slates with Republicans against their common foe, the Democrats. Faced with this threat, southern Democrats responded viciously. For example, in North Carolina where the Republican-Populist alliance was strong, Democrats struck back, denouncing this alliance as a tool of "Negro domination."[56] Democrats sponsored "Red Shirt Clubs" of "respectable" citizens who terrorized black voters, burned the offices of an African American newspaper, and killed twelve blacks. The campaign of terror shattered the Republican-Populist Alliance in North Carolina. To ensure that black voters would not be mobilized in the future, a poll tax and literacy test were enacted into law. In the Midwest, Populist candidates did not fare much better.[57]

As the presidential election of 1896 approached, the call for fusion with the Democratic Party gained momentum within the People's Party. This was a matter of political expediency. Fusion sentiment appeared especially strong among southern Populists who saw that an alliance with the small Republican Party in the South was a political dead end. At the same time, the call for fusion was also especially strong in western mining states in the belief that the Democratic Party was the best instrument for achieving a bimetallic gold-silver standard. In Congress, the thirteen members of the Populist caucus came out in favor of fusion, with the exception of U.S. senator Peffer of Kansas and House member Milford Howard of Alabama. Peffer warned that the People's Party was now at the mercy of "trained politicians."[58] Peffer was joined in his opposition to fusion by others, such as Henry Lloyd, Tom Watson of Georgia, Ignatius Donnelly, and Mary Lease, who saw fusion as a "sellout" of the Populist cause. They believed Democrats were untrustworthy allies. Lloyd called for a presidential ticket headed by Eugene Debs, a union leader recently arrested for his involvement in a national railroad strike, and Jacob Coxey, who had organized a national march (Coxey's Army) on Washington by unemployed workers—which showed just how out of touch Lloyd was with political reality.[59] He became convinced that the party had become "clique-ridden and machine ruled" as well as "buried, hopelessly sold out."[60]

In 1896, the People's Party faced the dilemma that confronts all grassroots movements when they transform themselves into political parties: how to win election without compromising on principles? For Populists in 1896, this problem became especially acute when the silver wing at the Democratic Party National Convention nominated silverite William Jennings Bryan as their presidential candidate. Bryan had won election to the U.S. House in 1890, which allowed him a national stage for his great oratory skills. His "Cross of Gold" speech at the 1896 Democratic convention embodied his anti-elitist and anti-Eastern financial sentiments, while speaking a religious language to a still largely Protestant nation. (Bryan was a devout Presbyterian). After winning the nomination, Bryan made a concession to the eastern wing by selecting as his running mate Arthur Sewall, a wealthy Maine shipbuilder. The silver takeover of the Democratic Party stunned the Democratic eastern gold wing of the party. As one Democrat supporting Grover Cleveland declared, "For the first time I can understand the scenes of the French Revolution."[61]

When the People's Party convention convened a short time later in St. Louis, delegates were confronted with the basic proposition: back Bryan or die. As Henry Lloyd observed, "If we fuse, we are sunk; if we don't fuse, all the silver men we have will leave us for the more powerful Democrats."[62] Most western delegates were for fusion with the Democrats. Southern delegates, too, were overwhelmingly in favor of fusion. Anti-fusion forces attempted to rally by targeting Sewall as a secret "gold bug," a supporter of a single monetary standard based on gold. Fusionists undercut this attack by offering a compromise: Populists would nominate Bryan as the People's Party candidate, while selecting Tom Watson, a radical Populist from Georgia, as his running mate. After nominating Bryan as their presidential candidate, Populists offered voters a choice of voting for a Democratic ticket of Bryan-Sewall or a People's Party ticket of Bryan-Watson. What would have happened had the Bryan-Watson ticket won on Election Day proved to be moot.

At their convention, Republicans selected William McKinley from Ohio as their candidate. The lines were clear: gold versus silver, stay the course financially or experiment with change. While the lines seemed clear, confusion prevailed in the ranks of the Democratic-Populist slate. Tom Watson spent the first days of the campaign assailing Bryan's running mate, Sewall, as a phony reformer and a "wart on the party."[63] Only Bryan's direct intervention stopped Watson's attacks. At the same time, many newspapers asked if Bryan won the election, would he appoint a Democrat or a Populist to head the Treasury Department?

Manufacturing and large business rallied to McKinley. Through his campaign manager, Mark Hannah, huge sums of money were raised to support the most expensive campaign in the nation's history up to that time. McKinley, a Civil War veteran and an adroit politician, embraced traditional Republican values of sound money and a high tariff to protect American manufacturing. He was not a reactionary, however. In Ohio, he rightfully earned a reputation as a friend of labor, and as governor he pushed through legislation protecting workers in industry, including a bill that punished employers who refused to permit employees to join unions. He favored labor arbitration, and as governor a new state arbitration board settled fifteen of the twenty-eight strikes and lockouts it dealt with.[64] He won the nomination fighting the big-business eastern wing of the party and its boss machines.

Well funded and well organized, Republicans flooded the country with speakers and pamphlets lauding their candidate and warning of inflation, factory shutdowns, and massive unemployment if Bryan got his way. With a campaign war chest of over $3.5 million, Republicans sent out 250 million pieces of campaign literature. McKinley hit hard on the gold question by explaining that "gold has not opened up the wheat fields of Russia, India, or the Argentine Republic."[65] Republicans caricatured Bryan as a radical hick full of hot air. Although in later years he grew fat and bald, in 1896 the thirty-six-year-old Bryan was the youngest presidential candidate in the nation's history and was strikingly good looking and charismatic. With his powerful voice, he reached crowds of thousands without a microphone. His appeal was authentic, and convinced of his righteousness, he hammered home the message that average Americans were having to bear the cross of the gold standard to the benefit of the rich.

Bryan undertook a feverish campaign, traveling more than 300,000 miles by train across the country. He made 249 major campaign stops, focusing primarily on eight midwestern states. Everywhere he went, he spoke on one issue, free silver. Free silver, he said, promised to liberate the masses from Wall Street and foreign financiers who controlled government in Washington to benefit their class interests. He tied low farm prices to the appreciation value of gold. Republicans countered that overproduction was the cause of low farm prices. In the early stages of the campaign, Bryan appeared to gain momentum. A poll in early September by H. G. McMillan, chairman of the Iowa Republican State Committee, showed that 20 percent to 25 percent of Iowa Republican farmers favored free silver.[66] McKinley, however, remained confident that the more Bryan only talked about silver, the more tiresome he would become to voters. McKinley was convinced that in the end voters would choose head over heart. The Republican strategy of focusing on winning the laboring classes in the East and Midwest by campaigning on sound money and protective tariffs paid off.[67]

McKinley routed Bryan on Election Day, winning the popular vote with 7.1 million votes to Bryan's 6.5 million. McKinley won the crucial north-central states of Iowa, Minnesota, Wisconsin, Illinois, and Michigan.[68] Industrial workers in Chicago, Indianapolis, Milwaukee, and Detroit went

Republican. Irish Catholic workers left their traditional Democratic enclave to vote Republican. Bryan's evangelical Protestantism and his enthusiasm for alcohol prohibition repulsed them. Republicans retained the House and the Senate. Both parties endorsed the income tax and regulation of railroads.

By the summer of 1897, business confidence returned, ending the depression of the 1890s. With a brief interlude of Woodrow Wilson's administration from 1913 to 1920, Republicans controlled the White House until the Great Depression. The Republican Party became the party of business and economic prosperity. McKinley understood that the trust problem remained, declaring in his annual message to Congress in 1899, "Combinations of capital organize into trusts to control the conditions of trade among our citizens, to stifle competition, limit production and determine the prices of products used and consumed by the people are justly provoking public discussion, and should early claim the attention of Congress."[69] The trust problem became particularly severe for the Republican Party in the next decade, as it did for Democrats who could not decide whether it was best to bust the trusts or regulate them. Whatever the case, both parties agreed that government needed to be involved. Few, if any, argued for laissez-faire competition. Grassroots agitation in the nineteenth century changed the discourse and involvement of government in the new corporate order.

Measuring Populist Success

Bryan's defeat marked the death of the People's Party. A futile attempt was made in 1900 to run a People's Party campaign, but it failed miserably. Once-avid Populists deserted the party and headed in different directions. A few joined the newly formed Socialist Party. Others, such as Annie Diggs, convinced themselves that the Democratic Party had undergone a significant conversion. To hold onto its Populist wing, the Democrats nominated Bryan two more times, and he lost two more times.

Electoral failure notwithstanding, the dynamics of grassroots agitation in the late nineteenth century leading to the formation of the People's Party gave impetus to reform within both the Democratic and Republican Parties. This reform impetus was neither complete nor without reaction, but the age of reform had begun.[70] From 1900 through 1915, the budget of the U.S. Department of Agriculture grew by more than 700 percent, and with a staff of more than 19,000 people, it became one of the largest departments in the federal government. The enactment of the Federal Reserve Act of 1913 helped meet demands for a more expansive currency. Both parties, although not without division, accepted greater federal regulation of business, the recognition of labor rights, the direct election of U.S. senators, women's suffrage, a federal income tax, and clean government measures.[71] On the state and local levels, Populist agitation led to many reforms, including the expansion of public schools and public libraries. In these measures, new government agencies were required. This meant the expansion of the administrative state, a fact the Populists understood when they called for the federal bureaucracy to be staffed by experts "placed under a civil-service regulation."[72]

Although defeated at the polls in 1896, reform sentiment could no longer be contained as the nation entered the twentieth century. In the next decade and a half, reform spirit erupted in a crusade-like fashion not seen since Civil War Reconstruction. Reformers enacted measures on the municipal, state, and federal levels to enhance democracy, while erecting new agencies on every level in the name of the people. These measures strengthened the voice of the people, even while bureaucratic government muted the timbre of popular democracy.

The reforms enacted were breathtaking in their range, intended to foster democracy in an age of industry, urbanization, corporatization, and diversifying population. On the municipal level, citizens experimented with new structures of government, municipal ownership of public services, fairer tax assessments, and new land use and property laws. States enacted measures allowing voter initiatives and referenda, greater railroad and corporate regulation, environmental conservation, campaign finance transparency, protections for women and child labor, labor arbitration, and expanded suffrage.

On the federal level, progressive reform incorporated Populist demands for an income tax, direct election of U.S. senators, railroad regulation, currency reform, banking regulation, and protections for labor and consumers. The electorate expanded with the ratification of the Nineteenth Amendment, which provided women with the right to vote. Anti-monopoly and anti-trust policies were pursued. Laws were enacted to protect the environment, expand national parks, and develop water resources in the West.

The Centrifuge of Progressivism: Partisan Politics

In this era of progressive reform, both parties faced internal division between recalcitrant old guards representing well-oiled local and state political machines and special interests aligned with party factions. Partisan politics, however, created clashes over strategy, principle, and personality. For Republicans, these divisions were especially pronounced because of the strength of an old guard, represented by such senators as Nelson Aldrich from Rhode Island and insurgent reformers, such as Robert La Follette, Hiram Johnson, and George Norris. These divisions became all too apparent in the presidential election of 1912, when Theodore Roosevelt decided to challenge his selected heir to the presidency, incumbent president William Howard Taft, for the nomination of the Republican Party. Taft, with remarkable political ineptitude, had alienated the progressive wing of his party during his three years in the presidency. Roosevelt took personal insult in Taft's inability or unwillingness to press more aggressively on a reform agenda.

Viscerally angry at Taft and his attempts to appease the old guard, Republican progressives looked initially to Governor Robert La Follette of Wisconsin as the savior of their party. In November 1911, six hundred men and women identifying themselves as the insurgent-progressive wing of the party, met at San Francisco's Palace Hotel to launch the La Follette League. Even while lining up behind "Fighting Bob," many secretly hoped that Roosevelt might be persuaded to challenge Taft for the Republican nomination. Their hopes were fulfilled when Roosevelt, after lunching with Hiram Johnson in New York, announced he had decided to take up the challenge of defeating Taft. With Roosevelt in the race, La Follette supporters quietly began to desert him. The evening of Roosevelt's announcement, La Follette's campaign fell to pieces when the Wisconsin senator gave a rambling two-hour speech in New York. Morning newspapers reported that La Follette had a "breakdown." The La Follette bid for the presidency collapsed overnight.

The primary campaign proved nasty. Roosevelt personally attacked Taft, and Taft returned insult with insult. For all his popularity, though, Roosevelt failed to win the GOP nomination. (Only one incumbent president, Franklin Pierce, had ever failed to win his party's nomination, and Roosevelt failed to break the pattern.) Taft deftly lined up party regulars and southern delegates to win. When it became evident that Taft controlled the convention, Roosevelt made a fateful decision: he declared he would run as a third-party candidate on the Progressive Party ticket. Roosevelt stormed out. Meeting with his lieutenants at the Congress Hotel in Chicago during the Republican convention, Roosevelt was assured of financial support from newspaper and magazine owner Frank Munsey and J. P. Morgan associate George Perkins. The Progressive Party convention was held in Chicago that August with the enthusiasm of a religious revival attended by moral crusaders out to change the world. Indeed, the convention opened with the singing of an old-time gospel song, "Onward, Christian Soldiers." After Jane Addams seconded his nomination, Roosevelt accepted the party's nomination. Hiram Johnson, U.S. senator from California, joined the ticket as his running mate. Roosevelt declared that the campaign was "the battle of Armageddon" and that he would battle for the Lord.

And battle Roosevelt did. He brought his signature vigor to the campaign. He assailed the Democratic nominee, Woodrow Wilson, and Republican rival, William Howard Taft, equally. His speeches often seemed without restraint. Even after being shot by an assassin in Milwaukee near the end of the campaign, Roosevelt insisted that he deliver his address as scheduled. He attacked Wilson's proposal for breaking up large corporations as "rural toryism" and characterized Taft's policies as the tools of big business. Instead, he called for a "New Nationalism" in which large corporations were regulated by government. Here, the divisions within the reform movement, represented by Wilson and Roosevelt, as well as by Taft, whose administration had filed more anti-trusts suits than had Roosevelt's, revealed the sharp division within anti-monopoly ranks. Attacking monopolies had provided fodder for various grassroots reform activists since the late nineteenth century. But what was to be done with corporations?

Divisions within the Republican ranks in 1912 provided Woodrow Wilson with the margin to win the election. Following Roosevelt's loss, the Progressive Party quickly fell apart in all but name only. In 1916, Roosevelt returned to the folds of the GOP, making peace with Wall Street financiers. The old guard reasserted its control of the party by nominating a moderate reformer, Charles Evans Hughes, to head the presidential ticket. The election proved close, with Wilson barely scratching out a narrow victory. On Election Day, only three percentage points divided the two candidates in the popular vote, and only twenty-three votes separated them in the Electoral College. A shift in California's thirteen electoral votes would have given Hughes the election. And, indeed, California proved decisive. Hiram Johnson contributed to the loss by urging his supporters to vote for Wilson.[73] Independent progressives continued to hope for the emergence of a third party to challenge the established parties. Isolated, dismayed by what they perceived as the ignorance of the masses, and given to their own factionalism, independent progressives personified activists with a cause but without support from the masses they claimed to represent.

If progressive reform appeared to be only sporadic and regional in the 1920s, both political parties, Republican and Democrat, accommodated calls for reform emanating from late nineteenth-century agitation. Both parties accepted the need for corporate regulation, as well as protections for labor, women, children, and consumers. Both parties agreed that governmental powers should be expanded and that it was necessary to provide measures to offer a greater voice for the people and a restraint on special interests in government. Republicans and Democrats responded to demands for reform and the necessity of reform to address real problems. Of equal importance, both parties accepted the construction of the new regulatory state. The era of big government had begun.

Postscript

The Single Tax movement faded into a distant, cultish memory. Henry George died of a stroke in 1897 while campaigning for the mayor's office as an Independent Democrat. Henry Lloyd's hopes for a vibrant and gradualist Fabian socialism were left in ruins. The dream of a socialist America was shattered by sectarianism and suppression under the Wilson administration during World War I and in the Red Scare of 1919. The Socialist Party of Eugene Debs shrank in membership, replaced by an impotent Communist Party in the 1920s that looked to the Bolshevik Soviet Union as a model for the socialist dream. Lloyd's son, William Bross Lloyd, helped found and lead the Communist Labor Party, which would be merged into the faction-ridden Communist Party. Edward Bellamy died broken-hearted with the failure of the People's Party. His novel, *Looking Backward,* having become a standard in American literature, was no longer a blueprint for activism.[74]

By the 1920s, among many former reform activists who had lived through the heydays of Populism and Progressivism, there was a profound sense of failure. This failure they felt was of the limitations of the masses—those very people they had rallied to their causes. Some concluded that they had asked too much of the people. William Allen White, an articulate voice of Progressivism in Kansas, captured this sentiment when he concluded that political power handed over to the masses benefited them little "except to make them responsible for their own mistakes." Reformers, he declared, should lead the masses "in a slow tedious process of education," but "we can no longer be sure that they are capable of political education."[75]

Writing in 1925 in his memoir, certain that his political life had come to an end (not realizing he was to find a minor role in the New Deal), Frederic Howe concluded, "I believe in reform, but prefer the reform that is taking place within myself."[76] Instead of great reforms having been accomplished, Howe learned from experience that what had been created was a huge administrative state, a state he described as one that often "shapes political action, that conspires with congressmen. . . . America created an official bureaucracy moved largely by fear, hating initiative and organized as a solid block to protect itself and its petty unimaginative, salary hunting instincts."[77] The reformer who reacted perhaps most bitterly to the masses and the new administrative state was once an ardent Single Taxer, Albert Jay Nock, author of *Our Enemy, the State* (1935) and *Memoirs of a Superfluous Man* (1943). Declaring himself an "individualist," he inspired a new generation of reformers and activists, except this time on the libertarian right, which viewed the progressive state as the enemy of freedom.

Progressive reform mostly languished in the 1920s, except for a few hot spots in the Midwest, replaced by Republican "efficiency and economy" in government. The economic crisis in the 1930s revived progressive reform and completed much of what had begun at the turn of the century. With the crash of the global economy in 1929, grassroots activism found new life, new leaders, and new causes.

2 The New Deal, Social Protest, and the Administrative State

Two observations can be made about grassroots activism during the Progressive Era and the period of the New Deal. First, grassroots agitation forced both political parties, Democrats and Republicans, to respond to demands for reform. In this respect, grassroot activists succeeded. As America entered World War II, corporations were regulated; the monetary system reformed; farmers and workers better protected; and welfare for the poor, children, and the elderly was much improved. Progressive and New Deal legislation had not created the perfect society. Much more needed to be done, and the end result might not have achieved all that the grassroots movements had demanded or envisioned. Nonetheless, progress had been made through legislation prompted in large part by the politics of the street.

The second observation suggests an irony in another result of grassroots activism: the emergence of the administrative state. Reform, encouraged by grassroots mobilization along with the inevitable result of the complexities of an industrial society, led to the creation of a regulatory and welfare administrative state, overseen by a vast bureaucracy of civil servants and experts. These administrators and experts pronounced themselves guardians of the republic. This was hardly the intention of grassroots reform movements that called for more democratic rule. Demands for popular reform, espoused by grassroots activists in the late nineteenth century and reignited during the 1930s, coincided with an educated elite that believed nonpartisan expertise was needed in government. As a result, activists' demands for democratic revival were channeled by those who called themselves "scientific" reformers—social scientists and business leaders—who sought the depoliticization of the political process.

Those Progressive and New Deal reformers who rallied to the call of expertise in government sought to create an administrative state overseen by a new class of well-educated experts. While accepting the need for democratic reform, many expressed anti-majoritarian sentiment. For example, writing in 1901, Woodrow Wilson captured this ambivalence toward democracy when he observed, "It is no longer possible to mistake the reactions against democracy." He continued, "The nineteenth century was above all others a century of democracy; and yet the world is no more convinced of the benefits of democracy as a form of government than it was at the beginning." He called for the "best men"—educated professionals—to be placed in government. He proclaimed, "Representative government has its long life and excellent development, not in order that the common opinion, the opinion of the street, might prevail, but in order that the best opinion, the opinion generated by the best possible methods of general counsel, might rule in public affairs."[1]

In this way, the politics of the street—democratic agitation—was transformed into the deadening shuffle of papers and studies by government administrators, who asserted themselves as representatives of the public interest. Grassroots activism encouraged, if not compelled, the two parties to accept reform agendas; the unforeseen consequence of popular reform, though, was the creation of more distant government, arguably one less responsive to the demands of the people. Those Progressive and New Deal office seekers—Theodore Roosevelt, Robert La Follette, and Franklin Roosevelt among them—sincerely espoused democratic values, and on the local, state, and federal levels, genuine reforms were instituted extending and ensuring democratic rights, including the ratification of the Nineteenth Amendment giving voting rights to women. These politicians responded to popular demands for reform, yet the confluence of popular democratic reform and the call for expertise in government established an administrative state, albeit one within a democratic regime, that distanced itself from the general electorate.

Progressive reform triumphed under the administrations of Theodore Roosevelt, William Howard Taft, and Woodrow Wilson, laying the foundations for the later expansion of the modern regulatory and welfare state in the 1930s. Then, in response to the Great Depression, grassroots activism erupted with volcanic intensity, channeling labor radicals, the elderly, disenchanted working-class and lower-middle-class Catholics, and midwestern and southern farmers. Grassroots movements attracted millions of Americans who demanded reforms to relieve the suffering of the unemployed, the poor, the farmers, and women and children. The rich were assailed for having too much; big business was accused of placing profits above humanity; and Wall Street financiers were caricatured as guys in top hats and tails manipulating markets for their own selfish gain. Grassroots agitators attacked the rich, the moneylenders, the gold interests, and political lackeys.

Movements led by Francis Townsend for old-age pensions; Father Charles Coughlin for monetary inflation and an isolationist foreign policy, and Huey Long and his successor Gerald L. K. Smith for wealth distribution were anti-Roosevelt and anti–New Deal, especially in 1935 and 1936, but all called for activist government to remedy the problems caused by economic crisis. Townsend, Coughlin, and Long attracted the largest followings and drew the greatest attention because they posed a threat (it appeared) to Franklin Roosevelt.[2] But their movements were not the only ones that sprang up in these years. James R. Cox tried to organize the Jobless Party in Pittsburgh. William H. "Coin" Harvey, now long in the tooth from his Populist heyday, organized the Liberty Party. In California, socialist Upton Sinclair won the Democratic Party's nomination for governor in 1934 under the banner of "Ending Poverty in California." Across college campuses, students organized against war. Right-wing grassroots movements also emerged, often led by women, which attracted tens of thousands of people to their causes.[3]

The schemes offered by grassroots movements—socialism, guaranteed incomes, monetarization of silver, public ownership of basic industries, and massive redistribution of wealth—did not lead directly in most cases to specific legislation. Nor did these movements lead to viable third parties. These reform movements nonetheless mobilized millions of Americans who demanded radical reform. These movements thus helped provide New Deal liberals with cover to enact more modest, yet meaningful reform legislation.

Grassroots movements in the 1930s wielded varying degrees of power on the national and state levels. For example, Coughlin's mobilization of voters was decisive in defeating a pending congressional bill in 1935 in support of the United States joining the World Court. Similarly, Francis Townsend, who organized millions of Americans in support for old-age pensions, pressured Congress and the Roosevelt administration to place a high priority on addressing the needs of the elderly. The Social Security Act of 1935, for example, provided more benefits for the elderly than it did for aid to women with dependent children. His movement's support for later Social Security amendments, especially in 1939, provided political cover for these expansions.

Grassroots activism contributed to the leftward drift in the country that was already occurring. Although resisted initially by many business interests and reactionary elements within the Republican Party, the modern regulatory and welfare state was well established by the time America entered

World War II. Although conservatives did not make a complete concession to the modern welfare-regulatory-administrative state, in the end they accepted its basic parameters. Republicans, for example, after expressing modest opposition to Social Security, voted for it in 1935. By 1950, however, the GOP called for the liberalization of Social Security benefits and expanded the rolls. Opposing benefits was just bad politics. In the postwar period, some of the largest expansions of the regulatory state came from Republican administrations.

In the 1930s grassroots activists demanded that government take a larger role in people's lives. Yet in this call for government action, ideological distinctions between left and right in this period are difficult to parse when the criterion is larger government. Socialists clearly stood on the left. On the other hand, radical movements that formed around Townsend, Coughlin, and Long employed patriotic and anti-communist rhetoric, often not associated with the left, even while these leaders denounced Wall Street, financiers, and political elites. Moreover, Townsend, Coughlin, and Long in their different schemes all presumed a more active role by the federal government and entailed a massive expansion of centralized government power. This was stuff of the left, but Coughlin, Townsend, and Long by 1935 were decidedly anti–New Deal. These leaders presented themselves as speaking for the common people against the economic and political elites.

Staying Barely Alive: Radicals in the 1920s

Political understanding of the outburst of social protest in the decade of the 1930s needs to be placed within a context of the general collapse of radicalism in the years that preceded the Great Depression. Progressive reform at the turn of the century absorbed agrarian and labor radicalism. As a consequence, radicalism as a political movement seemed all but dead as America entered into the generally prosperous years of the 1920s. Neither established party, Republican or Democratic, therefore was fully prepared for the radical outbursts that came in the 1930s, and neither party understood organizationally or ideologically how to translate grassroots protest into electoral victories. The radical Industrial Workers of the World (IWW) had been smashed and the Socialist Party left in disarray by repression during World War I and sectarian division over the Bolshevik Revolution. Meanwhile, liberal reformers were flailing in the wind trying to resuscitate a third-party movement. Progressive reformers saw glimpses of hope in sporadic labor strikes in the

1920s, Native American policy reform led by John Collier, and activism in the Women's Bureau, a federal agency created in 1920. Overall, though, these activities did not offer much given the general conservatism of the decade.

The decade of the 1920s appeared to mark the triumph of capitalism, although expressions of moderate reform continued in these years of Republican dominance of the White House. Republicans became once again the party of pro-business, high tariffs, and low taxes. Although later caricatured by New Deal historians as a party of reaction, Republicans undertook important reform initiatives in executive budgeting, American Indian tribal reorganization, prison reform, state highway development, and placement of women in government positions. Republicans backed federal anti-lynching laws. The Republican administrations of Warren G. Harding, Calvin Coolidge, and Herbert Hoover took credit for this prosperity, ensuring control of the White House throughout the decade. As Coolidge famously said, "The business of America is business." Hoover was Coolidge's secretary of commerce, a powerful position in the 1920s. He was the only secretary of commerce to succeed to the presidency. In this way, Republicans translated progressive reform into scientific management, efficiency and uplift, and government reorganization, enhancing executive powers and expertise in government.

Anti-corporate sentiment found expression in Congress through maverick Republicans, such as Robert La Follette (and later his son) from Wisconsin, George Norris from Nebraska, William Borah from Idaho, Hiram Johnson from California, and a few others. Most of them had been part of Teddy Roosevelt's Progressive insurgency in 1912. Grassroots radicalism continued in the 1920s, but it was generally weakened, finding sporadic and regional expression in the rise of the Farmer-Labor Party in Minnesota, the Nonpartisan movement in North Dakota, and a last national gasp in Robert La Follette's failed third-party run under the Progressive Party banner in 1924. La Follette won few Republican votes, but he did get the votes of Progressive Democrats who were disenchanted with their party's nomination for president, John W. Davis, a reactionary Wall Street lawyer. La Follette ran second to Coolidge in a few states with Progressive traditions but carried only his home state of Wisconsin, and the Progressive Party disappeared.

If genuine mass radicalism appeared alive, it was in Minnesota, where a third party, the Farmer-Labor Party, won control of the state in the 1922 election. The rise of this party turned the state Democratic Party into a third party throughout the 1920s and 1930s, while Minnesota's long-dormant Republican Party struggled to find a place as the second largest party. The

Farmer-Labor Party, with its deep cooperative and socialist roots, appeared to fulfill the promise of a true labor-farmer alliance.[4]

The formation of the Minnesota Farmer-Labor Party came directly out of the efforts of a brilliant organizer, Arthur Charles Townley, who began his efforts with the North Dakota Socialist Party when he was assigned the task of enlisting farmer support for the party platform without necessarily signing them up as party members. Townley deftly began enrolling farmers into a Nonpartisan League.[5] Within months, thousands of farmers enrolled. Fearing that a party within a party was being created, Socialist Party leaders ordered Townley to shut down the League. An angry Townley resigned from the party and undertook to make the League into an organization capable of taking over the North Dakota Republican Party. Socialists such as Arthur Le Sueur were enlisted as leaders in the new league.

Townley was a mastermind at organizing. He engaged organizers to spread across the state to build membership, paying a commission for each member they signed up, just like the Rotary Club and the Ku Klux Klan did. Most organizers were politically committed to the cause; others saw easy money. If organizers met their quota, the League provided a Ford automobile to extend their territory.[6] In 1916, Nonpartisan League–endorsed candidates within the Republican Party won control of the state. From this point through 1921, the League dominated state politics in North Dakota. Under Progressive Republican leadership, backed by the Nonpartisan League, the state established government-owned and -operated grain elevators, a government crop insurance company, and a state-owned bank for farm loans. Later, it set up a state health insurance plan. German and Russian immigrant farmers used to government-provided services played a big role in North Dakota's brand of prairie radicalism.[7]

An ambitious Townley undertook to extend the League to the neighboring state of Minnesota, which seemed ripe for political change. Since the 1850s, Minnesota had been dominated by a conservative, business-oriented Republican Party led by Minnesota corporations backed by the votes of Protestant Scandinavian farmers. In 1917, Townley moved the headquarters of the Nonpartisan League to St. Paul. Townley's goal was to once again infiltrate the Republican Party from within. Unlike North Dakota Republicans, the Minnesota GOP, with Twin Cities money and urban middle-class support, proved more adept in fending off a takeover. Ginning up patriotic support for World War I, Minnesota Republicans launched a counterassault on German immigrants and radicals. A legislative-backed Commission of Public Safety was used to attack the League, radicals, and organized labor. The crackdown was so severe that antiwar socialists, labor organizers, and most important, Scandinavian and German farmers reacted at the polls in 1918 to defeat many establishment-backed Republican Party candidates.[8]

The success of the Nonpartisan League candidates in 1918 led William Mahoney, a former Socialist candidate and president of the St. Paul Trades and Labor Assembly, to call for the formation of a third party. St. Paul was a Catholic city dominated by Irish and German immigrants who had traditionally voted Democratic. No one from St. Paul had ever won statewide office. Republicans tried to adjust to the radical upsurge by presenting a reform agenda, but this turn came too late. By 1920, the Farmer-Labor Party emerged as a distinct and well-organized political party able to challenge both established parties in the state. Farmers and urban workers flocked to the new party in droves. They were drawn by different means and with different agendas. The rural counties, heavily influenced by the cooperative movement in Scandinavia, stressed locally owned nonprofit general stores, banks, and grain elevators. The urban part of the party was union based. In St. Paul, Mahoney worked closely with Communist trade unionists in the machinist locals and others in labor to form a Farmer-Labor Association, in effect, a party within a party. He and his band hoped that this association would lead to a national third-party movement. Mahoney's Farmer-Labor Association became a base for the left-wing contingent in the Farmer-Labor Party. This activist base created tensions within the party among those who wanted to win election and those seeking to radically transform society.[9]

Townley, the man who organized the Nonpartisan League in the first place, now found himself on the outs. He saw the movement toward a third party as a takeover by the extreme left. Factionalism within the League was already apparent by the time Townley broke with the group. In 1919, Arthur Le Sueur had split with Townley, whom he accused of being in bed with the Republicans. In 1922, Townley resigned from the League—humiliated, embittered, politically impotent, and seemingly unaware that revolutions eat their own.[10]

La Follette's Failed Third-Party Effort

In his aspirations to form a national Farmer-Labor Party, Mahoney reached out to U.S. senator Robert La Follette from Wisconsin to join a Conference for Progressive Political Action meeting scheduled in St. Paul in mid-July 1923. Mahoney planned to make this conference the launching pad for the establishment of a national Farmer-Labor Party. La Follette's ambitions to run as a third-party presidential candidate were well known. La Follette stood as a hero to many progressives. As governor of Wisconsin from 1900 to 1905, he pushed through the state's first workers' compensation bill, a minimum-wage bill, railroad regulation, and the first state income tax. La Follette's support for the direct election of U.S. senators and women's suffrage won national applause from progressives. Elected to the U.S. Senate in 1906, he joined progressive insurgents in challenging congressional leadership. His bid to receive the Republican presidential nomination in 1912 was undermined when Theodore Roosevelt entered the race. Angered by what he saw as betrayal, La Follette refused to endorse Roosevelt or his Progressive Party. Instead, he threw his support to Democratic candidate Woodrow Wilson.

La Follette stuck by Wilson as best he could to any politician, but his loyalty was ultimately to his ideas. Their break came with World War I. La Follette's fierce and outspoken opposition to the war, which was especially unpopular among Wisconsin's German immigrants, caused many to loathe him, including many progressives, but in 1922 La Follette easily won reelection to the Senate. His reputation as a principled and courageous reformer was restored when he revealed on the Senate floor corruption within the Warren Harding administration.[11] La Follette saw 1924 as his last, best chance to save the nation from corporate control. Self-righteous, egotistical, given to hypochondria, he represented an old-style reform politics and nineteenth-century oratory style that seemed alien to a new age of radio and a decade of general prosperity.

Thus, Mahoney's invitation to La Follette to attend the St. Paul convention appeared to be a natural: enlist La Follette, and a huge first step toward a national Farmer-Labor Party would have been taken. La Follette, however, wanted nothing to do with Mahoney, whom he saw as too tightly tied to the Communists. He rebuked Mahoney publicly by calling the conference a mischievous effort to "deceive the public."[12] Hardheaded and not easily embarrassed, Mahoney went ahead with the conference only to find that La Follette's warning about Communist influence was true. Under orders from the Soviet Union, American Communists were directed to take over the conference to move it toward a revolutionary position, which excluded serious electoral politics.

La Follette was then nominated to head the Progressive Party. He made anti-monopoly the theme of his campaign. His speeches, denouncing monopolies, big business, and political opponents, often went on for two or more hours. When the final votes were tallied, he won only 4.8 million votes out of an estimated 28.6 million cast. He appeared to take more votes from

the Democratic presidential candidate than he did from the Republican presidential incumbent, Calvin Coolidge. In the end, he performed worse than
did his nemesis Theodore Roosevelt in 1912. La Follette carried only his
home state of Wisconsin.[13] A few diehards saw La Follette's 4.8 million votes
as a positive sign, but less ideological enthusiasts accurately saw the defeat as
the end of the dream of a national third party.

In Minnesota, while keeping its distance from La Follette's Progressive
Party, the Farmer-Labor Party in the state elections in 1924 preserved a
unified slate and sent three candidates to Congress. Further momentum came
with the onset of the Great Depression. In 1930, the party elected longtime
reformer Floyd B. Olson to the governor's mansion. Able to unite farmers,
especially the Norwegian vote and the urban labor vote, Olson swept into office. Although conservative Republicans still dominated the state legislature,
Olson pressed forward with reforms. In 1932, he easily won reelection, while
Farmer-Labor candidates swept other state offices.

In office, Olson faced, as did other governors across the nation, massive
unemployment, business bankruptcy, and home and farm foreclosures. Olson
pushed through an aggressive agenda that included homestead tax reform, a
state tax on chain stores, ratification of a national child labor amendment,
minimum hours for female workers, and state old-age pensions. At the same
time, he used a spoils system that led to the wholesale firing of state employees at every level of government who were not aligned with the party.
A weekly round of firings began based on reports from local party officials,
some with personal grudges. While doing this, he confronted outbreaks of
farmer and labor strikes.[14] Agrarian radicals, militants within organized labor,
and political revolutionaries found opportunities to organize.

Organizing the Unemployed

As Olson and other governors learned, massive unemployment offered an
opening for radical grassroots activists to organize protests for employment
opportunities, better housing, and welfare benefits for those displaced by an
economic crisis of national and international magnitude. Especially effective
in organizing the unemployed was A. J. Muste, a former Dutch Reformed
minister, who in the 1920s had become a militant labor organizer.

In 1929, Muste played a key role in organizing the Conference on Progressive Labor Action (CPLA), an educational organization formed in opposition to the conservative American Federation of Labor. Two years after

its establishment, in the midst of the Depression, the CPLA rejected the gradualism of the Socialist Party by calling for direct involvement in labor organizing with the ultimate goal of creating a "workers republic."[15] Muste used as his organizing base the Brookwood Labor College, established in 1919 in Katonah, New York, about forty-five miles north of New York City. The college fashioned itself as the nation's foremost labor school, enrolling around forty students each year to be trained in militant industrial unionism. With the onset of the Depression, Muste used the school to form a revolutionary cadre. As a consequence, the American Federation of Labor launched an investigation of the school in 1929, charging that it was a hotbed of Communist activity. The charge was unfair; Muste stood in opposition to the Communist Party, but there is no doubt that he wanted the college to translate its educational mission to direct political action.

Relying on a network of Brookwood students, alumni, and other radicals he had met over the course of a decade, Muste undertook direct organizing of the unemployed by forming the Unemployment League. Through the league, Muste sought to develop a revolutionary cadre for the formation of a new radical socialist party. The Communist Party, too, undertook a campaign to organize the unemployed through its own organization, the Unemployment Council. Although the Communists had some success in organizing mass demonstrations, Muste's Unemployment League excelled at grassroots organizing.[16] An early effort to organize the unemployed in Seattle in 1931 suggested the potential for this kind of organizing. In Seattle, a CPLA member joined with students and teachers at the Seattle Labor College in forming the Unemployed Citizen's League that attracted several thousand who were jobless. By 1932, the Seattle league had organized 6,000 families into what was labeled the "Republic of the Penniless."[17]

Unemployment Leagues sprang up in Ohio, Pennsylvania, West Virginia, and North Carolina. The League claimed 100,000 national members in 187 branches operating throughout the country. Witnessing this growth, Musteites began believing that "the nation was in a state of civil war."[18] In 1933, the CPLA was dissolved and relaunched as the American Workers Party.

Leaders in the Communist Party saw the growth of the Muste movement as a serious threat. Their own attempts at forming Unemployment Councils generally met with little success, although initially they attracted considerable public attention. Local Unemployment Councils organized hunger marches and protests against tenant evictions. Although active in major cities, the Unemployment Council failed to rival Muste's early efforts at grassroots organizing, with the council meetings often attended mostly by party members.[19]

In Minneapolis, the Communist Party undertook through Unemployment Councils to organize neighborhood block clubs to fight evictions and protest cutbacks in relief. Whatever success party organizers were having in the neighborhood was undermined when the party decided to shift its organizing focus from neighborhoods to male transients found in unemployment camps and hostels. Transients failed to provide the basis of a steady membership, so this shift away from neighborhood organizing ensured failure. In Minneapolis, Communist Party activists also attempted to organize public-relief recipients. This effort failed as well, as did the party's attempt to organize women against high meat prices.[20]

Franklin Delano Roosevelt's administration undercut the revolutionary goals of militant grassroots organizers. In response to the unemployment crisis, the New Deal launched relief and public works projects. The Federal Emergency Relief Administration provided state and local governments with relief funds, while the Civil Works Administration employed more than 4 million people in work relief.

Farmers' Holiday: Farmers on Strike

As grassroots activists tried to organize the unemployed, Midwest farmers, too, became increasingly militant. This militancy was represented in the Farmers' Holiday, a movement to prevent agricultural goods from reaching market. The strike turned violent in many parts of the Midwest.

The Farmers' Holiday Association drew national attention and had the most direct influence on shaping national policy. The movement began in Iowa as a grassroots effort and quickly spread to other midwestern states. It called for agricultural strikes to raise commodity prices and stop farm foreclosures. This movement was a direct result of falling prices in wheat, hog, and dairy prices that began in the 1920s and collapsed with the onset of the world-wide Depression in 1929. After World War I, American wheat farmers faced intense competition from Canadian and Argentinian wheat growers, while hog production in Germany and Denmark, American producers' two major European competitors, drove prices down. Furthermore, the high value of the dollar in the 1920s hurt American agricultural exports. Restrictive tariffs added to American farmers' woes. Germany by the early 1930s had increased a lard tariff to almost twice the value of the product, and England imposed import quotas on hog products. By 1933, wheat exports had fallen to a little more than 4 percent of the total crop production of American farmers, while pork exports accounted for only 1.7 percent of total American production.[21]

The crash in commodity prices led Milo Reno, an Iowa farm activist, to organize the National Farmers' Union. He joined John Simpson, another experienced veteran of farm struggle from the Populist days and a spellbinding speaker who built the Oklahoma Farmers' Union to 23,000 members. Reno, an ordained minister who traced his family roots back to the Greenback Party days, had been active in the Bryan movement. Reno first called for a farmers' holiday—a boycott by farmers taking their products off the market to drive up prices—but it was not until 1931, when he gained the support of Minnesota and Iowa farmers, that his call for a farmers' strike caught fire. The strike began in Iowa in early August 1932 and spread to neighboring states.[22] The movement quickly turned militant, then violent.

In Sioux City, pickets attacking 250 local milk producers appeared on the highway, stopping traffic. Reno and Simpson had not expected the picketing of highways. Meanwhile, an interstate freight train was stopped in Nebraska, with railcars broken into and ransacked. By late August, violence was spreading. In Council Bluffs, Iowa, 500 protesters seized the courthouse to prevent the arraignment of a group of Farmers' Holiday protesters. Threatened with the intervention of the National Guard that had been called out by the governor, the protesters agreed to abandon the courthouse. As violence spread, South Dakota governor Warren Green and Minnesota governor Floyd B. Olson issued statements declaring sympathy for the strikers but warning of martial law unless order was restored. Ironically, the one dissident governor who condemned the strike outright was Charles W. Bryan of Nebraska, the brother of William Jennings Bryan.[23]

As the crisis escalated, midwestern governors sought to address the situation. In addition to low farm prices, farmers were unable to pay the mortgages on their farms. In February 1933, Iowa Democratic governor Clyde Herring signed a bill permitting distressed farm owners to appeal for continuance of foreclosure action. In Minnesota Farmer-Labor governor Floyd Olson used executive action to declare a one-year moratorium on foreclosures. When this action was deemed unconstitutional, the Minnesota legislature pushed through a statute imposing a moratorium on foreclosures. In an important decision, the U.S. Supreme Court upheld this legislation in *Home Building and Loan Association v. Blaisdell* (1934), which judged the moratorium a valid exercise of state power in an emergency situation.

Franklin Roosevelt thus stepped into the White House confronted with this crisis in the agricultural hinterland. He faced an agricultural bloc in Congress calling for rapid inflation, led by Montana senator Burton Wheeler and Oklahoma senator Elmer Thomas. They embraced old Bryan ideas, seeking to remonetize silver, lower the gold content of the dollar, and issue more printed money. Exerting political pressure, Roosevelt prevailed upon these Democratic senators to back down for the moment on pressing for inflationist legislation. At the same time, White House pressure was applied to Governor Olson to get Milo Reno to call off the Farmers' Holiday, which he did in May 1933. To address the monetary crisis, Roosevelt undertook a gold-buying program to inflate the depressed economy. Agriculture secretary Henry Wallace, an Iowan, devised the Agricultural Adjustment Act (1933), which sought to boost commodity prices by subsidizing farmers *not* to raise crops and bring livestock to slaughter. The act won over farmers and dissipated the Farmers' Holiday movement. Reno found himself a leader without a movement.

1934: Shifting Left

While New Deal measures had a modest impact, the Depression continued into 1934, and the country appeared to turn left. A textile strike involving 400,000 workers in the Mid-Atlantic and southern states lasted twenty-two days before it was finally broken. In May, longshoremen on the West Coast went out on strike, closing all the major ports. The strike culminated in a general strike in San Francisco that led to the unionization of all Pacific Coast ports. Many disgruntled Americans openly spoke of revolution. As one Los Angeles businessman warned, "There'll be a revolution, sure. The farmers will rise up. So will labor. The Reds will run the country—or maybe the fascists. Unless, of course, Roosevelt does something."[24]

Class warfare in 1934 coincided with rising radical politics. Social discontent expressed itself in the California gubernatorial election in 1934 when socialist Upton Sinclair surprised everyone by winning the Democratic Party primary for governor. Sinclair's nomination to head the Democratic ticket seemed to have come out of nowhere. Author of *The Jungle* (1904), which exposed foul practices in the meatpacking industry, Sinclair had moved to Southern California in the 1920s. In response to the worsening 1930s Depression, Sinclair, then in his fifties, produced a series of self-published pamphlets, reissued into a book, *I, Governor of California and How I Ended Poverty*

(1933), in which he outlined a socialist scheme to restore the state's economy. Sinclair's plan called for California state government to take over unproductive factories and turn them over to the workers, who would produce goods for consumption and trade with agricultural cooperatives. His End Poverty in California (EPIC) plan drew wild enthusiasm from distressed Californians. EPIC clubs sprang up spontaneously throughout the state. Sinclair produced in effect, after years of socialist agitation, a genuine grassroots movement. After switching his party affiliation from Socialist to Democrat, he declared his candidacy for governor in 1934 and then went on to win the primary over his closest rival by more than 150,000 votes.[25] Sinclair won by carrying Los Angeles and Long Beach by three-to-one margins. Close to fifty other EPIC candidates running for the state legislature won their primaries as well.

Sinclair's nomination threw Republicans and the Democratic establishment into turmoil.[26] Sinclair had polled 436,200 votes, amounting to almost 90,000 more votes than the Republican incumbent governor Frank Merriam, a former Long Beach assemblyman and state senator aligned with the progressive wing of his party, received in his primary race. In one of the most expensive and vicious campaigns up to that point in California history, the 1934 gubernatorial race revealed the power of mass media in shaping an election's outcome. Frank Merriam proved to be better on the campaign trail than his opponent expected.[27] Republicans understood that more was needed to defeat Sinclair than just traditional clichés. As a result, the 1934 Republican state platform called for more unemployment relief, collective bargaining rights for labor, a thirty-hour work week and six-hour workday, and consideration of a national social security program. Equally important, Merriam endorsed Townsend's plan for a guaranteed income for those older than 60 years of age.[28] California had a lot of Democrats who disdained radicalism, and on Election Day, Sinclair was trounced. Merriam won 1.1 million votes to Sinclair's 879,537. This disappointment was tempered, though, by the election of EPIC-backed congressional Democratic candidate Jerry Voorhis, who won his race in Whittier, California.

This shift to the left nationally was further evidenced when A. J. Muste, stirred by his success in organizing unemployment leagues, set out to organize a revolutionary party, the American Workers Party. Rejecting his pacifist past, Muste declared a workers' revolution necessary to overturn the ills of an unjust and failed capitalist system. His newly organized party became involved in the strike at the Electric Auto-Lite Company in Toledo, Ohio, in April 1934.[29] Muste emerged as a key negotiator in the strike, which concluded when company officials capitulated under the threat of a general strike. Following this, Muste merged his party with a Trotskyist group to form the Workers Party of the United States. (Trotskyists were a small sectarian grouping that had broken away or had been expelled from the Communist Party for being followers of Leon Trotsky, Stalin's opponent from the left. Trotskyists proclaimed themselves the true Marxist Leninists and called for world revolution.) In the new formation, Muste quickly found himself embroiled in party factionalism. Within a year, Muste resigned from the party, announcing he was returning to his radical roots as a pacifist. Not deterred by the Muste loss, Trotskyists went on with their cytokinetic history of factional division in the name of purity. A common joke about Trotskyists at the time was, "What do you call two Trots in a phone booth? Two factions, a phone call away from a third faction."

In Minnesota, Governor Olson declared, "I am not a liberal. I enjoy working on a common basis with liberals for their platforms, etc., but I am not a liberal. I am what I want to be—I am a radical. I am a radical in the sense that I want a definite change in the system. I am not satisfied with tinkering. I am not satisfied with patching." He called for the creation of a vague "cooperative commonwealth," but at the Farmer-Labor Party convention in 1934, the party's left faction pushed through a platform for state ownership of banks, mines, hydroelectric plants, transportation, communications, packinghouses, insurance, and all factories except those cooperatively owned.[30] Olson downplayed his party's radical platform in his bid for reelection, when in the midst of the campaign one of the bloodiest conflicts in state history erupted. The trouble began when a small teamsters' local, led by a tiny Trotskyist grouping, went out on strike in the spring and summer of 1934.

The strike pitted resistant Minneapolis business owners, organized into the Citizens Alliance, against Teamsters Local 574, which was under the leadership of the Dunne brothers (Vincent, Miles, and Grant) and Carl Skoglund. As Trotskyists, they saw the union as a means to revolution, not class accommodation.[31] They were revolutionaries leading a grassroots labor movement. As faithful followers of Lenin and Trotsky, they envisioned workers' councils (soviets) being formed to spark a revolution—just as had happened in the Bolshevik revolution in Russia.

After Local 574 of the Teamsters Union won a strike against coal-yard operators in 1934, membership swelled to 3,000 members within a matter of months. At the time, the Minneapolis city government was totally under the control of conservative Republican business interests. In May, Local 574 took its next major step to bring business to heel by calling a strike against all city trucking operators after they refused to negotiate with the union. The strike turned violent when skirmishes broke out between the strikers and city police, augmented by special deputies supported by the Citizens Alliance. On May 22, full-scale violence erupted on the streets of Minneapolis in what became known as the Battle of Deputies' Run. Two strikebreakers died after being severely beaten. On July 20, known as Bloody Friday, police opened fire on strikers attempting to stop a truck delivery. Sixty-seven were wounded. As violence continued to escalate and federal arbitration went nowhere, Governor Olson declared martial law, finally forcing employers to accept an agreement that ended the strike.[32]

Organizing the Elderly and Rallying Catholics

By 1936, many radicals felt betrayed by the Roosevelt administration. This was especially the case with Francis Townsend and Charles Coughlin, early supporters of Roosevelt's New Deal. Townsend's and Coughlin's break with the New Deal marked a major turning point for grassroots social protest during the Depression years. Both Townsend and Coughlin, as well as Huey Long, a U.S. senator from Louisiana, had built movements attracting hundreds of thousands of followers.

A sixty-six-year-old physician from Long Beach, recently removed from his position in the city as a health inspector, Townsend organized millions of followers adamant that his proposal to provide a guaranteed annual income to the elderly offered a panacea to the Great Depression. Unassuming, a poor public speaker, and elderly, Townsend was an unlikely leader of one of the most powerful social movements to be organized in the 1930s. On the surface, his proposal was quite simple: the federal government should pay every person sixty years or older $200 per month on the condition that they not work and spend their monthly stipend fully each month. At the time, the average monthly pay for workers was often less than $100 per month. Revenue for this program would come from a universal tax on all goods and services exchanged. His numbers never quite matched up with estimates as to the actual costs of the program, but this did not dampen the enthusiasm of his followers. Townsend was aided in forming national Townsend chapters through a partnership with a sharp, young real estate broker, Earl Clements, whom Townsend had met while trying to make a go of it by selling real estate.

Townsend was the genius behind the program; Clements was the brilliant organizer. Within two years the Townsend movement had enrolled more than 2 million members, nearly a fifth of Americans older than sixty. The size of the organization was larger than any civil rights or women's movement in the twentieth century.[33]

Joining forces with Clements and his assistant Thelma Morris, Townsend set out to organize a mass movement to pressure Congress to enact legislation for the Townsend plan. At the heart of the plan was what Townsend called a "revolving tax," a national sales tax on every business transaction.[34] Townsend proposed, in effect, that half the national income was to go to pensions. His revolving tax scheme of a 2 percent tax on all transactions projected revenue of only sixty-five dollars a month for 10 million people.[35] The elderly who were caught in an economic depression that had left them without pensions or prospects for employment did not care about the fine points of finance, however. They wanted relief. Within months of Townsend's announcement of the plan, Townsend Clubs sprang up like mushrooms across the state. At the center of the organizing drive lay the *National Townsend Weekly*. The first issue sold 37,500 copies; the second, 50,000 copies; and the third, 75,000. By 1935, circulation reached 250,000. Clements and Townsend arranged for revenues from this and other publications to go into a separate for-profit corporation they formed.

Townsend set a sharp contrast to his young, shrewd, enterprising partner Clements. He had moved with his wife to Long Beach after an uneventful life as a country doctor in South Dakota. He found setting up a medical practice difficult even in the flush days of the mid-1920s. He turned to selling real estate for the young Earl Clements before gaining employment working in the city health department in 1930 at the outset of the Depression. When a new administration came into office and at age sixty-six he found himself out of a job, Townsend and his wife knew that their life savings were not going to last long. It was at this juncture, as if by heaven sent (his followers claimed), that he struck upon the idea of a pension plan for the elderly. The Townsend Plan was born.

The growth of the Townsend movement astounded its founders and outside political observers. In San Diego alone, eighty clubs formed with membership reaching 30,000 in a city population of 150,000. The movement spread from California into Idaho, Oregon, Nevada, and Colorado. Within a year, Clements had created a smooth-working organization. By 1936, the

Townsend movement reached the East Coast, able to run political campaigns in many of these states. In upstate New York, for example, Townsend Clubs waged strong political campaigns in thirteen of the state's forty-three congressional districts.[36]

The political power of the movement expressed itself in helping defeat Upton Sinclair, the insurgent Democratic nominee for the California governorship in 1934, when Sinclair refused to endorse the Townsend Plan. Sinclair had EPIC, his own plan to cure the ills of the Depression in California. Sinclair lost the election for many reasons, including a poorly organized campaign, Franklin Roosevelt's refusal to endorse him, and a well-organized and well-financed opposition that eviscerated him. It did not help, though, that Sinclair refused to endorse the Townsend Plan, while his Republican opponent, incumbent governor Frank Merriam, did endorse it.[37] After the election, Merriam backed a relatively meaningless state legislative resolution sent to Congress to act on the plan. Other state legislatures joined in petition of their state congressional delegations to enact the Townsend Plan. Western members of Congress were deluged with thousands of petitions from Townsend supporters calling for the plan to become law. The Roosevelt administration took the steam out of the Townsend campaign when the president proposed a social security program, the Social Security Act of 1935, that provided benefits for the elderly, widows, poor women with children, the unemployed, and injured workers. Townsend's followers denounced Social Security as "chicken feed," "a disgrace to the fathers and mothers of America," and a "starvation subsidy."[38] They continued to press forward with the Townsend Plan.

If Townsend was an unlikely guru to lead a mass grassroots movement, Charles Coughlin appeared even more unusual. In the 1930s, his weekly radio program attracted hundreds of thousands of listeners, Catholics and Protestants, who heard the parish priest's increasingly vitriolic screeds against the New Deal, financiers, and money manipulators.

Born in Hamilton, Ontario, in 1891 and raised in a devout Roman Catholic family, Charles Edward Coughlin grew up an only child. Following graduation from college, Coughlin entered St. Basil's Seminary in Toronto. The Basilian Order taught the beauties of a medieval church opposed to banking and usury. This critique of modern capitalism relied heavily on the social justice teachings of Thomas Aquinas and the papal encyclical *Rerum novarum* (Rights and Duties of Capital and Labor) issued by Pope Leo XIII in 1891. The encyclical condemned capitalist greed, while recognizing the right of labor to form unions and the right to private property.

Coughlin brought this social justice message to a Detroit working-class parish, Royal Oak, where he was assigned in 1926. Offered an opportunity to broadcast a weekly radio program, "Golden Hour," Coughlin seized on it. The opportunity came only four months after he began offering masses at the Shrine of the Little Flower. Within a year, Coughlin's broadcasts had been picked up by other stations across the Midwest. In 1932, after establishing his own independent chain of stations, Coughlin's audience reached from Kansas to Maine.

Radio was a new, exciting industry. NBC, the first national radio network, had only been formed the same year Coughlin appeared on the airwaves. Speaking in a clear and well-modulated voice, Coughlin rose to national fame. His first radio sermons focused largely on Christ's message of mercy for the downtrodden, but with the onset of the Great Depression he became increasingly political. He latched onto monetarization of silver, the old populist cry, as the means to economic recovery. The money question, he claimed, lay at "the bottom of poverty, unemployment, and confiscation."[39] Like the older populists before him, he blamed the economic crisis on international financial interests. This was a first step toward anti-Semitism, a leap he made in the next few years.

Later critics attributed much of Coughlin's success to his natural radio voice and slight Irish brogue.[40] (For example, he pronounced "misery" as "mazzery.") Without doubt, radio made Coughlin into a national figure, drawing millions of listeners. More important, his appeal came from his message. He called for the people to exert "agency" through the ballot box, not the bullet. He denounced "ungodly" communism that placed man, not Christ, at the center of the universe. As he became more hostile to the New Deal, Coughlin grew increasingly anti-Semitic by equating "moneylenders" with Jews. His claim that he was not anti-Semitic was especially hollow. He argued that because Jews had been oppressed historically, they had been driven to moneylending; therefore it was not their fault. Like some early nineteenth-century Populists, the money question led him to virulent anti-Semitism.[41] In 1934, Roosevelt decided to break with Coughlin, even while reassuring the priest that he was a welcome voice in his administration.

In November 1934, Coughlin announced the formation of a national "people's lobby" called the National Union for Social Justice, which eventually claimed a million followers. (In February, Louisiana senator Huey Long had announced his Share Our Wealth organization.) The National Union for Social Justice offered sixteen principles, populist in spirit, vague in policy.

The sixteenth point captured the spirit of the entire program: "Human rights to be held above property rights; government's chief concern should be with the poor; the rich can take care of themselves."[42] Coughlin's message appealed to class resentment.[43]

Coughlin became increasingly convinced he could make or break politicians and legislation. His confidence increased when he mobilized his listeners to defeat pending congressional legislation in 1935 that would have enabled the United States to join the World Court. After receiving tens of thousands of telegrams, the Senate defeated the bill. Coughlin endorsed candidates, such as Herbert Bigelow, running for the Cincinnati City Council, who appeared to win election because of Coughlin's support.[44] Thus when Coughlin joined Townsend and Smith in forming the Union Party to challenge Roosevelt in 1936, Coughlin believed he had become America's kingmaker. From the outset, though, this alliance was fraught with tension as these three men with oversized egos clashed in their quixotic crusade to defeat the devil, Franklin Roosevelt, and his wimpy, as they saw it, New Deal reform program.

While railing against privileged elites and Roosevelt's New Deal, and presenting themselves as the voice of the common people, Townsend and Coughlin offered programs—pensions for the elderly and monetarization of silver—that entailed greater government involvement in the economy. For all their complaints against capitalism, their programs projected, without intention, a new state formation: state capitalism in which government became essential to the market and in which government administrators held more power.

Third-Party Radicalism

By 1935, both Townsend and Coughlin had grown tired of what they considered to be Roosevelt's merry-go-round. They found an ally in the flamboyant populist Huey Long. Long formed his own grassroots movement through Share Our Wealth chapters, mostly based in the South. Long's call for "Share Our Wealth" was demagogic to the core, intended to generate class resentment. The plan proposed that every American family receive a $2,000 to $3,000 annual income, financed by taxing millionaires out of existence. The Townsend, Coughlin, and Long alliance that took shape was little more than a grouping of political discontents who shared populist rhetoric. Long's assassination in late 1935 did not stop Townsend and Coughlin from organizing a third-party challenge to Roosevelt's reelection.

Townsend's break with the New Deal began when Congress rejected his proposals for a pension plan for the elderly. Townsend was convinced of his plan and believed that the strength of his movement would force Congress to enact it.[45] By the end of 1935, Townsend claimed there were 2,000 clubs, although later estimates put it more likely around 1,000 clubs heavily based in California.

Townsend prevailed on Long Beach congressman John S. McGroarty to submit a Townsend bill, which quickly ran into political difficulties on all sides. McGroarty's bill went nowhere in Congress, and when a Townsend amendment to the administration's Social Security bill was offered, it did not make its way out of the House Ways and Means Committee. Townsend responded by mobilizing the estimated two million members of his clubs across the country. By 1936, he began to see himself as a prophet of a mass movement and a kingmaker who could make or break a president. He sought to transform the Townsend Clubs into an organization like Coughlin's National Union for Social Justice. By early 1936 there were an estimated 8,000 Townsend Clubs, more than double that of six months earlier. The Townsend movement was at its peak, but things began to fall apart when Earl Clements tried to take control of the movement.

While dealing with these internal problems, Townsend was called before Congress about his financial dealings. The hearings were called by Representative C. Jasper Bell, a Democrat from Kansas, at the urging of the White House. At the hearings, Bell revealed that Clements had netted $50,000 in stock transactions from the Prosperity Publishing Company. Dissident Townsend members testified that the Townsend movement was little more than a "racket." In May, Townsend was called before the committee. Over the course of two grueling days, he found himself fumbling over the details of his plan.[46] On the third day of hearings, Townsend had had enough. He stormed out of the hearings, refusing to testify further.[47]

If egos could be accurately measured, Father Charles Coughlin's far surpassed Townsend's. This parish priest from an obscure Detroit suburb had attracted a national following, which misled him to think he was as powerful as any member of Congress, cabinet member, or standing president of the United States. The initial enthusiasm that Coughlin had displayed for Roosevelt in 1932 soured into an equally intense hatred by 1935. Much like Townsend, Coughlin believed that Roosevelt had beguiled him into thinking he would have influence in the White House. Roosevelt never fully trusted Coughlin but understood that many Americans listened to him. Coughlin, for his part, began sending the White House notes that he was available to meet with Roosevelt when he was next in Washington. Coughlin's informal, chit-chatty, condescending tone amazed Roosevelt. Although Roosevelt at first strung Coughlin along, he never considered the Detroit radio priest a friend or a natural ally.

Coughlin overestimated his political power, but in 1936 he was not alone in this estimation. Indeed, Republicans believed that Coughlin was a threat to Roosevelt's reelection and tried to coopt him. They failed. Coughlin believed he was a power broker who could make or break candidates. In the 1936 Michigan Democratic primary, he backed his right-hand man and Washington lobbyist, Louis Ward, who challenged standing Democratic U.S. senator James Couzens. Ward surprised political pundits when he lost the primary by only 3,799 votes. (Ward reentered the fall general election as a candidate for Coughlin's Union Party, only to win 50,000 votes out of a total of a million cast.)[48]

Long's assassination should have ended hopes of a successful third-party movement. Nonetheless, Townsend and Coughlin, joined by Gerald L. K. Smith, the self-proclaimed successor to Long, went on to back for president, running under the Union Party, William Lemke. He was a fairly obscure populist Democratic congressman from North Dakota. Lemke's selection was announced by Coughlin without the pretense of a party convention.

Lemke proved to be a particularly dull campaigner, easily caricatured in the press as a hick. Smith undertook his own national tour to add life to the campaign and to enhance his national status.[49] Townsend, for his part, never showed real enthusiasm for the campaign, however. The highlight of the campaign came when Coughlin appeared at a mass rally in Chicago that drew 80,000 people to hear the priest denounce Roosevelt as a fraud.[50] The problem for Coughlin was that most of his listeners actually liked Roosevelt and the New Deal. On Election Day, Lemke won less than 2 percent of the popular vote, a percentage point more than that of Socialist Party candidate Norman Thomas or Communist Party candidate Earl Browder. This paled next to Roosevelt's 61 percent of the popular vote or even Republican Alf Landon's 37 percent.

Backlash

The uneasy alliance between Townsend, Coughlin, and Smith, already cracking in the last days of the campaign, fell apart totally after the election. Townsend denounced Smith as an opportunist, then broke with Coughlin, whom he never liked much anyway. The Townsend movement continued, but the election showed the limits of his power. For Coughlin the election was a disaster. He returned to the air as a diehard isolationist. He began ranting about Wall Street and London financiers leading America to war. He overstepped, however, when he began linking these financiers to an international Jewish cabal. When his protector in the Church, Detroit's bishop Michael Gallagher, died in 1937, the Catholic hierarchy, at the prompting of the Democratic establishment, moved to silence Coughlin. He was instructed that he could no longer make public statements on political matters.[51] His day in the spotlight was over. Gerald L. K. Smith's time at the heights of power was over as well. After the election, Smith turned to the far right, emerging in the 1950s as a spokesperson for anti-communist, anti-Semitic, and white supremacist extremism.

In Minnesota, the Farmer-Labor Party remained strong, but it too was about to peak.[52] In 1936, Elmer Benson won easy election to the governor's mansion to replace Olson, who had died earlier from cancer.[53] Benson was well-known for his leftist sentiments. He campaigned as a moderate, but once in office he veered sharply to the left by aligning himself with the Communist Party faction within Farmer-Labor.[54]

Benson hired Ruth Shaw, the wife of a leading Minnesota Communist, as his secretary. In addition, he appointed Orville Olson, a secret party member, as personnel director to the Minnesota Highway Department. He was joined by another secret party member, John Jacobsen, as assistant personnel director. The Highway Department served as a conduit for patronage jobs and highway contracts.[55] Benson's close relations with the Communist Party elicited attacks from the anti-Communist faction within the party, as well as from the non-Stalinist left. Trotskyists accused Benson and the Stalinists of using Farmer-Labor "strictly for their own ends."[56] There were to be many ironies in this factional warfare. Trotskyists joined anti-Communists within the Farmer-Labor Party in charges that the Popular Front faction members were Stalinist "Communist stooges."[57]

In 1937, Benson and his advisers proposed a comprehensive legislative program that included financing a state-owned cement plant and electric power system. They called for expanded benefits to the aged and unemployed and sharp tax increases on mining companies and incomes. When his program failed to win full legislative support, Benson became increasingly truculent. Known for his blunt, bellicose rhetoric, he threw his support behind a march on the state capitol by telling the marchers that "reactionary legislators" constituted the "most dangerous element in government and society."[58] At the capitol, two hundred demonstrators laid siege to the Senate chamber. They only disbanded the next morning after a personal appeal from Benson. Public reaction to this seizure of the state legislature was severe, and Benson never recovered politically.

Meanwhile, the Minnesota labor movement found itself involved in a factional war involving the Communist Party, the Trotskyists, and the national American Federation of Labor. By 1938, Teamsters Local 544, under the control of Trotskyists, had become the largest union in the state. In 1938, Trotskyists following the directions of their leader, Leon Trotsky—who was to be assassinated shortly afterward—decided to enter the Farmer-Labor Party. Here they confronted a small, although extremely active, Popular Front faction of Communists. International events added to this ideological confusion. Tensions between isolationist neutrality and interventionism fell heavily on elected Farmer-Labor politicians. They were caught in an ideological scissors of demanding an anti-Fascist foreign policy while still supporting anti-interventionist isolationism.

As the 1938 election approached, Benson tried to backtrack from his leftist positions by aligning himself with the Roosevelt administration. He retreated from his previous calls for public ownership of banks and industry. His attempt to throw off his Communist overalls for a two-piece New Deal suit did not fool many.[59] Matters grew worse for Benson when six members of the Minnesota Farmer-Labor Party stepped forward in congressional hearings in Washington to testify against Communist penetration in the state party.[60]

On Election Day, Benson and other Farmer-Labor candidates went down in a devastating defeat. Around the country, a conservative reaction set in as the economy suffered a recession within the Depression. Harold Stassen, the Republican gubernatorial candidate, won close to 60 percent of the vote. Of the five Farmer-Labor incumbents in Congress, only one survived. As Dave Lundeen, the U.S. senator from Minnesota, declared at a contentious meeting of the Hennepin County Farmer-Labor Association, "We lost because they [the voters] were sick of Communists running the show while the old time Farmer-Laborites couldn't even get into Governor's office."[61] The backlash was replicated in other states. Republicans made their first step toward a political comeback by picking up seventy-two seats in the House and making gains in the Senate. As a consequence, Congress swung in a more conservative direction, with influential conservative southern Democrats joining conservative northern Republicans in a coalition that ran Congress for decades.[62]

When the Soviet Union announced in August 1939 that it had entered into a pact with Nazi Germany, the American Communist Party abruptly changed its position from intervention on behalf of the anti-fascist cause to complete nonintervention. In September, Germany invaded Poland from the west while the Soviet Union attacked from the east. World War II in Europe had begun. The Soviet Union's invasion of Finland in November 1939 alienated American Finnish support within the Farmer-Labor Party. Isolationists within the Farmer-Labor Party joined Communists in a popular front opposing American aid to England. In Minneapolis, the Trotskyist-led Teamsters Local 544 opposed U.S. intervention in the war as "a war of imperialist bandit nations" who were fighting for "the right to exploit the peoples and resources of the world."[63] In June 1940, Congress passed with overwhelming support the Alien Registration Act (the Smith Act).

On June 27, 1941, five days after the German invasion of the Soviet Union, the Federal Bureau of Investigation raided the Socialist Workers Party headquarters in downtown Minneapolis. Evidence from this raid provided the basis for a federal grand jury indictment of twenty-nine Local 544 officers on charges of sedition and conspiracy to overthrow the government. The employment of the Smith Act against the Trotskyists drew the support of the international president of the Teamsters Union, Daniel Tobin, who had long opposed the Trotskyist local. (The Communist Party welcomed the prosecution of the Trotskyists under the Smith Act, a position it later regretted.)[64] In a subsequent trial, eighteen defendants, including Local 544 leaders Vincent Dunne, Farrell Dobbs, and Carl Skoglund, were found guilty and sent to prison. The clang of the jail door sounded another toll for grassroots radicalism in Minneapolis.[65]

Following the Nazi invasion of the Soviet Union, the Communist Party in the United States abruptly dumped its isolationist position. Communists called for the United States to join the war against fascism. The popular front against war collapsed overnight. Isolationists such as Benson found themselves increasingly isolated politically.[66] America's entry into the war following the attack on Pearl Harbor on December 7, 1941, put the final nail in the coffin of the isolationist cause. By 1946, Farmer-Labor had been fully absorbed into the Democratic Party in Minnesota as the Democratic Farmer

Labor Party (DFL). Under the leadership of up-and-coming Democratic star Hubert Humphrey, the new party would purge Communists in 1947.[67] Humphrey and others within the Democratic Party carried the banner of New Deal liberalism into the postwar period. In 1948, Humphrey became the first Democrat elected by the voters of Minnesota to the U.S. Senate.

In retrospect, grassroots activism in the 1930s imparted a sense of power in the midst of economic and social despair to millions of people who joined the Townsend, Coughlin, and Long movements, as well as third parties such as the Farmer Labor Party, insurgent campaigns such as Upton Sinclair's End Poverty in California campaign, and social protest causes such as the Unemployment Councils. While not directly affecting legislation, these movements gave impetus to New Deal legislation. As the decade drew to a close, legislation had been enacted that provided welfare to the elderly; benefits to women with children, widows, and the unemployed; and compensation to those injured on the job. Farmers were provided with federal subsidies. Monetary reform had been undertaken, and corporations, including Wall Street, were now regulated.

Both political parties, Democrat and Republican, accommodated to these demands for reform. Neither party called for the overturning of Social Security, the scrapping of farmer subsidies through the Agricultural Adjustment Act, or the disbanding of the Securities and Exchange Commission or the National Labor Relations Board. Conservatives might complain, but there were few who called for revolution to overthrow the empowered federal government.

New Deal liberalism institutionalized the regulatory and welfare state, and Republicans swallowed hard and either accepted it or complained helplessly. Thus, one of the great ironies of Progressive and New Deal reform was that grassroots demands for an emboldened democracy was translated into the language of an administrative state. Demands that the voice of the people should be heard in government—the cry of grassroots activists in the late nineteenth century through the 1930s—had given rise to a more distant government, one in which administrators and bureaucrats stood in for the people or their elected representatives.

Postscript

Francis Townsend died in 1960, a forgotten crusader for the elderly. Following the 1936 election, his movement underwent a slight revival in membership, and during World War II, he continued to campaign for increased benefits for the elderly. But his popularity as a leader of a national movement no longer existed. Charles Coughlin, following orders by the Catholic hierarchy forbidding him from public speaking, retreated into his duties as a parish priest. His congregation remained loyal until his death in 1979. One of those attending Coughlin's weekly services was a young boy, Tom Hayden, who grew up to be a leader of the New Left student movement in the 1960s.

3 | How Grassroots Mobilization Changed Postwar Civil Rights

Grassroots mobilization by African Americans after World War II transformed American politics and society. This struggle to achieve black political equality proved to be the most successful grassroots mobilization in U.S. history. The battle for legal black equality—the ending of segregation in public places and ensuring black voting rights—came through the courts, the legislative process, and the politics of the street. Resistance to racial integration and black voting rights brought violence, including the murder of civil rights activists, beatings, fire bombings of churches and homes, imprisonment, and police and state intimidation.

The black civil rights movement of the 1950s and 1960s is not usually framed in the American populist tradition. Nonetheless, it drew tens of thousands of grassroots and community activists, as well as average Americans, into a struggle to achieve fundamental rights as citizens. Beginning with the Montgomery bus boycott, led by Martin Luther King Jr., in 1955 to 1956, black citizens were mobilized. And although King emerged as the spokesperson during the boycott, most of the day-to-day operations were handled by black women. As the struggle to overcome segregation in the South continued, civil rights activists organized demonstrations, boycotts, and voter registration. In doing so, civil rights protest challenged the established political elites to reform.

As a consequence, the Democratic and Republican parties incorporated strong civil rights positions into their platforms.[1] In addition, both parties sought to incorporate black leaders into party structures and as elected officials. Furthermore, federal, state, and local governments, as well as public institutions and private business, established policies and institutional structures to enforce black civil rights. In this way, civil rights became bureaucratized into the larger administrative state. Bureaucracy creates rationality, as the

German sociologist Max Weber observed a century earlier. Yet bureaucratic rationality necessitates routine, and in this case, black civil rights became a natural part of American administrative life. Yet, in the process of bureaucratic implementation and administrative oversight (however necessary), the history of the struggle for black civil rights became more remote for many people.

The major black civil rights organization, the National Association for the Advancement of Colored People (NAACP), beginning in the 1930s pursued a largely legal strategy to challenge racial segregation, which culminated in *Brown v. Board of Education of Topeka* (1954). NAACP leadership pressured activists to not engage in social protest out of fear of a backlash in the courts, but activists protested nevertheless.[2] In this way, popular mobilization and legal strategy challenged elite political leadership on multiple levels. The end result was that the two political parties responded under pressure by endorsing and absorbing the basic goals of the movement. Concrete policy proposals and black leaders emerged within both political parties. In this regard, the black civil rights movement represents a case of popular mobilization successfully challenging established political elites within both parties and effecting legislative and social change.

Those grassroots activists who engaged in the struggle to achieve the American creed that all men and women are created equal showed courage by putting themselves on the line. Even more courageous were the local residents, clergy, and average folks who enlisted in the struggle for their rights. The struggle was not without internal division, and many local projects failed more often than they succeeded. Confronted by racial violence and massive resistance, many young black and white activists turned in the mid-1960s to more radical agendas and rejected King's call for nonviolent struggle.

In the halls of Congress, the passage of the Civil Rights Act of 1964 and the Voting Rights Act of 1965 provided legal protection for black Americans, as well as other groups faced with discrimination, including women, ethnic minorities, the aged, and religious groups. A broad rights revolution blossomed in America as other groups engaged in grassroots struggles to achieve their rights. The politics of the street set the context for legislative achievement and applied pressure on politicians, Republicans and Democrats alike, to support civil rights legislation. By the end of the 1960s, both political parties had endorsed civil rights in various ways. The northern-based Republican Party endorsed black civil rights earlier than did the southern-based Democratic Party, but under pressure exerted by civil rights activists, both parties stood in favor of black civil rights.

The struggle for civil rights at midcentury had deep roots in modern America. At the turn of the century, such black leaders as Harvard-educated W. E. B. Du Bois joined other activists to form the Niagara movement to protest passage of Jim Crow laws in the South in the 1890s, which disenfranchised black voters and legalized segregation of blacks in public places. In the 1920s and 1930s, activists protested racism in Hollywood, lynching in the South, and mistreatment of black Americans generally. World War II brought further struggle for black civil rights. Threats by A. Philip Randolph, founder and head of the Sleeping Car Porters, to organize a march on Washington demanding the end of discrimination in defense industries led President Franklin Roosevelt to respond by issuing Executive Order 8802 banning employment discrimination in wartime industries. In 1942, white and black civil rights activists involved in the pacifist organization Friendship of Reconciliation, in which A. J. Muste played a leading role, formed the Congress of Racial Equality (CORE). The new organization pledged to use nonviolent resistance to end racial segregation.

The onset of the Cold War raised further questions about the meaning of democracy and racial inequality in a self-proclaimed "free" society.[3] Ending racial segregation became the central goal of the NAACP and CORE. Under pressure from these groups, President Harry S. Truman issued an executive order 9981 ending segregation in the armed services. Though conservative southern Democrats controlled Congress and refused to pass antidiscrimination legislation, they did not roll back Truman's executive order because the military did not fully enforce it.

Meanwhile, the NAACP intensified its campaign to challenge segregation in the courts. Headed by Howard University–educated Thurgood Marshall, the NAACP Legal Defense Fund pursued a vigorous legal strategy by bringing civil rights suits. The NAACP's first victory came in 1938 when the Supreme Court defined "separate but equal" to mean that states had to admit blacks to graduate programs at white colleges if black colleges did not offer the program. Marshall's team won other major victories in *Smith v. Allwright* (1944), which outlawed a Texas law that allowed Democratic Party white-only primaries, and in *Shelley v. Kraemer* (1948), which prohibited racially restrictive housing covenants. In 1946, the Supreme Court banned segregated railroad cars on interstate railroads. The most significant victory came with *Brown v. Board of Education* (1954), ending segregation in public education. After *Brown*, CORE intensified its direct-action strategy to end employment discrimination and public segregation through sit-ins. President Dwight D. Eisenhower and Senator Lyndon B. Johnson, a Democrat from Texas, pushed through the first major piece of civil rights legislation since Civil War Reconstruction, the Civil Rights Act of 1957.

Court decisions and federal legislation ending discrimination looked good on the books, but implementation proved to be another matter. Many white southerners adopted a strategy of massive resistance. In the face of this challenge, on-the-ground activists pushed the campaign forward. Without their commitment, black civil rights in postwar America would not have been achieved, and the political parties would have remained complacent. Neither did the movement remain static. Within a period of about a decade, beginning from the Montgomery bus boycott in 1955 through the formation of the Student Nonviolent Coordinating Committee (SNCC) in 1960 to the rise of black power in the late 1960s, the civil rights movement underwent distinct phases. Martin Luther King's call for nonviolent resistance remained a persistent force within the black civil rights movement, but as younger black activists from the North entered the movement, nonviolent resistance was supplanted by calls for armed self-defense; demands for racial integration were exchanged for black separatism.

Thus, within the ten-year period from the mid-1950s to the mid-1960s, the black civil rights movement shifted in the eyes of the public from a movement of nonviolent protest led by Martin Luther King Jr. to a revolutionary Black Nationalist movement personified by Stokely Carmichael. This perception mischaracterized the importance of both leaders, especially in terms of support within the general white and black populations. King continued to be lionized by the general black population, while Carmichael and Black Nationalism, in general, garnered less widespread support among average blacks. Nonetheless, factional divisions within the activist civil rights movement were seen early. Although King was just a bit older than the new generation of black activists, by 1960 when SNCC was established, he was being criticized as too moderate and representing the older black establishment.

This factionalism can be seen as a generational conflict, divisions having less to do with age than with psychological points of division in which older leadership within a social protest movement is challenged.[4] What began as a movement to appeal to the conscience of society for social transformation within existing structures became a movement for complete social transformation.

Grassroots civil rights activism raises important questions as to the effects of social mobilization for political change. Would civil rights legislation have been enacted without social protest? Do social movements inevitably become revolutionary movements when change does not occur quickly enough for activists? Do social movements organized around an egalitarian ethos of leadership inevitably turn to authoritarian charismatic rule? More than any other figure, Martin Luther King Jr. personified these struggles within racial justice activism in post–World War II America.

Martin Luther King: Prophet

In 1955, Martin Luther King Jr., a twenty-six-year-old Baptist preacher recently arrived in Montgomery, Alabama, to assume his first pulpit after receiving his doctorate in divinity, was hurled into a struggle that would change his life and the nation's. Over the course of the next twelve years, before his assassination in 1968, King played a pivotal role in building a mass movement in the South for racial justice in America. He elicited both praise and abuse in this role. In December 1964, just short of his thirty-sixth birthday, King won the Nobel Peace Prize for his espousal of nonviolence and social justice. Hated by white supremacists and confronted by massive white resistance to racial integration, King experienced arrest, the bombing of his home, continued threats, and ultimately assassination.

As violence against civil rights activists increased and civil rights progress remained painfully slow for those seeking it, King found that his ability to retain support among young civil rights activists began to decline. Black leaders such as Malcolm X, a major spokesman for the black separatist Nation of Islam, captured this resentment against King when he declared that King and his call for nonviolence was little more than "just a twentieth-century Uncle Tom." When King appeared at a church rally in Harlem in June 1963, some of Malcolm X's followers threw eggs when King arrived in the church.[5] Many within SNCC condemned King's Montgomery March in 1965 as a wasteful distraction from the real struggle.[6] Criticism of King by young black activists reflected impatience with social change in racial relations in America and deep anger over abominable violence inflicted on civil rights activists in the South. King, a student of the Bible, experienced what Job observed in the Old Testament: "Upon my right hand rise the youth; they push away my feet, and they raise up against me the ways of their destruction."[7] By the time of

King's murder in April 1968, militant black activists had rejected King as a hero of the civil rights movement.[8] Meanwhile, many white liberals within the Democratic Party, the Johnson wing, also distanced themselves from King because of his opposition to the Vietnam War.

King's powerful eloquence captured the aspirations of African Americans to live as equals in a nation that proclaimed liberty as its foundation. He drew on a prophetic radicalism distinctive in the African American political-religious tradition.[9] In this way, his eloquence resonated with the larger public, necessary for support for a popular social movement. He entered into an environment in which elite opinion was divided on how to proceed with the advance of civil rights.

King's emergence as a national leader came from his ability, a natural talent for oratory within the Baptist tradition, and circumstance. King's destiny was set in Montgomery in 1955; before this, nobody envisioned the young preacher as a national leader and later an American icon. King arrived in Montgomery with a fine family and an educational pedigree.[10] His father, Martin Luther King Sr., headed the Ebenezer Baptist Church in Atlanta, Georgia. King Sr. had assumed his father-in-law's pulpit at Ebenezer in 1932 in the midst of a financial crisis for the church. A local bank had placed a padlock on the church doors for not paying its bills. Earthy, energetic, a natural leader, King Sr. turned around the fortunes of the church by growing the congregation and centralizing finances. Two years after arriving, the church was so prosperous that King asked his membership to send him on a summer-long tour of Europe, Africa, and the Holy Land. While in Germany, King Sr. (born Michael King) announced he was changing his first and middle names to Martin Luther.

Martin Luther King Sr. was strict, opinionated, and determined that his son, Junior, born on January 15, 1929, succeed. The young Martin was sent to the Atlanta University Laboratory, headed by Dr. Benjamin Mays, a prominent theologian and president of Morehouse University, funded by John D. Rockefeller, a northern white Baptist. He entered Morehouse College intent on becoming a doctor but switched to religious studies. His close friends at the all-black college were surprised when King in his second year announced he wanted to be a preacher. King was only eighteen when his father recommended him as assistant pastor of Ebenezer. King's trial sermon, delivered in a deep baritone, persuaded doubters as to his ability as a preacher.

In the late summer of 1948 King entered Crozer Theological Seminary outside of Philadelphia. He was admitted to the previously all-white school as part of the effort by the administration to expand its racial and recruitment bases. Crozer's reputation was theologically liberal. King was introduced to social gospel theology, which emphasized social ethics and the church's role in social change. At Crozer, King became a pacifist. In his last year of study, however, he was introduced to the work of theologian Reinhold Niebuhr's *Moral Man and Immoral Society* (1932). In this short, powerful book, Niebuhr articulated a full-throated criticism of Social Gospel theology and perfectionist social schemes. Niebuhr offered liberals a realist theology that embodied Christian orthodoxy and democracy. King did not understand the full nuances of Niebuhr's theology, but it tempered his social gospel impulse.[11] His study of Mahatma Gandhi's use of nonviolence to force social change affirmed his belief in this approach.

While at Crozer, King decided to pursue a doctoral degree in divinity to the chagrin of his father. King enrolled in theology at Boston University, a center for a theological school of thought called "personalism." Personalism combined a variety of continental philosophical currents, but its importance to King was its assumption that all humans have individual dignity. His study at Crozer and Boston University deepened King's understanding of Christianity's ironic and tragic view of the human condition and human frailty.

As a graduate student, King's reputation as a preacher grew. He received frequent invitations to speak at black churches in the East and the South. In doing so, he enlarged his church networks. His father encouraged him to return to Atlanta to assume his role at Ebenezer and establish his place in the community. In particular, he urged King to find a wife, an important step to social respectability. When young Martin announced to his family that he was marrying Coretta Scott, the daughter of a small cotton farmer in rural Alabama, his father was distraught. Senior thought his son should marry a more socially prominent Atlanta woman. Coretta had relatives, though, who were Baptist ministers, and she had studied music at the New England Conservatory, a white institution. When King Sr. and Coretta met, she showed she could hold her own with her future father-in-law.

King's decision to accept the pulpit at Dexter Baptist Church in Montgomery distressed his young wife, who had moved to Boston to pursue a classical musical career and to escape the South. In accepting the position in Montgomery, King turned down attractive positions in the North and a professorship at a theological school. The events in Montgomery in 1955 propelled King into the national spotlight. What followed over the next year were hardships, imprisonment, and terrorism.

Montgomery Bus Boycott: Civil Rights and Mass Mobilization

In 1955, many civil rights activists held hope that racial justice could come through moral persuasion and nonviolent demonstration. This hope expressed itself in full optimism when blacks organized a massive boycott of city buses in Montgomery, Alabama. The Montgomery bus boycott, which began when a politically involved black seamstress, Rosa Parks, refused to yield her bus seat to a white passenger and was subsequently arrested on December 1, 1955, arousing the black community. Parks, an active member of the NAACP, had just returned from a Highlander Center civil rights workshop led by Ella Baker, a longtime black civil rights activist who called for grassroots organizing.[12] Parks's refusal to relinquish her seat and subsequent arrest presented black clergy members such as Ralph Abernathy and black civil rights activists such as E. D. Nixon, a railroad porter, with the opportunity they were looking for to challenge bus segregation. Hearing of the arrest, Parks's mother phoned local activist E. D. Nixon for help. Initially, Nixon and other activists thought only in terms of a legal challenge, but after discussions a proposal was made to initiate a bus boycott. About fifty black leaders met in the basement of King's church to organize a mass meeting calling for the boycott. The meeting, which lasted through the night, showed divisions within the clergy, as well as concern that Nixon might be chosen to head the boycott. Many thought Nixon crude, ill mannered, reckless, and not a good face for the movement. There was also the practical matter that Nixon's job required him to be out of town much of the time, and many established black preachers in the city neither liked nor trusted one another. Thus when a motion was made to elect Martin Luther King president of what would be called the Montgomery Improvement Association, he won easily. He was too new to town to have created enemies; he was tied to the black elite in Atlanta, held a doctoral degree from a northern university, and had shown himself to be a powerful speaker. He proved exactly the right choice to lead the movement.

At one of the first mass meetings, King exhorted the audience, "Now let us say we are not here advocating violence. We have overcome that. I want it to be known throughout Montgomery and throughout this nation that we are a Christian people." He concluded, "And we are determined here in

Montgomery—to work and fight until justice run down like water, and righteousness like a mighty stream!"[13] He spoke of righteous relatable justice for his people and the nation. He was an idealistic twenty-six-year-old.

The launching of the boycott against the privately owned bus company at first threw little fear into the company or the city's white power structure, even though most bus riders were black. The city council continued to resist any compromise proposed in negotiations by bringing up wording problems for a new policy. Indeed the council's position hardened as negotiations broke down. Even a sharp decline in Christmas purchases downtown did not create much alarm among Montgomery store owners. Few believed that with the limited car ownership in the black community, the boycott could be sustained, even though daily fares had fallen by 30,000. Montgomery police tried to break the boycott by stopping carpool drivers for slight infractions. Any driver who took money for providing a ride was arrested for operating a taxi without a license. In January, King himself was arrested for going thirty in a twenty-five-mile-an-hour zone. Before King's arrest there were signs that the movement was beginning to lose some steam. King's arrest revived it.[14]

King's arrest outraged and mobilized his supporters. Over the next several days, seven overflowing mass meetings were held in King's church to protest the arrest. That the church could be seen from the state capitol steps meant everyone who was politically powerful in Alabama could see what was happening: King was leading a movement. The Montgomery Improvement Association board escalated the campaign by filing a federal suit to end bus segregation. Those around King agreed that it was not safe for him to drive and that he needed bodyguards. His mood swung between fear and inspiration.

Shortly after his arrest, King found himself alone late one evening. He began praying silently. When he was finished, an inner voice told him that he walked with God and to do what he thought was right. This transcendental moment, the first in his life, gave King the courage to continue to step forward as a leader for his people. His moral courage was tested almost immediately. While preaching at Ralph Abernathy's church, King was informed that his house had just been bombed. A month later a bomb exploded in E. D. Nixon's yard. Three days after this bombing, white students rioted at the University of Alabama over the court-ordered admission of the first black student, Autherine Lucy, to the university. The university responded by suspending her for her own "safety." That same month, the segregationist White Citizens' Councils drew tens of thousands of people to the

Montgomery Coliseum, where they heard U.S. senator James Eastland, a Democrat from Mississippi, encourage them not to let the NAACP control their state and urge southern whites to "organize and be militant."[15]

Escalating violence shook the Eisenhower administration. The president requested FBI director J. Edgar Hoover to present a classified briefing about racial violence in the spring of 1956, an election year. Eisenhower was concerned about pushing forward Attorney General Herbert Brownell Jr. and Vice President Richard Nixon's plans to get Congress to pass a civil rights bill, the first such legislation since 1875. Whispers that Eisenhower planned to move forward with the bill led ninety southern Democratic members of Congress and all but three Democratic senators to issue a manifesto declaring opposition to racial integration. Lyndon Johnson dissented from the "Southern Manifesto," arguing that as majority leader he could not be expected to sign a regional proposal. Johnson, who was looking ahead to a presidential run, knew that no one who signed the manifesto would be nominated for president. When Eisenhower's civil rights bill came before Congress in 1957, Johnson played a key role in winning Democratic support by watering down the enforcement section of the original bill, much to Eisenhower's chagrin.[16]

Before the vote on Eisenhower's bill, on June 1, 1956, Alabama state attorney general John Patterson obtained a court order banning most NAACP activities within the state because the organization was supporting and financing an "illegal boycott" in Montgomery. Three days after Patterson's ban, on June 4, a three-panel federal court in a two-to-one ruling struck down the city's segregation ordinances. The year-long boycott had won a surprising victory. King's leadership proved critical to the movement's success by inspiring average people to step forward for the cause of justice. They endured hardship, intimidation, arrest, and violence. King and his fellow ministers, including Ralph Abernathy, appealed to common Americans about the injustice of racial segregation. Their call for racial justice, deeply rooted in a black religious tradition dating back to slavery, also resonated with whites who shared the Christian vision of equality in God's eyes. In 1957, the white evangelist Billy Graham invited King to deliver a prayer during his sixty-eight-night revival held in Madison Square Garden.

After Montgomery, King hoped for racial reconciliation in the South. His dream was quickly shattered when, on Christmas night of 1956, fifteen sticks of dynamite exploded in Fred Shuttlesworth's parsonage in Birmingham, Alabama. A wave of bombings followed.

The Southern Christian Leadership Conference
and the Student Nonviolent Coordinating Committee

King understood that while the courts had ruled against desegregation of Montgomery buses, the battle for black civil and voting rights was far from over. He decided on the advice of Abernathy, Bayard Rustin, and Stanley Levison to form a new organization, the Southern Christian Leadership Conference (SCLC), in 1957. This was not a general membership organization; rather membership was by invitation. Most of the members were southern Baptist preachers strongly drawn to civil rights.[17] The involvement of Rustin, a longtime black socialist activist and pacifist, and Levison, whose communist affiliation was well known, gave rise to accusations that radicals had infiltrated the civil rights movement.[18] King publicly disassociated himself from both Rustin and Levison on a number of occasions, even while relying on them for advice, often over the phone, and for opening doors to northern donors, including left-wing donors. King, though, had become a national figure immune from charges of radicalism. His speaking schedule often involved appearing at four events a week, about two hundred a year.[19]

The SCLC represented a generation of black southern ministers, but in 1960, a new generation of young black activists emerged, inspired by King's nonviolence. In February 1960, four black first-year college students decided on the spur of the moment to sit in at the Woolworth's department store in Greensboro, North Carolina, to desegregate lunch counters.[20] Throughout the South, department stores such as Woolworth's had separate lunch counters for whites and blacks or no counter at all for blacks. The Greensboro protest began on a Monday. By Thursday, hundreds of black students had been drawn into the expanding protest. Although the Greensboro sit-ins were temporarily discontinued to give city leaders a chance to find a solution, the sit-in movement exploded across the South. Radio and television news coverage spread the word. In Chattanooga, Tennessee, a two-day riot involving an estimated thousand whites had to be quelled by the police using fire hoses. As the movement spread, it affected a hundred cities and involved tens of thousands of students. By the end of the election year in 1960, about 70,000 black students were involved in demonstrations across the South.

Seeking to channel student enthusiasm, NAACP activist Ella Baker organized a conference under the auspices of the SCLC to be held at her alma mater, Shaw University, in Raleigh, North Carolina, on Easter weekend of 1960.[21] King and Baker attended the meeting as observers. King hoped that students could be directed to organize a youth chapter of the SCLC. Baker had other ideas in mind and encouraged students to form an independent organization. What emerged was the Student Nonviolent Coordinating Committee. (The organization was abbreviated as SNCC, pronounced "snick.") Most of the members were college students in historically black colleges, but white and black students in the North were also drawn to the movement. If Baker was the organizational genius behind the formation of SNCC, James Lawson, a divinity graduate student, was its inspirational voice early on.[22] During the Korean War, Lawson went to prison rather than serving in the military. Following his parole, he spent three years in India as a missionary, where he studied Mahatma Gandhi's use of nonviolence as a means of political change. His commitment to nonviolence provided the core principle behind early SNCC. He returned to study theology at Oberlin College in Ohio and then became a field organizer for A. J. Muste's pacifist organization, Fellowship of Reconciliation.

After enrolling in the theology program at Vanderbilt University in Nashville, Lawson organized workshops on nonviolent resistance. Nashville had a significant black middle class. Students attending these classes became leaders within SNCC and American politics, including John Lewis (later elected to Congress from Atlanta), Marion Barry (later mayor of Washington, D.C.), Dianne Nash (a formidable SNCC activist), and James Bevel (a key organizer in Birmingham and later Chicago before he became a Reagan Republican). In 1959 these students under Lawson's leadership launched sit-ins to integrate lunch counters in Nashville stores.

Lawson's call for a "nonviolent army" for the "moral" transformation of American society inspired students within SNCC. He spoke of redemptive suffering. He emerged as the star of the Shaw University conference. He declared that the student activist movement was not just against segregation but "against the NAACP's over-reliance on the courts, and against the futile middle-class technique of sending letters to the centers of power."[23] Lawson's attack revealed early fissures within the civil rights movement and criticisms of King, whom SNCC activists began calling "De Lawd" behind his back. Lawson's Nashville students formed the early core of SNCC.

A permanent structure for SNCC, organized around a coordinating committee composed of one representative from each southern state, emerged in late 1960.[24] Local groups were allowed autonomy, and local leaders could speak as SNCC representatives. At its national headquarters, largely run by Ella Baker in Atlanta, SNCC began work with a staff of 16 people who lived on subsistence wages. By 1964, the staff had grown to 150 full-time workers, most of whom were black. James Forman became the executive secretary for an organization whose members shared a "generalized disdain for 'leadership.'"[25] From 1961 through 1964, SNCC launched dozens of community-organizing projects throughout the South to organize the grassroots. Violent white segregationists responded with church bombings, beatings, and murder; civil rights activists made courageous decisions to put their bodies on the line in the struggle for social justice.

Freedom Rides

SNCC activists became, in effect, the shock troops of the civil rights movement, entering areas considered dangerous.[26] In 1961, SNCC joined CORE in a campaign to force racial integration of interstate buses in the South. The Supreme Court had ruled in *Morgan v. Virginia* (1946) and again in *Boynton v. Virginia* (1960) that interstate racial segregation in transportation was unconstitutional. Nevertheless, buses in the South continued to require black passengers to sit in the back and had separate waiting rooms and restrooms. The first ride began on May 4, 1961, when thirteen Freedom Riders (seven blacks and six whites) boarded Greyhound and Trailways buses in Washington, D.C., to ride through southern states to arrive in New Orleans.[27] The riders experienced minor trouble in Virginia and North Carolina and got police escorts across Georgia and South Carolina. As the first bus crossed into Alabama, all hell broke loose. Northern Alabama was run by the Ku Klux Klan (KKK), who prepared for a violent welcome. When the first bus arrived on May 14, Mother's Day, in Anniston, Alabama, a white mob slashed its tires. Several miles outside of town, the crippled bus was under full attack by a mob following in automobiles. When the bus pulled to the side, a firebomb was thrown into the bus as the mob held the bus doors shut to keep the riders inside. They escaped through an emergency exit, only to have the club-wielding mob attack them. Warning shots from a highway patrolman prevented the riders from being lynched.

When the second bus arrived in Birmingham, police were nowhere to be seen, and a white a mob carrying baseball bats, iron pipes, and bicycle chains surrounded the bus. White riders were singled out for especially brutal beatings. James Peck, a pacifist who had served two years in prison as a conscientious objector during World War II, required more than fifty stitches. He never really recovered from the beating, physically or emotionally. Police arrived only after the melee was in full force. Birmingham public safety commissioner Bull Connor later told the press that he had not posted police protection for the riders because it was Mother's Day and he wanted his men to spend time with their families. In Birmingham, civil rights activist Reverend Fred Shuttlesworth organized several cars of black citizens to rescue the injured Freedom Riders. The attacks made national news, but CORE called off the Freedom Ride, fearing that someone was going to get killed.

SNCC activists were ready to die for the cause. Dianne Nash called for the Freedom Rides to continue. She feared that if the terror campaign succeeded, the civil rights movement would be set back years. On May 17, 1961, ten SNCC activist students set out from Nashville to continue the Freedom Ride. Among the ten was John Lewis, who had already been beaten by whites when he entered a whites-only restroom in Rock Hill, South Carolina. They arrived in Birmingham, where they were arrested by Bull Connor and jailed. Released, they set out to resume the ride, but a mob surrounded the depot and prevented the bus from leaving the station. At this point, U.S. attorney general Robert Kennedy intervened. Greyhound was forced to provide a driver to carry the riders from Birmingham to Montgomery. Kennedy was assured by Alabama governor John Patterson, who had won election running on a white supremacist platform (defeating George Wallace), that the bus would be protected from mobs and snipers. Outside the city limits, the state highway patrol abandoned the bus and its riders. At the Montgomery station, a mob awaited them. An assigned Justice Department observer, John Seigenthaler, was beaten unconscious. Local black residents rescued the riders. They were taken to Ralph Abernathy's First Baptist Church. Federal officials watched the events from their offices overlooking the riot. They recognized Seigenthaler but did not dare try to rescue him.

Martin Luther King Jr. arrived to celebrate the riders at a Sunday night rally. More than 1,500 people filled the church, when a white mob gathered outside and threated to storm the church or firebomb it. Kennedy, who had promised to protect the riders, realized that he had been betrayed by Governor Patterson. Threatening to send in federal troops, Kennedy ordered Patterson to act. It was touch-and-go all night long, and the feds put out the false statement that King had left the church. Instead they forced King to leave the pulpit, vanish from sight, and hide in the basement. King was furious. He was less afraid of dying than looking like a coward. He vowed never to retreat that way again. Only the arrival of the Alabama National Guard forced the mob to disperse the next morning.

Freedom Rides continued and were met with a consistent and shocking pattern of violence and arrests. Quakers, college professors, rabbis, priests, ministers, unionists, communists, and students flooded in from throughout the country.[28] Violence against the Freedom Riders became international news and made for easy propaganda by the Soviet Union. Under pressure to protect the Freedom Riders, Robert Kennedy ordered federal protection from violence, but the riders continued to be arrested by local authorities and placed in jails and prisons with abominable conditions and to experience abuse from jail and prison officers. In November 1961, the Interstate Commerce Commission mandated the full integration of all interstate travel facilities.

The Freedom Rides inspired student activists, but it created a backlash from the general public.[29] A Gallup poll in June 1961 reported that 63 percent of Americans disapproved of the Freedom Rides because of the violence that came with them.[30]

Albany, 1961

Paralleling the Freedom Riders, SNCC organizers found themselves in a full-scale, violent struggle in Albany, Georgia, in the first mass protest campaign following Montgomery. Albany was a totally segregated city with a black majority, both a white and a black working class, and an African American college, Albany State.

In late 1961, SNCC field secretaries Charles Sherrod and Cordell Reagon went to Albany to bolster local efforts at community organizing.[31] They sought to build a base among ordinary people in the community through a local umbrella organization that included the NAACP, which had been active in the area for years. SNCC escalated the anti-discrimination campaign by organizing street protests and launching a bus boycott and consumer boycotts. The campaign brought arrests and escalated racial tensions between black activists and recalcitrant white business owners and white city officials. Black college students understood the importance of nonviolence, but Albany's black working class was more militant. Matters became more difficult when high school students unexpectedly joined the protest. They were impulsive and hard to control. The local sheriff, Laurie Pritchett, however, was determined not to be another Bull Connor. Roy Wilkins, head of the NAACP, complained that SNCC was being unnecessarily provocative. In December 1961, a short time after the arrival of SNCC workers, a local leader of the Albany movement, a doctor, invited Martin Luther King Jr. to visit the city to highlight the struggle. SNCC opposed the invitation because they believed it was yet another example of King parachuting in to gain attention for his organization. After being arrested, King accepted bail (secretly paid by the mayor) and encouraged city leaders to negotiate an end to the protests. The NAACP was rattled dealing with both SNCC's activism and King's appearance. Vernon Jordan, a black attorney working for the NAACP, was dispatched to take charge of the situation. When a riot broke out on July 24, National Guard forces were sent to Albany to restore order. By the time King and his SCLC associate Ralph Abernathy were convicted of disturbing the peace, with suspended sentences, the back of the Albany movement had been broken.

The struggle in Albany lasted over a year and half with more than a thousand activists arrested. In the end, few tangible results came out of the struggle in terms of ending segregation. Moreover, tensions increased between SNCC, the SCLC, and the NAACP, indications of growing factionalism within the movement.[32] Albany marked a defeat for SNCC, King, and the NAACP because the goal of integrating the buses had failed. King left Albany depressed. The *New York Times* described Albany as "one of the most stunning defeats" in King's career to that point.[33]

King learned two important lessons about organizing from the Albany experience. First, local leaders needed to have a disciplined movement in order to win. Second, Albany was beyond the range of national television coverage: news showing blacks under violent attack built support for the movement in the North, and the Albany movement did not warrant that kind of coverage.

Birmingham and the March on Washington

In 1963, the SCLC decided to target segregation in Birmingham. For King and the SCLC, Birmingham was an ideal city for confrontation. Locally, Reverend Fred Shuttlesworth had developed an activist base. Violence in the city had already drawn national attention with the bombing of Shuttlesworth's church in 1956 and the beating and branding of his associate pastor, Reverend Charles Billups. The home of a declining steel industry, the city was already famously called "Bombingham." The KKK played a large role in the city and intimidated the white business community as much as it did the black community. Furthermore, the city's white leadership was divided on how to confront segregation. The newly elected mayor Albert Boutwell wanted to avoid violence. Leading the extreme segregationist cause was Police

Commissioner Eugene "Bull" Connor, who presented to the northern public and press a stereotypical image of white southern racism. Connor had ties to the local Klan. Some suspected that he actually ran it.

The purpose of King's assault on Birmingham was to force the Kennedy administration to move forward with civil rights legislation through a national, media-oriented campaign.[34] The movement gained national attention, and for sixty-five consecutive weeks there were nightly mass meetings. Protesters began to fill the jails after being arrested for "disturbing the peace." On Palm Sunday, 1963, King called for a mass march. Bull Connor responded, as King hoped, by unleashing police on the protesters. Photos of police with snarling dogs attacking peaceful protesters appeared in newspapers and network news.

Demands for federal intervention increased when King was arrested and jailed for disobeying a court injunction against marching. He later released his "Letter from a Birmingham Jail," in which he defended nonviolence. Further mobilization came when the SCLC called on high school students to join the protest, a campaign that became known as the Children's Crusade. By early May more than six hundred students had been arrested. The movement culminated in a mass march in downtown Birmingham. Connor responded accordingly by ordering the use of fire hoses and K-9 units to disperse the marchers. Finally, on Sunday evening, May 12, President John F. Kennedy announced that army units were ready to be deployed if further violence continued. Although an agreement was reached, the Birmingham Accord, which brought down "for white only signs," was not fully enforced. In this regard, the local campaign had mixed success. King's s goal, though, was national civil rights legislation.[35]

King's strategy worked. Following the Birmingham protests, President Kennedy decided to submit new civil rights legislation to Congress. Civil rights leaders called for a march on Washington to pressure the administration to act. In late June 1963, Kennedy met personally with thirty civil rights leaders, including the new SNCC chair, John Lewis. (Later, Lewis's meeting with Kennedy would be used against him by militants within SNCC.) At the meeting, Kennedy tried to persuade the leaders not to undertake a march. Philip Randolph, a longtime civil rights activist who had been involved in the movement since the 1930s, explained to him that blacks were already in the streets, and it would be better for everyone if they were led by organizations "dedicated to civil rights" rather than other leaders who cared neither about civil rights nor about nonviolence.[36] Kennedy agreed to cooperate.

To plan the march, civil rights leaders from the major civil rights organizations, including SNCC, formed a coordinating committee.[37] From the outset SNCC proved to be the *enfant terrible* within the committee. In meetings, SNCC representatives called for demonstrations at the Justice Department. This proposal was defeated by the committee. Further problems arose when Lewis, representing SNCC, released the text of his speech to the press the day before the march. The speech criticized directly the Kennedy administration, saying that it provided insufficient support to protect blacks from police brutality and that the administration's civil rights bill was "too little and too late." He charged, furthermore, that the indictment of SNCC activists in Albany was "part of a conspiracy on the part of the federal government and local politicians in the interest of expediency." Moreover, the speech declared that "the revolution is at hand" and was not going to wait for the federal government to act before "we will take matters into our own hands and create a source of power, outside of any national structure."[38]

Appeals to Lewis to temper his language were being made right up to the time of his speech. After reading the speech, the Catholic archbishop of Washington declared that he would not appear on the same stage with Lewis unless changes were made. Bayard Rustin, representing King, tried to negotiate a compromise. On the day of the speech, Rustin, Randolph, King, and Abernathy met in a room inside the Lincoln Memorial with SNCC leaders Lewis, James Forman, and Donald Cox. Randolph begged Lewis, "John, for the sake of unity, we've come this far. For the sake of unity, change it."[39] Lewis relented only at the last moment, deleting the word *revolution* and direct criticism of Kennedy from the speech. Nonetheless, the more radical version of the speech had been circulated in printed copies. In the speech he declared that American politics is dominated by "politicians who . . . ally themselves with open forms of political, economic, and social exploitation." Lewis's speech captured the sense of urgency within SNCC by speaking to the activists who rejected gradual change. King's speech, which followed, spoke to the conscience of the larger nation.

The March on Washington on August 28, 1963, drew an estimated 200,000 to 300,000 people. It was truly a mass gathering. About half the marchers were black. Northern Protestant and Catholic clergy, along with labor unions, bused in northerners. Southern black activists were joined by local residents. For those watching on their television sets, and for generations that followed, the highlight of the march was Martin Luther King's speech "I Have a Dream." King had begun using these words before the march, but on this day of mass demonstration—and the events that followed—his speech resonated with the deepest ideals of justice, fairness, and hope for all children to be equal. Kennedy's civil rights bill, however, remained stuck in Congress, and three months after King's speech, the president was assassinated.

Mississippi Freedom Summer, 1964

King's speech emerged as one of the immortal addresses in American history, subsequently becoming required reading in classes across the country. In 1963, however, racial segregation remained in place across the South, and federal legislation was stalled. The question confronting the civil rights movement was "What's next?" SNCC called for continued "direct action" in local communities. Others within the movement saw voter registration as the necessary step to overturning the system. (Kennedy's successor, Lyndon Baines Johnson agreed with the latter.) One of the problems faced by civil rights activists, especially within SNCC, was that voter registration looked like a means of channeling black protest into the established party system, thus defusing militant activism. SNCC director John Lewis warned that voter registration was "a trick to take steam out of the movement, to slow it down."[40] No doubt, liberals did want to channel SNCC activism into the Democratic Party.

Divisions within SNCC over whether to commit fully to voter registration had come to a head at an August meeting at the Highlander Folk School in Tennessee in August 1961. Passions ran high on both sides. Principle was at stake. Hours were consumed in debate, with both sides becoming increasingly intransigent. SNCC looked like it was on the verge of breaking apart when Ella Baker intervened to save the situation by raising a simple question: why not do both—voter registration and direct action? The decision to undertake both saved SNCC from collapse.[41] In the end, divisions between "direct action" and "voter registration" proved moot in the violence that followed in Mississippi.

Bob Moses, who had been working on civil rights in Mississippi for years, was assigned the task of heading up voter registration in the state. Moses, who had earned a master's degree in philosophy from Harvard University, was assigned by Baker to Mississippi soon after he joined SNCC. Under Moses's leadership, SNCC established nearly two dozen local projects in the ensuing years. In these projects, SNCC undertook to develop and build upon the efforts and knowledge of local community leaders. Most often these efforts in building local leadership failed, often because local activists were deterred by intimidation and violence they experienced from white racists. There were notable exceptions, however, as seen in Fannie Lou Hamer, who emerged as a leader in the drive to register black Mississippi voters in 1962. Hamer came from an impoverished family of sharecroppers. Deeply religious and simply tired of the injustices she experienced, she volunteered to help in the voter registration drive. After leading a group of blacks to register at the local courthouse, she was fired from her job that she had held for eighteen years, harassed, and shot at by local whites. She began working full time for SNCC. Hamer would become a leader in challenging the all-white Democratic Party hold in the state.

From the outset, Moses, SNCC organizers, and locals experienced baptism by fire. White resistance came from the White Knights of the KKK, United Klans of America, and Americans for the Preservation of the White Race. Estimates placed the White Knights at 100,000 members and Americans for the Preservation of the White Race at 30,000 members.[42] On a single night in May, the United Klans burned crosses in sixty-four of the eighty-two state counties as part of a recruiting drive. SNCC reported that between June 15 and September 15, black citizens and SNCC activists experienced more than a thousand arrests, eighty beatings, thirty-five shootings, thirty-five church burnings, and thirty bombings.[43] In 1961, a white state legislator killed a fifty-six-year-old married black farmer, Herbert Lee, who had registered to vote in Liberty, Mississippi. Even though the murder was witnessed by a dozen people, the all-white jury found the defendant E. H. Hurst innocent on grounds of self-defense. One of the witnesses who testified against the defendant was later murdered. Moses and fellow SNCC activists demanded federal protection, but the Kennedy administration refused to intervene on the grounds that it did not have jurisdiction.[44]

Before the official start of the summer voter registration program, local blacks had attempted to participate in 1,884 precinct meetings in the state, only to be excluded from most, with the exception of meetings in large cities, such as Greenville and Jackson.[45] By the end of 1963, however, only about 5 percent of the black voting-age population was registered to vote.[46] Clearly something more was needed. Moses sought to have SNCC give its highest priority to voter registration. Working with northern liberals such as Allard Lowenstein, Moses launched Mississippi Freedom Summer in 1964. More than 700 northern students, almost all white, descended on Mississippi. On June 21, as the project was being launched, three volunteers-- James Chaney, a local black Mississippian, and two white Jewish volunteers,

Andrew Goodman and Michael Schwerner--were reported missing on a trip to investigate a church bombing in Philadelphia, Mississippi. Six weeks later their decomposed bodies were found buried. An informant later reported that the three men had been stopped and jailed for a traffic violation. Shortly after their release from jail, they were pulled over by a patrol car that was followed by two cars filled with KKK members. The activists were beaten with chains, then murdered. Chaney had been castrated. The murders not only drew national press attention but also sent fear through the volunteers in Mississippi that summer. In the end, the project had mixed results. More than 80,000 blacks were registered but to little overall effect on Mississippi politics. Mississippi remained a one-party state—lily-white Democratic.

Mississippi Freedom Democratic Party and the Liberal Crack-Up

These efforts had no effect in opening up the all-white Mississippi Democratic Party. Blacks continued to be excluded from party precinct meetings, often through intimidation, economic threat, and procedural tricks. After four years of voter organizing, beatings, arrests, and murder, Moses concluded that the linchpin to breaking the segregationist hold on southern politics was to form a new party as a direct challenge to the white establishment. In August 1964, the Mississippi Freedom Democratic Party (MFDP) was announced. Freedom Summer volunteers began canvassing communities to elect their own delegates to the Democratic National Convention in Atlantic City in August. A full-scale effort was undertaken to ensure that MFDP delegates would be heard. Joseph Raul, a United Auto Workers union attorney and a member of the Americans for Democratic Action, volunteered to represent the MFDP at the convention. SNCC veterans Ella Baker and Marion Barry organized northern support for the challenge.[47] Meanwhile, SNCC compiled a list of violent incidents just from June 16 through mid-July that included sixteen bombings in churches and elsewhere.[48]

In the beginning, most white liberals in the Democratic Party supported the cause. In July, just before the convention, Lyndon Johnson had signed the Civil Rights Act of 1964. Johnson believed he had advanced the cause of black civil rights, but he feared further alienating the powerful southern wing of his party if he appeared to capitulate to the MFDP. At the preconvention credentials committee hearings, Fannie Lou Hamer, who had been chosen to head the delegation, made an impassioned televised speech pleading for

MFDP recognition. It did little good. Johnson was so alarmed by her appearance that he held an emergency press conference to push her off the air.

Johnson sought a compromise by assigning liberal Minnesota senator Hubert Humphrey to offer the MFDP delegation two nonvoting delegate seats. Martin Luther King Jr., Joseph Raul, and Allard Lowenstein urged the delegation to accept the compromise. Hamer spoke for the entire delegation, though, when she declared that "we did not come all this way for no two seats."[49] Moses, MFDP delegates, and SNCC activists saw the convention as a confirmation that white liberals in the Democratic Party could not be fully trusted. For them, the passage of the Civil Rights Act had come too late. In Alabama, it launched the Lowndes County Freedom Organization, taking as its symbol a black panther. After the summer of 1964, militancy within SNCC increased rapidly.[50]

Selma and Bloody Sunday

While the growing radical wing of the civil rights movement had come to see liberals as the enemy, Martin Luther King Jr. and others believed in 1965 that the next step in the struggle should be the passage of a voting rights law that would provide direct federal oversight in state elections. To get the Civil Rights Act passed in 1964, Johnson had been forced to appease southern Democrats by dropping voting rights from the bill. The more liberal Congress elected in 1964 gave Johnson a chance to pass the new bill. King sought to put political pressure on the Johnson administration to press forward on federal rights voting legislation. King found a perfect opportunity to do so in Selma, Alabama, in March 1965.

King's announcement of a major voting rights campaign in Selma drew a mixed response among SNCC activists. King had become increasingly militant in his use of nonviolent resistance as an instrument designed to draw northern attention to the violence experienced by southern blacks in their demands for basic constitutional rights. King remained committed to nonviolent resistance. He understood, however, that violence perpetuated by racists drew national attention to the cause. In this strategy, King sought to rally northern public opinion to pressure congressional action by their representatives.[51]

With the exception of Mississippi, the state of Alabama had the lowest proportion of blacks on the voter registration rolls.[52] Furthermore, Alabama, having elected George Wallace in 1963 on a segregationist platform, presented the image of a stereotypical Deep South state. Amid King's Birmingham campaign, four black girls in 1963 had been killed while attending Sunday school at a Birmingham church. In Selma, located in a black-majority county, city leadership was divided between white moderates and extremist segregationists. The newly elected mayor Joseph Smitherton hoped to attract northern business to create jobs, and he had appointed Wilson Baker to head the small city police force. Both men understood that the best way of defusing the movement was to deny them the publicity that came from mass arrests. Selma, however, was surrounded by Dallas County, run by Sheriff Jim Clark, a hard-line segregationist. The Selma mayor and police chief had little influence on the sheriff, whose vision of law and order was rooted in brute force. Following the shooting of Jimmie Lee Jackson on February 26, 1965, during a peaceful march in nearby Marion, SCLC director James Bevel called for a mass march from Selma to the state capital of Montgomery, covering seventy-five miles.

On Sunday, March 7, marchers who walked outside the Selma city limits into the county confronted a line of state troopers and the county posse, recently deputized by Jim Clark. Television cameras rolled, and one network even broke into a National Football League game to show what was happening. The posse stopped the demonstrators as they tried to cross the Edmund Pettus Bridge. Marchers were ordered to disperse, but before anyone had a chance to retreat across the bridge, state police using mounted troopers waded into the marchers using nightsticks and tear gas. National news captured the mayhem on camera. ABC News interrupted its Sunday night movie, *Judgment at Nuremberg*, to report on what became known as Bloody Sunday. President Johnson went on television to denounce the deplorable brutality inflicted on the black marchers. With northern public opinion inflamed by the attack, King led a second march to the Edmund Pettus Bridge. This time, thousands of white northern liberals, including nuns in habits, joined the march. At the front of the march, King's followers chanted "Freedom Now," but further back, militants from SNCC began to shout "Black Power." This time they were afforded federal protection. By pre-agreement, King at the bridge kneeled and prayed. The rest of the dangerous march to Montgomery continued without violence. The day ended with all seemingly having gone well, but that evening three white ministers who had participated in the march were brutally beaten by a small group of KKK thugs. One of the ministers later died from the beating.

On March 15, Johnson under public pressure convened a joint session of Congress to push voting rights legislation. Overwhelmingly passed by the

Senate and the House, the Voting Rights Act of 1965 was signed into law by President Johnson on August 6, with Martin Luther King and other civil rights leaders in attendance. In 1963 only 6 percent of black voters in the nine southern states were registered. By 1969, 59 percent of blacks were registered. The enactment of the Voting Rights Act in 1965 should be seen as a direct result of a social protest movement.[53] The mass movement embodied in the Selma march had translated to legislative reform.

Although the Voting Rights Act of 1965 proved to be a major turning point in securing legal protections for black voting rights, SNCC activists openly criticized King's tactics.[54] They disdained King's refusal to continue the march on to Montgomery. Many within SNCC believed appeals to northern conscience were useless. Surveys at the time showed, however, that racial attitudes in the North and the South were changing. Northern and southern support for abolition of the poll tax, anti-lynching legislation, and equal opportunity drew majority support.[55] Furthermore, in the immediate aftermath of *Brown v. Board of Education,* as many as four out of ten southern whites supported the decision. Editorials in liberal daily newspapers and religious bulletins across the South called for judicious implementation of the law and the need to protect minority rights. The *Miami Herald* declared on May 18, 1954, that desegregation should be "sanely, judiciously and humanely carried out," while the Nashville *Tennessean* stated on the same day, "The South is and has been for years a land of change. Its people—of both races—have learned to live with change. They can learn to live with this one. Given reasonable amount of time and understanding they will." Similar sentiments were echoed by Harry S. Ashmore, executive editor of the *Arkansas Gazette*, who wrote, "This is a great time of testing, a time when democracy has to protect the right of a minority. I think in the end our free institution will meet the test and be strengthened by it. . . . Integration will come—more slowly in some areas than others—but it will come."[56]

At the same time, however, surveys showed that both in the North and the South, there was a decided shift in public opinion from 1961 to 1963 that the struggle for racial integration, civil rights, and housing equality was moving too quickly. Civil rights had emerged by 1963 as a major concern for voters. Most Americans believed (85 percent in 1963) that blacks should have "as good a chance as white people to get any kind of job"; 79 percent opposed separate sections for blacks on streetcars and buses; and 77 percent had no objection to sending their children to schools with blacks. Nonetheless, in a poll taken in May 1962, Gallup showed that 32 percent of national opinion believed racial integration was proceeding "too fast," with 59 percent of southern whites concurring. By November 1963, 46 percent nationally and 73 percent of southern whites thought things were moving too quickly.[57]

This shift in public opinion, along with the continued fierce violence and white resistance in the South to civil rights activists, reinforced attitudes among young black militants that the answer lay in empowering black communities. While white liberals praised the Civil Rights Act of 1964 and the Voting Rights Act of 1965 as pinnacles of achievement, many black activists had become disillusioned about meaningful advancement in white America.

From Nonviolent Resistance to Armed Revolution

For many black activists, these legislative advances did not tackle systemic social inequality and racial oppression. White violence in the South led many activists to conclude that nonviolence only invited further violence without retribution. Blacks needed to arm themselves as a matter of self-defense. This sentiment was evident in the formation of the Black Panther Party in Lowndes County, Alabama, in 1965. The stated purpose of the party was armed self-defense. Robert F. Williams, a local NAACP organizer in Monroe, North Carolina, personified the call for armed self-defense. Williams always claimed he was not opposed to nonviolence as a technique, but he believed blacks needed to be armed to protect themselves from white KKK violence. His part of North Carolina had a long history of white on black violence. He warned that paramilitary extremist groups such as the Minutemen were being "armed and prepared for pogroms."[58] In a violent atmosphere Williams's rhetoric resonated among a growing number of militant blacks.

During World War II, Williams served briefly in the Marines before he returned home to Monroe, North Carolina. He became involved in the NAACP, often confronting its national leadership over its moderation. In 1959, he launched the *Crusade Weekly Newsletter* to counter the NAACP's moderation by calling for blacks to arm themselves against white supremacist violence. He became a frequent speaker at Malcolm X's Muslim temple located on 116th Street in Harlem. At the same time, Williams developed close ties with the Trotskyist Socialist Workers Party. He entered into public debates with pacifists, such as A. J. Muste and Bayard Rustin, over nonviolence as a political strategy. He openly courted northern money to buy rifles for the Monroe NAACP through his National Rifle Association chapter called the Black Guard.

In 1961, violence in Monroe and surrounding towns reached a fever pitch when white vigilantes attacked local blacks. White mobs raged through downtown Monroe, unable to be subdued by highway patrolmen and police. In response Williams ordered barricades to be built protecting the black portion of the city. Two machine guns were unfurled to show that blacks meant business. Amid this frantic scene a white couple drove into the black section of Monroe. They were surrounded by a black mob who were screaming to kill them. Shots were being exchanged with "night-riding" whites in cars. In this chaotic environment, the terrified couple entered Williams's home. State troopers surrounded the house with machine guns, even as roving bands of whites persisted in their attacks. In the chaos, Williams and his family somehow escaped, only to be charged with kidnapping. Williams fled to Long Island, then Canada, and eventually to Cuba. In Cuba he launched in 1962, with the Cuban government's support, a radio program, "Radio Free Dixie," which was beamed into the South. For some black activists, Williams emerged as a hero.[59] William's paramilitary organizational model and armed resistance was adopted by local black activists in Mississippi and Louisiana in the following years.[60]

By 1965, support for armed self-defense and black power had penetrated SNCC itself. Many within the movement concluded, as did Assata Shakur, a later Black Panther and member of the revolutionary Black Liberation Army, that "I still could not get used to the idea of letting somebody spit on me."[61] Underlying tensions within SNCC involved both nonviolent resistance as strategy and the role of whites within the organization. Some SNCC activists, especially those engaged in the struggle before Mississippi Freedom Summer, found many whites who came South that summer unnecessarily condescending and projecting a sense of "the anointed" sent to save blacks. In local meetings, whites raised questions about reform versus revolution, which left rural southern blacks confused. Black activists who had been working years in the South resented what they saw as do-gooder white students offering support, direction, or compassion before they returned to the comforts of the North and their affluent families and schools. Tensions were further exacerbated by white female students dating black men, which created anger among black women within the movement.[62]

In May 1966, SNCC field officers convened in Kingston, Tennessee, to discuss the future direction of their organization and to elect new officers. By 1964, SNCC had about a hundred paid staff, including about twenty whites. They shared a sense of community.[63] Local chapters often relied on charismatic leaders operating generally independently from the national office.

SNCC elections had been uncontroversial in the past, and few expected trouble. But matters were not made better when Bob Moses, a quiet, pensive, and natural leader, announced he was leaving SNCC and was changing his surname. He believed that his position in the organization had become too strong and too central. Throughout the week, discussions kept coming back to interracial democracy. Lewis, who had served as SNCC chair, spoke passionately for a strategy of nonviolence and keeping whites as members. As Lewis recalled, the discussion got "very low and nasty, very bitter and mean." Lewis was attacked for spending too much time speaking on campuses, for his involvement in the Washington march, for his allegiance to Martin Luther King, and for his religious orientation. In the first vote, Lewis defeated Stokely Carmichael, but when the vote was challenged, discussion continued into the wee hours of the morning. The meeting turned, as Lewis later said, into more of a mob than a discussion. In this heated atmosphere, Carmichael defeated Lewis for the chairmanship. James Forman, never a friend of Lewis's, was also forced out. Shocked, Lewis said that as much as he "tried not to feel it, this was a serious blow, a personal thing, and it affected me very much. My life, my identity, most of my existence, was tied up in SNCC. Now, so suddenly, I felt put out to pasture."[64] Lewis was twenty-five years old, tossed away by the movement he had helped build. Only a week before, he and King had celebrated the passage of the Voting Rights Act.

After his election as chairman of SNCC, Carmichael began espousing black nationalism.[65] He expressed the sentiment among some activists, especially in SNCC's Atlanta Project, that all links with whites be broken.[66] As one staff member of the Atlanta Project declared, "All white people are racists; that is, no white person (when you really get down to the nitty-gritty) can stand to deal with black people as human, as men, as equals, not to mention superiors."[67] The turn to black power within SNCC severed all remaining links with the white liberal left. Northern funding for SNCC dried up as foundations and white liberals withdrew their support. No better symbol of SNCC's turn from nonviolence came in April 1968 in New York at a dinner to honor the founding force of SNCC, Ella Baker. Only a few weeks before the dinner, the assassination of Martin Luther King Jr. had ignited riots across the country. The dinner was to honor Baker, raise funds for SNCC, and express a kind of unity. Carmichael was urged to offer a conciliatory speech. Instead, he entered the banquet hall flanked by bodyguards and an entourage of militant young blacks. In his speech he called for black power and black revolution.[68]

Stokely Carmichael and other black nationalists became associated with urban uprisings. Carmichael reinforced this perception when shortly after an incident in Cleveland, he told a crowd, "When you talk about black power, you talk about bringing the country to its knees. When you talk about black power, you talk of building a movement that will smash everything Western civilization has created."[69] In late 1966, Carmichael was arrested for his involvement in violent protests against police brutality in the black section of Summerhill in Atlanta. Julian Bond, recently elected as one of the first African Americans to be sent to the Georgia legislature in the twentieth century, publicly resigned from the organization he had helped found. Marion Barry, another SNCC activist who had moved to Washington, D.C., resigned his post as an independent organizer for the organization. SNCC had become too much of a liability for an aspiring politician.

As SNCC began to fall apart under attack from congressional investigators and the news media, SNCC leaders tried to partner with the newly formed, California-based Black Panther Party for Self-Defense. The founders of the Black Panther Party, Huey Newton and Bobby Seale, claimed to have been inspired by SNCC. Newton, who had been imprisoned in 1967 on charges of murdering an Oakland police officer, left negotiations for merging the two organizations to Eldridge Cleaver, who had become a major spokesperson for the party. Cleaver expressed admiration for Carmichael, who began appearing at Panther "Free Huey" rallies. Behind the promotion of Carmichael, however, there was not much to merge. SNCC was never more than a coordinating committee for grassroots action, and by 1967, it had fallen apart. Furthermore, the Panthers were experiencing their own troubles with police shootouts, federal investigations, and rivalry with other militant groups. In Southern California, violence erupted between Panthers and a Southern California–based nationalist group called US (that is, United Slaves) organized by Ron Karenga. In 1969, SNCC's total collapse came when the organization's leader, H. Rap Brown, who famously said violence was as American as cherry pie, was arrested on charges of having provoked a riot in Maryland. The day before the trial, two SNCC activists were killed in a car explosion when a bomb they were carrying went off prematurely.

Radicals Go Awry

The rise of the black power movement coincided with growing student protest across college campuses. From January to June 1968, demonstrations occurred at 101 colleges and universities involving over 38,000 students. Of these 221 demonstrations, 97 involved black power. Forty-five were related to the Vietnam War or anti-military protests.[70] The Vietnam War and militant civil rights protests gave impetus to left-wing radicalism in this period. In this ideological shift, older civil rights leaders were dismissed as having served their time. For example, Fred Shuttlesworth, who had put his life on the line in Birmingham and continued the struggle for black rights when he moved to Cincinnati, found young black militants telling him, "You go along home and pray, Reverend, and let us take care of it now."[71]

For young urban black radicals, Huey Newton, the founder of the Black Panther Party, became the symbol of revolutionary struggle for black liberation in racist America.[72] Newton and his friend Seale had formed the Black Panther Party for Self-Defense in 1966 in Oakland, California, with a core membership of fewer than a dozen members. By the fall of 1970, the Panthers had established chapters in thirty-five cities in nineteen states and the District of Columbia.[73] The majority of the leadership was between the ages of twenty-six and thirty-four, while those aged sixteen- to twenty-one years old composed the majority of the rank and file. The Panthers imparted to those young blacks, male and female, a sense of purpose. The Panther uniform, training for guerrilla combat and community self-defense, Maoist indoctrination, and assigned duties with rank gave young blacks a purpose beyond the street. The Panthers manifested violence. This infatuation with violence was captured at a play presented before a "Free Huey" rally held at the Fillmore Auditorium in San Francisco in 1967. At the rally, a black drama group from San Francisco State University, including a young actor who would later become famous, Danny Glover, performed a one-act play about two guerrilla fighters pinned down by police in an unnamed America city, heroically dying in the struggle for black liberation.[74]

Huey Newton and the Black Panther Party saw themselves as heirs to Malcolm X, who, following his murder in 1965, became nearly a mystical figure for many young black revolutionaries. As Black Panther leader Eldridge Cleaver declared in 1968, "Huey P. Newton, one of the millions of black people who listened to Malcolm, lifted the golden lid off the pot and blindly, trusting Malcolm, stuck his hand inside and grasped the tool. When he withdrew his hand and looked to see what he held, he saw the gun. . . . Huey P. Newton picked up the gun and pulled the trigger."[75]

Black Panther ideology and strategy garnered little support among the larger black population, but Newton and the Panthers attracted wide media attention and drew passionate young black militants to the party. Newton and Seale instinctively understood the appeal of Panther Party discipline. Unlike SNCC, the Panthers were centrally organized with a command structure. Those who dissented underwent self-criticism, were beaten, or were expelled. Later some were murdered. In a calculated media campaign, Eldridge Cleaver, the appointed minister of information, made the Panthers into front-page and evening television news. The Black Panther Party gained celebrity status on the radical left. Hollywood actors Marlon Brando and Ossie Davis and authors Norman Mailer, Susan Sontag, and Oscar Lewis proclaimed their support for the Panthers.

As Panther chapters appeared in American cities, chapters also emerged in Europe, Australia, and Hong Kong. The rapid growth of the party created organizational problems for the leadership, but as the party grew and funds flowed into headquarters through newspaper sales, contributions, and criminal activities, corruption developed. Party leaders were given houses and cars. As the FBI and local police launched investigations, undertook disinformation campaigns, and infiltrated the party with informants, paranoia seeped into party leadership. Beginning in 1969, party dissenters or critics of party leaders were denounced as informants and treated, to use party language, as "jackanapes."[76] For all of the publicity generated by the Panthers, membership never reached more than 2,000 people.

In 1967 Huey Newton was arrested following a shootout during a police stop in Oakland, leaving one officer dead and Newton severely wounded in the early hours of October 28. After his conviction for voluntary manslaughter in September 1968, party leadership fell to Bobby Seale. For the next two years, until the Alameda County Superior Court finally dismissed the charges following a court order for a new trial, Newton tried to direct the party from his prison cell. His word remained law. Day-to-day decisions were being made by Seale, who was quick to expel members who threatened his leadership.

Meanwhile, Eldridge Cleaver expanded his own influence in the party. Cleaver turned to supporting the Peace and Freedom Party, formed in 1966 by radical antiwar and civil rights activists. Communist Party intellectual Herbert Aptheker ran for a congressional district in New York under the party's banner, while two other candidates were placed on the Washington state ballot. Combined, they received about 50,000 votes. The party received new life when voter registration drives among young whites and African Americans led to ballot status in California and thirteen other states the following year. The plan was to put Martin Luther King Jr. on the ballot for president, but King proved difficult to recruit and was then assassinated in April 1968. At a national convention, Cleaver received the presidential nomination, and Kennedy assassination conspiracy theorist Mark Lane got the vice-presidential nod. However, because of Cleaver's felony conviction and the fact that he was not eligible to run for president owing to his young age, the party placed various names for presidents and vice presidents on different state ballots. The party was an odd amalgamation of revolutionaries, far-leftists, and a smattering of libertarians, such as the economist-historian Murray Rothbard, who called for victory for North Vietnam. The party attracted its share of other oddballs. In the Bay Area, Robert Avakian, son of a local judge and later founder of the Revolutionary Communist Party, became the Peace and Freedom Party's chief spokesperson. After much campaigning and intense media coverage, the Peace and Freedom Party received nationally a little more than 100,000 total votes in November 1968.

Seeing the riots that followed King's assassination in April 1968, Cleaver concluded that the revolution was now at hand. Panthers, he insisted, must set a revolutionary direction for the masses. On April 6, he and fourteen other Panthers ambushed two Oakland police officers. The shootout left two officers wounded, Cleaver shot in the leg, and one Panther, seventeen-year-old "Lil Bob" Hutton, dead. On September 27, Cleaver's parole was revoked. The judge gave him a sixty-day stay before he had to turn himself in. Less than a month later Cleaver and his wife, Kathleen, who had emerged as a major force in the party in her own right, fled the country, first to Cuba and then to Algeria.

Newton, who had grown increasingly hostile to Cleaver, was outraged by this ambush. He denounced Cleaver as an ultra-leftist. While in prison, Newton concluded that Black Panther violence and its reputation for armed violence had alienated the party from the community. From the fall of 1967 through 1969, nine police officers had been killed and another fifty-six wounded in shootouts with the Panthers. Ten Panthers were killed in these confrontations. In 1969, close to 350 Panthers had been arrested in Panther–police confrontations. Most notorious was the December 4, 1969, shootout at the home of Chicago Panther Fred Hampton. Who fired the first shot during this raid remains in dispute. Not disputed, however, is that the police blasted the apartment with ninety-four shots, killing Hampton and fellow Panther Mark Clark and seriously wounding four other Panthers.[77]

During Newton's incarceration, the party fell into complete discord over Bobby Seale's arbitrary and authoritarian leadership. When Seale was indicted with seven others on charges of conspiring to cause a riot at the Chicago Democratic Party National Convention in 1968, day-to-day operations fell to David Hilliard, a Newton loyalist. Seale's disruption at the "Chicago Seven" trial led presiding judge Julius Hoffman to order him shackled and gagged during the trial, which inspired revolutionaries such as the newly formed Weather Underground revolutionary faction, led by Bernardine Dohrn and Bill Ayers, to see Seale as a hero. While serving a four-year sentence following the Chicago trial, Seale was indicted by New Haven, Connecticut, authorities for involvement in the torture and murder of Alex Rackley, a Black Panther accused of being a police informant. Seale's pretrial hearings led to social protests across the country declaring him a "political prisoner." Panthers converged on New Haven and drew the enthusiastic support of Yale University students who forced university president Kingman Brewster Jr. to issue a statement declaring that he was skeptical that black revolutionaries could get a fair trial anywhere in the United States. In the end, the judge in the trial dismissed the charges against Seale. By 1970, the Panther leadership was in disarray.

Many rank-and-file Panthers hoped Newton's release from prison and resumption of direct leadership of the party would bring order. Newton sought to turn the party back to community projects by establishing free breakfasts, health clinics, and educational programs.[78] Working with the white radical David Horowitz, Newton started a community educational school in Oakland. While regaining control of the party, however, Newton became increasingly erratic in his behavior. Drugs were suspected. He moved into a luxury apartment on Lake Merritt in Oakland, naming it "the Throne." He kept changing his title: first supreme commander, then servant of the people, followed by supreme servant of the people. He began drinking and using cocaine. Rank-and-file Panthers found their once-imprisoned hero to be a letdown. Always a poor speaker, Newton was given to long-winded, abstract speeches that left audiences bewildered. His purge of critics within the party escalated. In 1971, the Newton-Cleaver split aired publicly when the two appeared on an early morning radio show. Newton was in the studio, while Cleaver phoned in from Algeria. Cleaver stunned Newton by openly attacking Hilliard's leadership. Immediately after the program, both stayed on the phone. The exchange turned into a prison-yard showdown—two ex-cons, two street fighters, two immense egos, and both self-proclaimed leaders of the vanguard.[79]

NEWTON: You dropped a bombshell this morning.

CLEAVER: I hope so.

NEWTON: Well, it was very embarrassing for me.

CLEAVER: Well, it had to be dealt with.

NEWTON: Well, I have to deal with it too because I think it was unfair because when you say things like that it should be to the Central Committee and discussed openly and not outside, you know?

NEWTON: Hello. You listening? The Intercommunal Section is expelled.

CLEAVER: If that's what you want to do, brother. But look here, I don't think you should take such actions like that.

NEWTON: As far as I'm concerned you can go to hell, brother.

CLEAVER: Say, Huey—

NEWTON: I'm going to write the Koreans, the Chinese, the Algerians and tell them to kick you out of our embassy.

CLEAVER: Say, Huey—

NEWTON: And to put you in jail. You're a maniac, brother.

CLEAVER: Say, Huey—

NEWTON: Like Timothy Leary [LSD guru]. I think you're full of acid this morning.

CLEAVER: I think you should slow down, brother, because that's not going to work.

NEWTON: Well, I think it will. . . . You know I'd like a battle, brother. We'll battle it out.

CLEAVER: Say, Huey, that's not the best way to deal with it.

NEWTON: We'll battle like two bulls; we'll lock horns . . . but I think I've got the guns.

CLEAVER: I got some guns, too, brother.

The conversation continued with Newton calling Cleaver "a punk." Cleaver replied, "I think you've lost your ability to reason." Newton ended the conversation with, "You heard what I called you and that's what I feel about you now. You're a punk!"[80] The war was on.

Cleaver took most of the national chapters with him, except the Oakland chapter. Cleaver's appeal was to revolutionary action. Fratricidal violence erupted. In New York, pro-Newton Panthers shot Cleaverite Robert Webb, who had begun arguing with them on 125th Street in Harlem. Six weeks after Webb's death, the charred body of Samuel Napier, a pro-Newton Panther from Queens, was discovered. He had been bound, gagged, and shot six times. A few days later the remains of Fred Bennett from the Oakland chapter were found in the Santa Cruz hills. Cleaver, operating in Algiers, directed his supporters to form a new underground organization, the Black Liberation Army.[81]

Following his acquittal in New Haven in the spring of 1971, Seale returned to Oakland to resume his position as party chair, but it became a glorified position. David Hilliard was convicted for his involvement in the April 6, 1968, Oakland police ambush orchestrated by Cleaver and began serving time in July 1971 for attempted murder. Elaine Brown became the new party chair. By 1972 the party was down to about 150 core members. Brown turned the energy of the party to Oakland politics. A Panther slate won six seats on the West Oakland Planning Committee, the citizen's board of Oakland's Model Cities program, financed by the U.S. Department of Housing and Urban Development. The board directed how $4.9 million of federal funds for urban renewal and social services should be spent.

Out on bail for threatening to kill two plainclothes officers, Newton became involved in an altercation with two prostitutes on the streets of Oakland, leaving one, Kathleen Smith, fatally shot. A few days later, Newton severely beat a tailor who had come to his apartment. Indicted for the murder of the prostitute, Newton fled to Cuba. While Newton was in Cuba, Elaine Brown consolidated her power as party chair. In early 1975, the body of Betty Van Patter, an aide to Elaine Brown, washed up in San Francisco Bay. She had been recommended to the Panthers as a bookkeeper by David Horowitz.[82] (Shortly afterward, Horowitz broke with the Panthers and began his political march to the right.) In 1976, Brown won appointment to the powerful Oakland Council for Economic Development. The following spring, she marshaled Panthers to help elect Lionel Wilson as mayor of Oakland. Key party members were placed on Wilson's staff and various state commissions. Public funds through grants were directed to Panther projects. Following the election of Wilson, Newton returned to Oakland. He set up an elite security force, named the Buddha Samurai, which became his bodyguards, party enforcers, and "tax" collectors on the street.[83] Violence and party purges continued under party chair Elaine Brown, and Newton's life continued to revolve around drugs and alcohol.

On October 24, 1977, the Richmond police received a frantic call from Mary Matthews that her house was being broken into. When the police arrived, they found one member of the Black Panthers dead from two shots that Matthews had fired through her back door. Evidence found by police—overalls, an M-16 rifle, and two pairs of gloves—suggested a hit team. A couple of days later a doctor treated Panther Flores Forbes for a gunshot wound. Fearing arrest for his involvement in the attempted murder, Forbes fled to Las Vegas with another Panther, Nelson Malloy. While in Vegas, Malloy was shot by two Panthers who were instructed to remove any witnesses to the crime. Malloy was discovered in the desert by two tourists. He was left paralyzed from the neck down. Fearing for her own safety, Elaine Brown left Oakland in the dead of night. Ongoing federal investigations revealed that funding for Panther programs had been misappropriated. By the fall of 1982, the Panther Party had collapsed. The state of California seized Newton's home and garnished other assets in its embezzlement case against him. After another prison term for violating his parole, Newton returned to the streets of Oakland. On August 22, 1989, in the early morning, Newton was assassinated by two street thugs acting on a contract Oakland dealers had placed on Newton's head. Newton was dead, but the party had already died.

Writing in 1993, David Hilliard captured the disillusionment of the left in his memoir:

> I don't want to hear any of this madness.
> Party history.
> Personal history.
> Let me smoke. I don't want memories. I want oblivion.

Neither he nor Newton nor the Panthers disappeared totally into historical oblivion. Huey Newton became a much-romanticized figure in progressive circles.

Political Transformation

One of the great ironies of the revolutionary turn among militant black activists was that at the same time, blacks were making strides in established political institutions.[84] Both Democrats and Republicans endorsed civil rights. Reliant on the black vote, Democrats became the party of civil rights. Republicans responded by criticizing forced school busing, affirmative action, and Great Society anti-poverty programs. Nonetheless, a political transformation occurred as a result of social protest. Within a decade of the Voting Rights Act of 1965, eligible blacks registered to vote in the South had risen from 2 percent to close to 60 percent.[85] In 1965 there were six blacks in the House of

Representatives. By 2018, there were 52 black congresspeople. By the end of the 1960s there were only a little more than a thousand black elected officials across the country. Two years after the first black American, Barack Obama, was elected to the White House, there were more than 10,000 blacks elected to public office, with a high percentage located in the South. These gains brought a new kind of politics to the South and the North.[86] Black voters became powerful forces in northern urban cities and in the South. In the late 1960s and early 1970s, black mayoral candidates won victories in Cleveland, Newark, and Gary, Indiana. Atlanta elected its first black mayor, Maynard Jackson, in 1973. A year before that, black civil rights activist and King ally Andrew Young was elected to Congress, winning reelection for two subsequent terms.[87] Black politics was moving beyond the politics of ideology and activism to the pragmatism of hard-hitting electoral politics.

This new politics was captured in the race for Georgia's Fifth Congressional District in 1986, which pitted two former SNCC activists and close friends, Julian Bond and John Lewis. Bond, who had served in the Georgia state legislature, believed that the district was his and was surprised when his friend Lewis announced he was going to seek the office as well. Bond and his wife had vacationed with Lewis and his wife. He tried to persuade Lewis to wait his turn. Lewis refused. The final confrontation came down to a run-off election, in which Bond fell a few percentage points short of winning the primary outright. Bond, the son of a distinguished university professor and well educated, faced John Lewis, the son of a poor black farmer and a graduate of American Baptist Theological School. Lewis organized a grassroots campaign, but the key turning point came down to a televised debate. Lewis had spent days with a professional coach prepping for the debate. When Bond suggested that Lewis had been paid off by a lobbyist while serving on the city council, Lewis struck back. Lewis had heard (and probably knew) that Bond and his staff had been using cocaine. He turned to Bond, camera aimed on both, and said, "My friend. My brother. We were asked to take a drug test not long ago, and five of us [in the primary] went and took that test. Why don't we step out and go to the men's room and take another test?" Bond fumbled, nearly speechless. On Election Day, Lewis won barely, putting together a coalition of black voters in the poorest Atlanta precincts and white suburban voters.[88]

Though systemic racial inequality remained, civil rights became institutionalized on the federal, state, and local levels—as well as in the private sector. Administrative structures were created to ensure and oversee fair election laws and fair employment and housing for blacks. Federal and state agencies provided grant and loan programs to encourage job training for minorities and educational and business opportunities for black Americans. The array of federal agencies involved in civil rights extended through every department.[89]

These achievements came through the sacrifice of activists willing to put their lives on the line to organize at the grassroots level. In the struggle, the nation was transformed, although not made perfect. Democratic aspirations remained, but much had been achieved. Activists created new opportunities for black Americans, and as had occurred in earlier social movements, the legislative changes wrought by a grassroots movement became institutionalized in the modern administrative state.

Postscript

Before Martin Luther King was assassinated on April 4, 1968, his most tangible achievement had been the enactment of the Voting Rights Act of 1965. A year before his death, he came out fully against Johnson's war in Vietnam. This alienated many pro-war liberals in the Democratic Party. Marginalized by the younger generation of black activists, King found himself a hero to much of the public but in a kind of no-man's-land politically. His attempts to address racial inequality in the North, including the "Open Housing" marches in Mayor Richard Daley's Chicago in the summer of 1966, failed to achieve much. King's essential role in leading a movement led not to a perfect nation but to one vastly changed since his arrival in Montgomery in 1955.

4 Second-Wave Feminism, Social Protest, and the Rights Revolution

The crescendo of postwar feminism gained intensity in the late 1960s and early 1970s, albeit with disconcerting dissonance within the movement's ranks and among the general public. The aftermath of the movement continued to reverberate in American politics and culture, as more women were elected to office, entered the workforce and college, and demanded respect in gender relations. A huge infrastructure protecting women's rights was created in government, corporate business, and colleges to ensure equal opportunity and action for advancement of women. A reasonable argument can be made that the feminist movement in this period—second-wave feminism—made the greatest gains for its cause than any other social movement in the postwar era.

Estimating with any precision the relationship of cause and effect of social movements and sociopolitical gains is always difficult. Although second-wave feminism had roots in labor organizing in the 1940s and the early civil rights movement, feminism as a mass social movement did not take clear formation until the mid-1960s. Even before this, however, state courts and the U.S. Supreme Court had ruled in a number of significant cases advancing the rights of women. Congress enacted the Equal Pay Act of 1963 aimed at abolishing wage disparity based on gender, and in 1964 Congress included discrimination on account of gender in the Civil Rights Act. Leaders in both the Democratic and Republican parties understood the importance of winning women voters, which suggests that protecting women's rights was going to advance with or without feminist social protest. There should be no doubt, however, that the feminist movement employed social protest to accelerate the advancement of women, and that this movement gained mass support—as well as conservative female and male reaction.

Although seriously divided politically and ideologically along a number of fault lines, second-wave feminists shared a common goal to challenge established male political, social, and cultural power. The movement was anti-elitist in rhetoric and substance. Early second-wave feminists sought egalitarianism within their ranks, and those claiming to be leaders or spokespeople for the movement came under heavy criticism from grassroots activists. Some feminist organizations sought to address the elitism issue by rotating leaders, lecturers, and those appearing before the press.

In its anti-elitism, feminism as a social movement reflected a populist sentiment within the American political tradition. Yet unlike late nineteenth-century populism, second-wave feminism was a movement that arose largely from the concerns of white, middle-class women. Most leaders of the movement came from privileged backgrounds. Thus to describe second-wave feminism as bourgeois populism presents a kind of oxymoron.[1] Feminists answered this quandary by offering greater inclusion to women of color and incorporating issues facing minority and working-class women. In addition, radical feminists maintained that sexual oppression in a patriarchal system extended beyond a simple matter of class or economics—capitalist or socialist—but reflected a deeper oppression found in essential male domination. They argued that trying to change male attitudes toward women, asking men to change to more enlightened and sensitive creatures or forcing them to share power, represented a misunderstanding of the causes of female oppression. The relationship of gender, class, and race remained elusive concepts then and later but did not distract from the growing power of the movement.

Feminism made significant political and social gains beginning in the 1960s and afterward, even as it confronted an anti-feminist backlash occurring around the battle to ratify the Equal Rights Amendment. Demands for women's equality continued to win bipartisan support, but the rise of the New Right in the mid-1970s provided an opportunity for Republicans to mobilize a counterrevolution, securing their own share of the women's vote. Political competition between the parties prevented feminists from achieving their full agenda, and this left many feminists disappointed and demoralized by the time Ronald Reagan, a conservative Republican, won in a landslide to gain the White House in 1980. Further disappointment came when Reagan won easy reelection in 1984, even though the Democratic Party nominee, Walter Mondale, placed the first woman, Representative Geraldine Ferraro, on the ticket as his running mate. The feminist movement faced its own internal and ideological contradictions: it called on government to redress social problems of women, even while promoting anti-statist politics; the movement adhered to highly egalitarian norms and organizational structures, which induced its own internal problems; and its attempt to replace older radical ideologies based on class led to identity politics and the subsequent splintering of identities (race, class, sexual preference) within the movement.[2]

Although claiming to represent all women, feminists remained divided throughout these formative years about whom they represented. The claim that women made up 51 percent of the population but were not proportionally represented in government, business, academia, or in the editorial offices of *McCall's* was fair enough. But polls showed that average American women were divided over the feminist movement. This gap between the movement and average American women allowed opponents to charge that feminists were extremists, out of touch with the people they claimed to represent. The defeat of the Equal Rights Amendment seemed to confirm this view. The larger problem of representativeness proved even more difficult for lesbians within the movement. At first lesbians were ignored, some said consciously excluded by movement leaders, only to find later a growing voice within the movement. The question of representation became even more pronounced when some feminist intellectuals and activists claimed that female-female relationships offered the only truly equal opportunity for women.

Divisions within the feminist movement focused on questions of how to best break male domination (described by feminists as "patriarchal control") of politics, society, and culture. Like similar past social protest movements, questions of gradual reform versus revolutionary change divided the movement. By 1977, though, greater unity was found in support of the Equal Rights Amendment (ERA), reproductive rights, lesbian rights, and a rich legislative agenda that included income equality, child care, health care, welfare, disability, and other issues involving women as workers, mothers, and citizens. This unity found expression at the National Women's Conference in celebration of International Women's Year held in Houston from November 18 to 21, 1977. The conference achieved remarkable unity among delegates over gay rights and abortion.[3] However, conservative "pro-family" women, led by anti-ERA activist Phyllis Schlafly, played upon the alleged radicalism of the conference that, they claimed, went well beyond equal rights for women.

Although the anti-ERA movement succeeded in defeating ratification of the Equal Rights Amendment, feminist activism helped enact state constitutional ERA amendments, liberalize divorce and abortion laws, and establish commissions and agencies overseeing the status of women. On the federal level the Equal Employment Opportunity Commission (EEOC) pressured private businesses and educational institutions to employ more women and so did the U.S. Department of Education. The Women's Educational Equity Act of 1974 provided federal protections against gender discrimination of women in education. Pregnant women were protected by the Pregnancy Discrimination Act of 1978. Throughout American universities and colleges, women's studies programs became common, and the curricula in the humanities, social sciences, and hard sciences gave more attention to gender issues.

Second-wave feminism coincided with other racial, ethnic, and sexual-identity movements demanding group rights. Arguably American politics has always been about "identity politics"—mostly along socio-religious lines until the twentieth century—but the emergence of identity politics revolving around racial, ethnic, gender, and sexual identity created a new political culture and an ongoing cultural debate. Traditionalists reacted to these changes by accusing radical movements of creating a cult of otherness, of dividing American politics and culture into a set of self-identified subgroups—persons of color, women, and homosexuals—who identified with their own cultures rather than any American culture and of dividing society into those enjoying "white male privilege" versus the oppressed. Supporters of the liberation movements responded by declaring that such criticism reflected an effort to preserve socioeconomic and cultural privilege and that a truly just America living up to its creed that all men and women are created equal needed to acknowledge and encourage diversity of cultures within the nation to further justice.

Later scholars looking at second-wave feminism maintained that opponents at the time exaggerated differences within the movement and unnecessarily highlighted the most radical expressions of feminism. There is some truth to this criticism. Conservative opponents such as Phyllis Schlafly did focus on the most radical expressions of women's liberation in these years. Nonetheless, looking at tensions within the movement allows for a more nuanced understanding of the historical dynamic of a social movement and an opportunity to generalize about social protest and democratic change. Second-wave feminism can be seen as occurring within three phrases, with the caveat that historical periodization has an arbitrary quality: 1963 to 1967, the liberal origins; 1968 to 1975, division and radical discord; and by 1976, unity and institutionalization.

The first expressions of second-wave feminism concentrated on economic and legal inequities experienced by women. These concerns were expressed by prominent organizations and groups, such as the National Organization for Women (NOW), the National Women's Political Caucus (NWPC), Federally Employed Women (FEW), and Women's Equity Action League (WEAL).

These organizations were run top-down, whatever the size of their member-ships. By the late 1960s, a burst of younger activists entered the movement, most lacking affiliation with national organizations. These younger activists injected new social and cultural issues into the movement and brought with them a new style and tone. Many of the new activists came out of the New Left and civil rights movements of the 1960s. They formed local activist or-ganizations, as well as "consciousness-raising" women's groups. Older activists such as Betty Friedan initially denounced publicly the style of these younger activists and the introduction of such sexual issues as lesbianism (although Friedan was a strong and early supporter of abortion). Even among the younger activists, those declaring themselves revolutionary socialists, criticisms were leveled against cultural feminists and those involved in consciousness-raising groups as distracting the movement from class revolution. Yet in the cacoph-ony of feminism in the 1970s and the hurling of political and personal accusa-tions, feminists of whatever orientation saw themselves as radicals challenging established politics, culture, and social norms.

Betty Friedan: From Small-Town Girl to Celebrity Woman

With the publication of *The Feminine Mystique* in 1963, Betty Friedan became the early face of the emergent feminist movement. This was a re-markable feat for a small-town woman who had grown up in Peoria, Illinois, forty-two years earlier.[4] Much as they had with Martin Luther King Jr., con-servatives derided her as a radical, while her opponents in her own movement turned on her within a matter of years, accusing her of being too accommo-dating, too soft, and out of touch with activists who demanded faster and more transformative change.

The Feminine Mystique, a national best seller, appealed to a generation of women who were coming into their own in post–World War II America. Her targeted audience consisted of college-educated and white suburban women whom Friedan claimed found themselves trapped as housewives. Speaking on their behalf and claiming to be one of them, Friedan declared that women had been sold a bill of goods that happiness lay only in defining themselves in one role: housewives and mothers. Having bought into this "feminine mys-tique," these women had sold themselves short by thinking fulfillment came through just housework, marriage, and children. This mystique left such women unsatisfied, unable to express their frustrations. She maintained that the feminine mystique was reinforced by the educational system, advertising, law, and custom. Friedan urged women to break through these stereotypes and realize self-actualization beyond marriage and motherhood. Specifically, she urged women to seek fulfillment in careers.

By 1964, the book had sold a million copies. It made Friedan a national celebrity and the voice of an incipient feminist movement. *The Feminine Mystique* was an exceptionally well-written and well-argued book designed to appeal to a mass audience. She wove into it poignant examples of how women were portrayed in the media, as well as introducing readings on Freudian theory and psychologist Abraham Maslow's hierarchy of needs. (She had majored in psychology at Smith College and won a graduate fellowship to study the subject at the University of California, Berkeley.)

Crucially, Friedan presented herself as a suburban housewife and mother trapped by the feminine mystique. Her claim to being just an average suburban wife and mother belied her own history as a professional labor journalist and longtime activist. Her assertion was similar to that of her later nemesis Phyllis Schlafly, who also claimed to be just an average American housewife and mother. However, both had a long record of political activism before stepping on the national state. Betty Friedan and Phyllis Schlafly, although polar opposites politically and ideologically, shared much in common. Both came from the Midwest and were raised in families with college-educated mothers. Both their families aspired to be among their town's elite—Peoria for Friedan and St. Louis for Schlafly. Both women excelled in high school and went to elite colleges (Smith and Berkeley for Friedan and Washington University and Radcliffe for Schlafly). The similarities do not end there, however. Both worked professionally before marrying successful men and raising large families. Among their children were sons who were mathematical prodigies, who coincidentally—or ironically—were in the same graduate student cohort at the University of California, Berkeley. Friedan emerged on the left, a leading spokesperson for feminism; Schlafly came out on the right as a crusader for traditional family values.

Only three years separated Friedan (b. 1921) and Schlafly (b. 1924) in age. Both came of age in the Great Depression of the 1930s. Friedan, who grew up in a large house with servants, including a chauffeur, was not affected much by the Depression until her final year at Smith College when her father fell ill. Schlafly experienced the full effects of the Depression when her father lost his job as an engineer and never found employment again. Her mother had to go to work in a department store as a clerk and later a librarian at the St. Louis Art Museum.

Friedan, born Bettye Goldstein, grew up in Peoria, Illinois' second largest city next to Chicago and home to the Caterpillar Tractor Company. Her father, Harry, immigrated to the United States from Kiev. His jewelry business in Peoria catered to the wealthy in the town, selling gems, silver, and china. Her mother, a daughter of Jewish immigrants from Hungary, grew up in Peoria, the daughter of a medical doctor and the city's health commissioner. Before marrying, her mother wrote for the society page for the local paper. The Goldsteins raised their family in a fashionable section of Peoria known as the Bluffs. They were not the wealthiest people in town, but they had a maid, an occasional butler and chauffeur, and a nurse when Bettye was younger. The Goldsteins were socially striving, secularized, and prosperous.

In high school, Bettye became the editor of the school's literary magazine and a school brain. Many of her peers found her arrogant and off-putting. Later she claimed she was socially ostracized because she was Jewish. Following graduation, she enrolled at Smith College in 1938. By her junior year she had become politically active in left-wing popular-front organizations opposing American intervention in Europe. She was an active campus member of the American Youth Congress, a Communist Party–aligned national student group. After the Hitler-Stalin Nonaggression Pact, signed on August 23, 1939, the Communist Party USA became as adamant as pacifists and isolationists in opposing American intervention by aiding Britain. Her position drew the ire of the new university president, a strong interventionist. By late 1939, public opinion in support of aiding embattled Britain had begun to change. In the summer of 1941, Friedan attended the Highlander Folk School in Tennessee, a school for labor organizers.

When Friedan enrolled in graduate school at Berkeley to pursue a degree in psychology, she was divided about activism versus academia. She lasted less than a year in the graduate program. During her year at Berkeley, 1942 to 1943, she became close to the staff of the *Communist Campanile*, although there is no evidence she was a member of the Communist Party while there. In 1943, Friedan left graduate school to move to New York City, where she became a popular front labor journalist, getting her first job with the Federated Press, a left-wing news service launched at the Farmer-Labor Party convention in 1919. In 1946, during a staff cutback, she was let go. She began work for the *UE News* at the age of twenty-five. *UE News* was the official publication of the United Electrical, Radio, and Machine Workers of America, a communist-controlled union that had come under heavy attack from within the Congress of Industrial Organizations (CIO) and from federal authorities. The major enemies of the newspaper were anti-communist liberals, such as President Truman, Hubert Humphrey, and United Auto Workers union president Walter Reuther. She worked at *UE News* until 1952.

Friedan married in 1947, becoming Betty Friedan in private life. In 1950, pregnant with her second child, she and her family moved to Parkway Village, a suburb of Queens. In this middle-class suburb she became editor of the *Parkway Village* newspaper and turned it into an activist publication. With the birth of their third child, the Friedans left Queens to move to Rockland County on the west side of the Hudson River. With the inheritance of her father and her husband's benefits from the GI Bill, they bought an eleven-room, three-bathroom, stylish Italianate house built in 1868. It took time and money to fix it up. In Rockland County, Friedan became friends with a group of radicals and public intellectuals, such as sociologist C. Wright Mills, historian Herbert Gutman, and others. They became involved in local school educational programs, which came under attack later in 1961 by local conservatives and the Rockland County American Legion. During these years, Friedan became a prominent freelance journalist. What began as a proposed series on middle-class suburban women became *The Feminine Mystique*. Friedan was forty-two years old at the time. Within just a matter of three or four years, she had become the doyen of second-wave feminists. Within another couple of years she had become the target of radical feminists who saw Friedan as old and out of touch.

Second-Wave Feminism Launched

The struggle for women's rights had a long history before Friedan wrote *The Feminine Mystique*. Female struggle for equality was not new to the country and had deep roots in the nation's history dating back to pre–Civil War reform movements. Feminist activism expressed itself in the suffrage movement at the turn of the twentieth century, the formation of the National Women's Party in 1920, welfare reform labor activism, support for an Equal Rights Amendment, and debates about gender equality among the pre–World War II left.[5] Feminism found new energy in the early 1960s in the fight for civil and employment rights for women; by the late 1960s the movement accelerated into direct, vocal, and angry challenges to patriarchal domination in politics, culture, and sexual relations. Second-wave feminism proved more transformative, however, politically, culturally, and socially. It arguably was the most successful social movement in modern American history in its effects on government policy, the workplace, and sexual and marital relations. The movement—or perhaps more accurately described as movements because of the multiplicity of female voices involved—became increasingly radicalized. This radicalization, however, coincided with more tempered, although no less significant, changes in popular culture, experienced by women and men mostly in the middle class, in social consciousness about the roles and place of women in society.

Women had found new opportunities in modern, industrial, and urban America at the turn of the twentieth century. Although employment opportunities remained limited, women gained political agency when they won the right to vote with the enactment of the Nineteenth Amendment in the 1920s. In the Roaring Twenties, young urban women smoked, wore short skirts, drank, and flaunted their disregard for Victorian sexual conventions. Many more women entered college and the workforce. These trends continued into the 1930s and further accelerated during World War II when the shortage of male workers required a greater reliance on female workers in war production.[6] The war, however, disrupted traditional patterns of behavior.[7] After World War II, many women left the workplace to return home, but large numbers continued to work. Support for work by married women was widely accepted by the public. By 1954, in families earning middle-class incomes of $6,000 to $10,000, both husband and wife worked. Increasingly women entered college; so by 1968, more than 43 percent of all bachelor's and professional degrees went to women. In this environment, times were ripe for the emergence of a revived and new feminist movement.

Equal rights for women took a major step forward in 1961 when Esther Peterson, head of the Women's Bureau in the Department of Labor, pressured President John F. Kennedy to create a special commission on the status of women in the United States. Many women, including former first lady Eleanor Roosevelt, were sorely disappointed in the failure of the administration to appoint more women to government.[8] Peterson was the highest-ranking woman in the Kennedy administration. Kennedy's reluctance to appoint women to higher positions in his administration drew inevitable criticism from women. Furthermore, Kennedy refused to endorse the Equal Rights Amendment guaranteeing equal protection for women under the Constitution. His signature had been included, without his permission, on a letter endorsing the ERA during the 1960 presidential campaign, but once in office he continued to oppose ERA. Many New Deal liberals, including Eleanor Roosevelt, along with organized labor, opposed the amendment, fearing that it would undermine protective legislation for female workers, which granted women special rights in setting hours and preventing them from engaging in dangerous occupations. In response, Kennedy appointed Peterson, an opponent of the ERA with a union background and a longtime advocate for equal pay for women. When released in 1963, the President's Commission on the Status of Women report reaffirmed the important role that women played in society as wives, housekeepers, and mothers, while offering striking statistics of inequities women faced in the workplace.[9] The report drew immediate press attention by making the front page of the *New York Times*. Eighty-three thousand copies of the report were distributed. Esther Peterson appeared on NBC's *Today* show, and the Associated Press ran a four-part series on the report. It caused dozens of states to establish commissions, and by 1967, all fifty states had done so.[10] One of the immediate results of the commission was the passage of the Equal Pay Act of 1963. The act was an important step forward for women's rights, although the act enabled employers to shift job titles, which allowed for female workers to be placed in lower-paid jobs, even though the jobs were comparable to those held by men.[11]

The commissions helped set the stage for the insertion of a non–sex discriminatory provision—Title VII—in the Civil Rights Act of 1964. Representative Howard Smith, a Democrat from Virginia, offered the provision in the employment section of the bill. Whatever Smith's intentions—some said he did so because he thought the provision was so absurd it might divide liberals—the provision was accepted, and the bill was enacted.[12]

Under Title VII, the Equal Employment Opportunity Commission was established as the federal enforcement agency charged with ensuring that job applicants and employees were treated without regard to their sex, race, creed, color, or national origins. From the outset, the EEOC was notoriously lethargic and at times hostile in its response to sex discrimination complaints. The EEOC's first director angered many activists when he described the sex discrimination clause as an accident, "conceived out of wedlock."[13] This attitude led directly to the formation of the National Organization for Women in June 1966 during the third conference of state commissions on the status of women. After the regular session, a group of women retired to Betty Friedan's hotel room, angered by the federal government's dismissive attitude to female discrimination in the workplace.

NOW organizers envisioned a kind of female NAACP to pressure the federal government for more equal opportunities and nondiscrimination against women. In October 1966 NOW was incorporated with three hundred chapters, but the organization was top-heavy from the outset and not a grassroots-based organization. The officers of the new organization reflected established leadership: Friedan was elected president, two former EEOC commissioners were vice presidents, and the secretary-treasurer was from the United Auto Workers Women's Committee. These were well-established and well-connected women, but with the exception of the labor representative, they lacked experience in developing a mass grassroots organization. NOW chapters operated basically on their own without clear direction from the national office.[14] This loose network did not allow for easy cooperation among chapters, and it created opportunities for some chapters to be taken over by radicals pursuing their own agendas.

Political Discord Within a Young Movement

In late 1967, NOW leadership sought to reach the larger grassroots by organizing a national day of picketing against the EEOC offices in New York, San Francisco, Pittsburgh, and Washington, D.C., for the commission's refusal to rule on gender-segregated "help wanted" newspaper job ads. The demostrations did not draw large numbers of picketers in most cities, but had their desired effect on the EEOC. Under pressure, the EEOC ruled in mid-August 1968 that separate want ads were a violation of Title VII. This was a clear victory for NOW, but within its ranks deep divisions were emerging over the ERA, reproductive rights, and lesbian rights. In 1967, women from the United Auto Workers left NOW because of its support for the Equal Rights Amendment. Reproductive rights created another fissure within the organization. A sizable number of members believed that NOW's support for repealing restrictive state abortion laws distracted the organization from focusing on legal and economic issues. In 1968, these dissidents broke from NOW to form the Women's Equity Action League to concentrate on employment and education.

Lesbian rights caused further division. In 1969, Friedan began warning against the "lavender menace." She remained convinced that "man-hating" lesbians provided an easy target for critics and might alienate legislators and policy makers. She refused to list the New York chapter of the Daughters of Bilitis (a lesbian rights organization) among the sponsors for the NOW-sponsored First Congress to Unite Women in 1969.[15]

Division over lesbian rights came to a head at the Second Congress to Unite Women in spring 1970. Friedan refused to place any lesbian on the program. The result was a backlash from activist lesbians. On the opening day of the Congress, a small group of seventeen demonstrators converged on the meeting wearing T-shirts inscribed "Lavender Menace" and carrying placards reading "Women's Liberation IS a Lesbian Plot" and "You're Going to Love the Lavender Menace." Karla Jay, one of the demonstrators, stood up in the middle of an audience of three hundred women and shouted, "Yes, yes, sister! I'm tired of being in the closet because of the women's movement." The demonstrators distributed a ten-paragraph manifesto, "The Woman-Identified Woman."[16] The demonstration had its desired effect. On the final day of the conference, the congress passed a pro–lesbian rights resolution advanced by former NOW staff member Rita Mae Brown.[17]

Friedan appeared to stand on the wrong side of history on this issue. At the 1971 NOW convention, delegates passed a resolution declaring that "a woman's right to her own person includes the right to define and express her own sexuality and to choose her own lifestyle; therefore we acknowledge the oppression of lesbians as a legitimate concern of feminism."[18] Two years later NOW passed a stronger resolution supporting civil rights legislation to end discrimination based on sexual orientation. A survey of NOW members in this period showed that only 8 percent described themselves as gay, while another 9 percent identified as bisexual.

After four embattled years as founding president of NOW, Friedan stepped down in 1970. She was not quite finished, however. In her lengthy farewell address to the convention, she called unilaterally for a nationwide strike against inequality as a means of commemorating the fiftieth anniversary of the Nineteenth Amendment. Many within NOW were reluctant to endorse the strike, but Friedan prevailed. The call for national demonstrations drew widespread support among feminist groups across the country. An estimated 10,000 to 20,000 women marched up Fifth Avenue in New York; in Boston, 5,000 women rallied in the Common; 2,000 congregated in San Francisco; and in Washington, D.C., female government workers rallied. Following the demonstration, NOW membership swelled. The demonstrations revealed NOW's potential as a grassroots social movement. The demonstrations fulfilled Friedan's wildest expectations, even though she had been pushed out of NOW's leadership.

She found herself under criticism within the National Women's Political Caucus (NWPC), an organization she had helped found a few years earlier to exert more feminist influence in politics. Her problems within NWPC came at the Democratic National Convention in 1972.[19] At the convention NWPC sought to test its political power within the Democratic Party.[20] Under new party rules the number of female delegates to the Democratic convention increased from 13 percent to 40 percent. Friedan and her allies pushed Democratic candidate George McGovern to nominate a female running mate. (Friedan preferred New York congresswoman Shirley Chisholm, who had run for the presidential nomination.) The NWPC took credit for placing on the Democratic Party platform support for federally funded child care and preschool and after-school programs. But activists failed to get a strong abortion plank, which led to accusations that Friedan and her cohort within the NWPC had been too coopted by Democrat Party leaders. Infighting between Friedan and Gloria Steinem and her ally, New York Democratic representative Bella Abzug, cemented factional differences.

A month after the convention, Friedan openly attacked Steinem in her monthly column in *McCall's* magazine. She accused Steinem and *Ms.* magazine of promoting female chauvinism under the guise of "sisterhood." She declared that it was untrue that "women have any moral or spiritual superiority as a class or that men share some brutal insensitivity as a class." To believe this, she said, is "male chauvinism in reverse: it is female sexism. It is, in fact, female chauvinism and those who preach or practice it seem to me to be corrupting our movement for equality and inviting a backlash."[21] The counterattack came shortly afterward. Calling a press conference, the former head of the NWPC, Brenda Fasteau, and the coordinator for the women's rights project of the American Civil Liberties Union and a member of the policy council for the NWPC, Robin Morgan, among others, dismissed Friedan as out of touch. Fasteau accused Friedan of being "severely myopic, a lesbianphobe, dyke-baiter" sellout and an obsolete figure in the movement.[22]

Friedan struck back. In March 1973, writing in the *New York Times* under the title "Up from the Kitchen Floor," she conjectured that militant lesbians within the movement were being used by the Federal Bureau of Investigation and Central Intelligence Agency to disrupt the movement and give it a bad image. In fact, she accused radical lesbian activist Ti-Grace Atkinson of having CIA connections. She maintained that everyone had a right to sexual privacy, but lesbians were "hurting and exploiting the women's movement to try to use it to proselytize for lesbianism because of the sexual preferences of a few."[23]

Steinem and Abzug exacted their vengeance on Friedan at the first national convention of the NWPC in Houston held that summer in 1973. At the convention, Abzug and Steinem teamed up to push Friedan out of leadership positions within the organization. Friedan later reflected she was hopelessly "out-foxed" by her rivals.[24] The Friedan-Steinem-Abzug fights reflected other divisions within the movement. These were the years of a boiling cauldron of feminist polemics.[25]

Intellectual Ferment

New York City remained the epicenter of polemical warfare.[26] The year 1970 proved to be a banner year for important feminist publications, including works by Anne Koedt, Shulamith Firestone, Kate Millett, and Robin Morgan. Koedt gained notoriety when she published an essay, "Myth of the Vaginal Orgasm," first in pamphlet form in 1968 by the New York Radical Women and then reissued as a book by the New England Free Press in 1970. Koedt argued that men were not necessary for female gratification, which drew umbrage from the well-known novelist and notorious womanizer Norman Mailer.

While the debate on the nature of female orgasm raged, Firestone released *The Dialectic of Sex: The Case for Feminist Revolution* (1970). The book envisioned a better world without men. Patriarchy—male domination—lay at the root of all oppression. The book became one of the primary required readings for feminists. *The Dialectic of Sex* maintained that oppression was historical because males sought domination. This was their nature. Firestone maintained that with new technology, sex could be separated from pregnancy and child-rearing. Through new technology, women could take control of their bodies and not rely on men for reproduction. She wrote that until "a certain level of evolution has been reached and technology had achieved its present sophistication, to question the fundamental biological conditions was insanity." Today, she said, women stood on the verge of a new epoch in human history in which culture could be reordered. Women now had the power to reclaim ownership of their bodies and exert feminine control over human fertility. She accused feminist socialists of ignoring that real revolution could only be based on sex, not class. She proclaimed that a "revolt against the biological family could bring on the first successful revolution. . . . We now have the knowledge to create a paradise on earth anew."[27] Firestone, it might appear, accepted Aldous Huxley's ironic description of fathers in his novel *Brave New World* (1932), when his character Mustapha Mond, one of the ten World Controllers, declared that the word *father* is "not so much obscene as . . . merely gross, a scatological rather than a pornographic impropriety."[28]

In *Sexual Politics* (1970), Kate Millett, a University of Minnesota and Oxford University graduate, brought to feminism a literary analysis of patriarchal sexism evident in male authors, most notably D. H. Lawrence, Henry Miller, and Norman Mailer. Her book, based on her doctoral dissertation at Columbia University, gained wide notice in feminist circles for her assertion that politics—and literature—was essentially sexual. She, too, demanded changes in family and gender roles. She gained celebrity status overnight—a recent PhD's dream come true. She followed this book with *The Prostitution Papers,* arguing that prostitution reflected only the most apparent degradation of women, not much unlike what wives suffered in traditional marriage. Her status, however, quickly drew criticism within New York feminist circles, even though she announced she was a lesbian. Denounced by New York Radical Women for allowing herself to become a spokesperson for feminism in interviews and on the lecture circuit, she withdrew from the organization, but her visibility as a feminist intellectual continued.

Robin Morgan's anthology of contemporary feminist writings, *Sisterhood Is Powerful*, published by Random House in 1970, struck the reading public like a bombshell and arguably did more to circulate second wave feminist ideas to the public than did any other book at the time. The intent of the volume was to radicalize women. Missing were dry, statistics-filled reports of women's exclusion or mealy-mouthed pleas for female inclusion. Instead contributions offered cutting and often personal portraits of women in television, the media, advertising, academia, medicine, the Catholic Church, and the "secretarial proletariat." Female sexuality, the politics of orgasm, birth control, and Madison Avenue "brainwashing" were explored. Mexican American women, black women, female high school students, and housewives were called to join the revolution. There were poems by Rita Mae Brown, Janet Russo, and Sylvia Plath. NOW's Bill of Rights for Women was included, but more radical manifestos were included as well, such as Valerie Solanis's SCUM (Society for Cutting Up Men), the Redstockings Manifesto, and the Women's International Terrorist Conspiracy from Hell (WITCH).

Firestone, Millett, Morgan, and others were published by major presses targeted at the mass market. The feminist book trade boomed. Academic publishers got on board, and over the next three decades a steady stream of books written from a feminist perspective flowed and never abated. Newspapers, national television networks and local channels, and night-time talk shows began covering what looked like the sudden arrival of "women's lib." The right for women to control their own bodies became a constant theme within the movement. In 1969, the Boston Women's Health Collective published *Our Bodies, Ourselves*, a short booklet that gained wide circulation. First published by the New England Free Press, the booklet was picked up by Simon and Schuster. With complete editorial control of the project, the twelve authors of the booklet expanded it into a three-hundred-page book that explored women's health and sexuality issues, including pregnancy, postpartum depression, contraception, abortion, male doctors, female health care workers, and a range of other subjects. The book inspired the growth of women's health centers that were being established across the country. It argued that women's control of their bodies should not be subjected to the narrow and often conscious and unconscious bias of male expertise.

The Movement Takes Shape

Reproductive rights—abortion—was central to the concept of women's right to control their bodies. Until the late 1960s abortion in most states was restricted to therapeutic abortions to save the life of a mother.[29] In 1969, New York State decided to reconsider its abortion law by calling legislative hearings to be held on February 13, 1969. Feminists were outraged when it was announced that fourteen men and one woman—a nun—were the only expert witnesses called to testify. NOW organized to picket the hearing. Militant feminists decided that more than picketing was needed. On the day of the hearings, after the first witness testified, Kathie Sarachild, a founding member of a radical New York feminist group, the Redstockings, stood up and shouted, "Alright, now let's hear from some *real* experts—women!" Stunned legislators adjourned the hearings. The Redstockings announced it would have its own hearings, a speak-out on abortion. In March 1969 around two hundred women gathered to convey their experiences of pregnancy and abortion. Testimony was made personal by focusing on the emotional and psychological effects of pregnancy and abortion. Politics expressed itself in the personal narrative.[30] One woman recalled how different her reaction was in discovering she was pregnant than that of her boyfriend: "I remember something about the guy's reaction. I mean, my first reaction was, 'Get this child out of me!' and his first reaction was, 'Isn't it romantic?' Like playing house, his mother wanted to buy me a maternity dress, and here, I mean, it was six weeks and he thought the whole thing was just beautiful and romantic." Personal power, as this woman stated, was found in the differing emotions experienced by men and women in a relationship. Male power, as others testified, was systematic domination. As explained by another woman testifying, "There's another point involved here that was brought up, and this is that women are used as tools in the power structure. Look, abortion, people don't want to legalize abortion because then there would be a breakdown in the power structure."[31]

Another point of contention within the movement was the emergence of "consciousness-raising" groups that had begun to spring up across the country. For feminists who believed in the politics of the street, consciousness-raising groups were a complete distraction from revolution. Often self-organized and without national coordination, these groups ranged in orientation from psychological support meetings to ideological collectives. Activist Susan Brownmiller recalled in her memoir *In Our Time* that many of these groups, often meeting in somebody's living room, asked women to speak "honestly about intimate matters in front of relative strangers." She observed that many of the "'naturals' had been in group therapy or just adored talking about themselves." Whatever its strengths or weaknesses as a political instrument, the consciousness-raising movement encouraged feminist discourse to reach into mainstream middle-class culture in these years.[32]

More divisive was the call for feminists to declare themselves lesbians and to separate themselves totally from men—politically, culturally, and socially. Lesbian separatism remained a minority viewpoint within the larger feminist movement but drew obvious dispute.[33] The importance of separatism proved to be twofold. First, it forced the larger heterosexual women's movement to recognize lesbian and gay civil rights. Second, separatists reinforced the belief within the larger movement that gender and sexual roles were a matter of social construction. Opponents of lesbian separatism within the larger feminist movement feared that the "anti-male" message being sent by gay female activists created an easy target for defenders of the traditional order.

However small their support in the beginning, radical lesbians gained increasing support within the larger movement for the recognition of gay rights.[34] Especially important in voicing the need for recognition was lesbian activist Rita Mae Brown.

She was theatrical, magnetic, often dogmatic, and extremely motivated. Her critics accused her of being self-serving and usually failing to listen to other people.[35] Whatever her personal faults, she presents an example of how a single activist can help inspire a larger movement. Charismatic and dramatic, Brown became a major force in the emerging lesbian rights movement. Brown believed homosexuality was a political choice necessary to overthrown male dominance.[36] Her stridency and personality led her in and out of a number of feminist organizations—NOW, the Redstockings in New York, and separatist collectives in Washington, D.C.—but she became a leading activist and voice within the radical lesbian movement. Radical feminists, including lesbian separatists, were important on the local level in creating alternative businesses, health care centers, rape counseling centers, women's shelters, and other institutions for women. These alternative organizations created a new set of problems as they often competed among themselves for public funds—local, state, and federal.[37]

Steinem and *Ms.* Magazine

Further evidence of feminism's growing acceptance in culture appeared with the founding of *Ms.* magazine in 1971. Aimed at a mass market, the magazine reached beyond the internecine factional struggle within the movement. In its trial run, the magazine sold 300,000 copies within its first week and drew an amazing 20,000 letters to the editor. *Ms.* was just one of about 200 feminist magazines being published by mid-1975, but no other feminist magazine compared in readership. By 1976, it had a readership of 2.1 million people, with an estimated 19 percent male readers.[38] Unlike many of these other publications, *Ms.* sought a broad readership of middle-class professional and working-class readers, whites and persons of color. Its readership, though, remained mostly younger, white professional women.

Steinem's prominence inevitably opened her to criticism from anti-feminists and some radical feminists who charged that she was little more than a media creation. Physically attractive, articulate, and a journalist practiced in writing clear and well-crafted articles, Steinem provided feminism in the mid-1970s with an opportunity to reach further into middle-class culture. A liberal Democrat, Steinem carefully threaded established partisan politics and radical feminism. She refused to talk about her personal life. Although not a lesbian, she spoke in favor of gay rights. Politically deft, she outmaneuvered rivals such as Betty Friedan as well as those on her left. She served as a liaison between grassroots feminist activism occurring on many fronts and the progressive left in the Democratic Party.[39] Her greatest skill and contribution to feminism came in the media arena, where her status as a chic, articulate feminist made her into a favorite of journalists and television show hosts.

Steinem imparted a middle-class respectability to the larger feminist movement. Under her guidance, *Ms.* sought to reach children and teenagers through its Foundation for Women. In 1972 the foundation released a record of children's music and short stories for children called *Free to Be . . . You and Me.* The brainchild of Marlo Thomas, a television actress and daughter of comedian Danny Thomas, the record showcased celebrities, including singer Harry Belafonte, actor Alan Alda, comic producer Mel Brooks, and Diana Ross of the popular female group the Supremes. One skit had two newborns, a male and a female, in a conversation reaching the conclusion that gender was a socially constructed idea. At the time, *Free to Be . . . You and Me* appeared quite radical, revealing how feminist sentiment was entering into the larger culture, albeit with varying degrees of success.[40]

Into the Political Mainstream and Out

By 1975, many activists believed that the movement had fallen into disarray. As Susan Brownmiller recalled in her memoir, "A profound sense of powerlessness and rage always drives revolutionary movements, often to the point of destruction." She believed that 1975 was one of those destructive years. "Those of us involved in the movement still kept trying to go on with our work, until one by one each of us arrived at our own pivotal moment when enough was enough."[41] This sense of despair experienced at the time, however, belied the clear gains women had made in politics and legislative reform.

Second-wave feminism, as it gained momentum in the 1960s, pushed the Democratic Party and the Republican Party to respond to women's demands for greater representation. Grassroots agitation over a range of issues placed further pressure on parties to respond to accommodate demands addressing a range of social issues. Political competition encouraged both parties to seek alliances with new social groups.[42] The progressive agenda proposed by feminists aligned most easily with the Democratic Party, especially its northern representatives, although Republicans, with a tradition of supporting the ERA, strove to accommodate itself to liberal-leaning feminism. The rise of the New Right and the religious right, however, provided an opportunity for Republicans to mobilize anti-feminist women and men.

In 1972, Title IX was added as an amendment to the Education Amendments Act, stating that no person on the basis of sex could be "denied the benefits of, or be subjected to discrimination under any education program or activity receiving Federal financial assistance." The act revolutionized women's athletics in high schools and colleges by requiring, in effect, equity in school funding for female athletic programs. Between 1971 and 1996, the number of females participating in high-school sports teams increased from 300,000 to 2.4 million. In 1974, Richard Nixon, after intense lobbying from NOW, organized labor, and feminists, signed the Equal Credit Opportunity Act, which criminalized discrimination of women by credit agencies.

The passage of the ERA by Congress in 1972 revealed that politicians in both parties were anxious to show that they stood on the side of women.[43] The amendment declared, "Equality of rights under the law shall not be denied or abridged by the United States or by any State on account of sex." The amendment had been floating around since 1923, when Alice Paul at the National Woman's Party endorsed it. At the time, some feminists, such as the National Consumers League's Florence Kelley, expressed opposition to the amendment, warning that it would undermine legislation protecting female workers. The amendment won endorsement within the Republican Party in 1940, and in 1944 the Democratic Party endorsed it. When a modified version of the amendment came up in 1950, Carl Hayden, a conservative Democratic senator from Arizona, tried to address the issue of female labor rights by adding a rider that the amendment should not be construed to impair any rights, benefits, or exemptions conferred by law upon persons of the female sex. Purist ERA supporters opposed any restrictions on the amendment. As a consequence, the amendment was defeated on the floor in 1950. The division over female labor rights carried into the 1970s for ratification, when some unions, such as the United Auto Workers and the International Ladies' Garment Workers, at first opposed the amendment. Under pressure from feminists, organized labor soon came on board in support of the ERA.

In 1967, the ERA continued to languish in Congress because the liberal chair of the House Judiciary Committee, Emanuel Celler, a Democrat from New York, continued to support women's protective labor legislation. In the summer of 1970, matters came to a head over the ERA when Representative Martha Griffins, a Democratic from Michigan, won support in the House to bring the amendment to the floor. After an hour-long debate, the House overwhelmingly approved the measure in a 352 to 15 vote. After the measure was held up in the Senate, the House again passed it, followed by the Senate in late March 1972, supported by Democrats and Republicans with the approval of the Nixon administration. Congress granted seven years for the amendment to be ratified by three-fourths of the states (thirty-eight states), as required by the Constitution.

Within the first year, women across the country mobilized to support the ERA. After thirty states ratified it, the amendment appeared headed for quick ratification. Any celebration was short lived after longtime conservative activist Phyllis Schlafly organized a movement to stop the ERA.[44] Schlafly brought to her successful crusade a number of advantages that revealed the limits of feminists as political strategists and, equally important, feminist overreach. Although the ERA failed to be ratified in the end, many states passed their own ERA laws and amendments. At the same time, radical feminists won within the movement support for gay and lesbian rights. This was no pyrrhic victory in changing American attitudes toward gay rights, including same-sex marriage. At the time, though, the feminist push for lesbian rights and reproductive rights appeared to have backfired, ultimately leading to the defeat of the ERA.

The winds appeared to be at the backs of the feminist movement and the ERA in 1972, yet whirlwinds of inner discord swirled as the drive for the ERA stalled. Establishment leaders of the ERA accused radicals of pursuing strategies bound to alienate state legislators and the general public. Radicals accused established leaders, in turn, of being too timid in their tactics. Thus, from the outset, the pro-ERA movement was divided on strategy and tactics. NOW refused to join the principal pro-amendment organization, ERAmerica, in the campaign for ratification. ERAmerica was an umbrella organization representing 130 groups, including labor unions, the ACLU, and religious and political organizations. ERAmerica, based in Washington, D.C., advised state coalitions on legislative lobbying, mobilizing public opinion and testimony at hearings. ERAmerica brought organization and money to the campaign. Cochaired by Democrat Liz Carpenter and Republican Elly Peterson, ERAmerica sought to replicate what they described as a candidate-like political campaign. As one ERAmerica strategist observed, "The name of the game is turning legislators and the general public around on ERA."[45] Movie and television stars Alan Alda, Carol Burnett, and Lily Tomlin joined other celebrities in supporting ERA. First Lady Betty Ford and Ronald Reagan's daughter Maureen Reagan spoke out on behalf of the amendment. Thirty-two magazine editors came together to promote pro-ERA articles in their publications.[46] Regional and state field organizers were deployed to direct lobbying efforts aimed at state legislators.

Meanwhile, NOW conducted its own separate grassroots campaign through state and local chapters, linking the amendment to legalized abortion and gay rights. NOW's ratification strategy differed from ERAmerica's approach. NOW chapters pursued a civil rights social protest struggle, that is, the politics of the street. NOW chapters organized rallies, marches, and guerrilla demonstrations to threaten legislators who did not vote for the ERA. Tensions between ERAmerica and NOW became pronounced when ratification of the amendment began to slow. ERAmerica leaders became convinced that NOW was only using the fight over the amendment to boost fundraising and membership for its own purposes. As relations between the organizations became more strained, ERAmerica leaders accused NOW of promoting social protest for its own purposes with total disregard to getting the ERA ratified. No doubt, NOW did use the struggle over the amendment to increase its membership and its financial coffers, which grew immensely during this period.

The larger issue, though, was more than just the contentious factionalism within the feminist movement itself; it was a dilemma faced by a social protest movement translating its demands into actual legislation. Achieving successful legislation usually involves compromise and not making too many enemies. For a younger generation of radical feminists represented by NOW, the Equal Rights Amendment was only a small part of the larger struggle for reproductive rights, lesbian rights, and transformative social change.[47] These younger activists abhorred ERAmerica's old-fashioned lobbying efforts and working within the traditional political system. These differences were captured by one ERAmerica lobbyist in Illinois who wrote to the national office, "You can imagine how the hard-nosed Cook County pols who inherited Mayor Daley's power have looked upon the 'braless, loud mouthed NOW women.'"[48]

During the ERA fight, NOW itself became increasingly radicalized. Its handbook, *Revolution: Tomorrow Is Now,* produced in 1973 to acquaint local chapters with national policy, expressed positions that distanced itself from its middle-class origins. The handbook declared that NOW supported the furthering of the sexual revolution by pressing for widespread sexual education, provision of birth control information and contraceptives, and the repeal of laws restricting abortion, contraception, and sexual activity between consenting adults in private. It called for sex education early in public schools to include "factual information on contraception and on the ecological crisis of overpopulation." NOW noted that "the lesbian is doubly oppressed both as a woman and as a homosexual." NOW also denounced women's work in voluntary community organizations as "another form of activity which serves to reinforce the second-class status of women, which is one more instance of the ongoing exploitation of women." NOW decried the "enslavement of the body and mind which the church historically has imposed on women," and for religious seminaries to "immediately stop and repudiate their propagation of sexist, male supremacist doctrine." All denominations, the handbook declared, should ordain women.[49] In its pursuit of equality, the organization demanded the end of preferential treatment of veterans in employment.

In 1974, NOW elected Karen DeCrow, a Syracuse, New York, attorney, as its president. DeCrow ran on the slogan "Out of the Mainstream, into the Revolution," arguing the NOW's major priorities should be jobs for women and homosexual rights. Friedan tried to stop DeCrow's election by accusing her of lacking any tactical sense, pointing out that DeCrow had given a speech in Illinois calling for abortion on demand a week before the ERA ratification came up before a vote in the state legislature.[50] Under DeCrow, NOW threw itself into support of homosexual rights legislation on the state and local levels. The organization pledged to work for a gay rights bill, introduced by Representative Abzug in Congress. In her keynote address at the NOW national convention, Abzug declared that her organization had launched its Day of Outrage campaign against "the Roman Catholic hierarchy's interference of the woman's right to control her own body." In the speech, she made a public apology to gay women and gay men for the previous "oppression of lesbians and gay men in NOW."[51]

Gloria Steinem echoed the left turn in NOW, even while adroitly keeping her connections with the liberal Democratic Party establishment. She denounced religion as a "con job" in a speech at Southern Methodist University; declared at Indiana University that "feminism should be valued above nationalism" and that she was a feminist "before I am American"; and speaking at a Jewish synagogue in St. Louis told the audience that women opposing the ERA were little more than slaves, declaring, "It's the ol' house n***** syndrome that came up in the civil rights movement when so many said our people did not care." She added that "the movement is in a serious sense a revolution not a reform."[52] She played a critical role in forcing the Carter administration to change the title of its conference on the family to "families" to include gay families. Such rhetoric, while reflecting genuine feminist sentiment (although perhaps not shared by more moderate feminists), played to her audiences but did little to expand support for the ERA.

This leftward turn by NOW in the mid-1970s, although appearing less radical forty years later, fed into a growing reaction against the ERA. By early 1973, the *New York Times* reported that the news media had begun detecting a rising anti-ERA sentiment across the nation.[53] The regional representative of NOW warned that "if we focus on lesbianism or minorities or peace or any other issue than feminism then we will be defeating ourselves."[54] ERAmerica organizers became increasingly aware that feminism, especially as projected by radical feminists, was alienating the general public, especially average American women. Legal counsel to ERAmerica Bonnie Cowan warned in 1976 that "women's groups are only now beginning to realize how little identification they have made with homemakers. And I, for one, prefer to try to keep homemakers from winding up either 1) alienated or 2) deprived."[55] The complaint that the pro-ERA movement was failing to reach Middle America became common. An Illinois organizer wrote to the national ERAmerica office in 1980, as it became clear that state ratification was going to fail: "We simply have to reach Mr. and Mrs. Mainstream. That has been our failure and unless we are willing to do whatever, spend whatever, we must awaken them or well forget the whole thing."[56]

State ratification for the ERA had begun to slow by the time Jimmy Carter, a Georgia Democrat, stepped into the White House in 1977. His presidency found itself caught in the rip tides of feminism. He found himself alienating conservative and moderate state Democratic legislators for his support for the ERA, while feminists accused him of not doing enough for their cause. He tried, however. He supported a $5 million appropriation of federal funds for the International Women's Year Commission, following the U.N. declaration that 1975 was the International Women's Year. Carter's predecessor in the White House, Gerald Ford, following the U.N. lead, appointed a U.S. Commission on International Women's Year (IWY). The commission called for a national conference to be held in Houston in 1977. Ford's and Carter's support for the conference indicated the gains the feminist movement was making in the established political arena.

Houston and the International Women's Year

The conference, however, proved to be a public relations disaster for the pro-ERA cause. More than 20,000 women gathered at the Albert Thomas Convention Center in late 1977.

The Houston IWY Conference cannot be compared quite to the Russian czar sponsoring a Bolshevik conference on "How to Make a Revolution," but nonetheless there is a certain irony in the federal government sponsoring a "radical libber" national meeting. As Gloria Steinem asked, "Could a government-sponsored conference really be populist and inclusive?"[57] Federal support for the International Women's Year showed the inroads the feminist movement had made within both parties. The conference marked a high point for feminism as a unified social movement, but also revealed its limitation to a broader appeal to the general American public.[58]

Delegates attending the conference voted on a multitude of resolutions to address economic, social, and racial disparities among women, embodied in a "Plan of Action." Equal pay for women, federally supported child-care centers, early childhood education, job training for minority women, and the expansion of social welfare programs fit within a broad liberal agenda. ERA opponents, however, gave little attention to this standard liberal fare. What drew attention were two resolutions—reproductive freedom and sexual preference.

The reproductive freedom resolution was extensive in its demands for federal and private insurance funding for abortion (on demand), family planning for teenagers, and sex education in all schools including elementary schools. It overwhelmingly passed in the conference vote. More controversial was the sexual preference resolution in support of gay rights. This plank emerged from a year-long grassroots campaign organized by lesbian activists. Lesbian rights had been excluded during the 1975 U.N. IWY Conference in Mexico City. Furthermore, the Ford-appointed commission report avoided any statement on sexual-orientation discrimination. Bella Abzug, presiding officer of the Carter-appointed commission, which took over in 1977, remained undecided on whether to include any resolution on gay discrimination. Martha Griffiths, the former congressperson from Michigan who had pushed the ERA through Congress, wrote to commissioners who opposed the inclusion of lesbianism in the Plan of Action for fear that it would undermine ERA support. She declared in her letter, "Homosexuality is a national issue of concern to men and women. . . . I see no evidence that lesbians are more discriminated against than male homosexuals. Discrimination because of sexual preference is *not* discrimination because of sex."[59]

The demand for inclusion of the sexual preference plank in the final Plan of Action provided an opportunity for gay activists to mobilize.[60] They were led by IWY national commissioner Jean O'Leary, who had briefly been a novitiate of the Roman Catholic religious order Sisters of the Holy Humility of Mary. After leaving the convent and with a degree from Cleveland State University, she moved to New York City in 1971, where she became a gay activist and helped form the Lesbian Feminist Liberation. As codirector of the National Gay Task Force, she worked with Carter White House staff member Midge Costanza to organize the first meeting with gay activists in the White House.

O'Leary used her position to urge that state coordinating committees planning for the national conference include workshops on "sexual or affectional preference." The inclusion of this topic allowed lesbian activists to organize in preconvention workshops and later in state conventions. As activist Charlotte Bunch recalled, "The lesbian community began bringing out large numbers of women to attend [state] conferences, especially in the big cities."[61] At the California state convention to elect delegates to the national conference and vote on the Plan of Action, large numbers of lesbian activists were mobilized. California sent the largest group of openly gay and lesbian delegates to the national conference. Lesbian activism was replicated in other state conventions. Lesbian rights resolutions were adopted in thirty states. These resolutions created tensions within the national commission, leading Deputy Coordinator Catherine East to resign because she believed that the inclusion of a lesbian plank would set back the ERA.

The sexual preference plank came up for a vote in Houston at the end of the Sunday plenary session. As one journalist said, "It was obvious to everyone that the lesbian issue had become the emotional focal point of the conference."[62] A fierce floor debate followed, with opponents declaring the plank was an "albatross" for the movement. Finally, Betty Friedan spoke. She had long opposed the inclusion of sexual preference issues in the feminist and pro-ERA movement. She now reversed positions with a declaration, "I am known to be violently opposed to the lesbian issue. . . . Now priority is in passing the ERA. And because there is nothing in it that will give any protection to homosexuals, I believe we must help the women who are lesbians." Activists carrying signs saying "We Are Everywhere" cheered in jubilation when the plank was endorsed.[63]

Opponents of the ERA seized on the lesbian and abortion issues in the final stages of the ratification battle. Phyllis Schlafly, leading the STOP ERA movement, declared that the Houston IWY Conference had become the "Midway" of the pro-ERA movement. "The Women's Lib movement has sealed its own doom by deliberately hanging around its own neck the albatross of abortion, lesbianism, pornography, and Federal Control." In the final death throes of the ERA, the Houston IWY resolutions became a centerpiece of opposition. As one anti-ERA organizer said, the Houston IWY resolutions are "the best recruiting tool I've ever had. I just spend twenty minutes reading the Houston resolutions to them. That's all I have to do."[64] At the conference, anti-ERA activists collected boxes of materials from exhibitors' tables, including lesbian magazines and a display of sex toys. Photos of these materials were put on sixty sheets of posterboard and shown at meetings in more than thirty states. Congressional supporters of the ERA extended the ratification deadline in late 1977 for a thirty-nine-month period, to June 30, 1982. (Whether Congress could extend a deadline contained in an amendment was not clear.) What was clear to most was that ERA ratification had become a lost cause.

Pro-ERA activists became increasingly frustrated. Steinem warned of massive civil disobedience if the ERA failed. Militant activists denounced ERAmerica leaders as too tepid. Activist attorney Florence Kennedy denounced Schlafly as a "pigocrat," and said, "I just don't see why some people don't hit Phyllis Schlafly in the mouth."[65] Pro-ERA activists were stunned by the failure to ratify the ERA. They spoke of a rising far right-wing movement that had caught them by surprise. The anti-ERA movement, they claimed, was racist; Schlafly, they said, was herself a racist. They tried to tie her and her anti-ERA movement to the Ku Klux Klan and the John Birch Society. At the same time, feminists blamed Democratic male leaders for not waging a tough enough battle on behalf of the ERA. President Carter came in for particular criticism, especially when he forced the resignation of Bella Abzug as cochair of the President's Advisory Committee for Women in 1979 after the committee criticized the administration's anti-inflationary policies as hurting women and then used a State Department mailing permit for sending a newsletter comparing the Mormon Church's policies on race to the Ku Klux Klan. When Carter came up for reelection in 1980, NOW refused to endorse him. NOW's opposition did not cost Carter the election; nonetheless, NOW's opposition to Carter in the face of a Ronald Reagan victory seemed odd even at the time.

The lesbian and abortion issues in themselves were not the cause of the ERA's failure. The nation was divided on the abortion issue, and the majority of Americans believed that sexual preferences should remain in the bedroom. The larger public relations problem was that the seemingly innocuously worded amendment was so open-ended that it allowed expansive interpretation. Any interpretation, opponents claimed, would come through the courts, and in the late 1970s there was growing opposition to what was described as "judicial activism." In addition, the tenor of the Houston IWY Conference projected a radicalism that contradicted supporters who claimed that the ERA was a modest amendment within the American tradition of equal rights.

The defeat of the ERA proved to be a setback psychologically for the feminist movement. Their claims to represent American women appeared tenuous, if not completely illusionary. As one feminist Sylvia Ann Hewlett concluded, "It is sobering to realize that the ERA was defeated not by Barry Goldwater, Jerry Falwell [leader of the religious right], or any combination of male chauvinist pigs, but by women who were alienated from a feminist movement, the values of which seemed elitist and disconnected from the lives of ordinary people."[66]

The Aftermath of Feminism at the End of the 1970s

The defeat of the ERA and Ronald Reagan's election in 1980 cast a dark cloud across the feminist movement. As one feminist activist, Karla Jay, concluded in her 1999 memoir *Tales of the Lavender Menace,* "Though the grand revolution we were expecting never came, we are all freer today because of the courage of many individuals who were willing to risk everything for gender justice."[67]

Jay was not an exception in feeling disappointment in the decades that followed. For many, the subsequent generations of younger women did not seem to appreciate the sacrifices and struggle of an earlier era that allowed the greater equality they enjoyed in the twenty-first century. Feminism itself seemed ideologically fragmented, having been transformed from a social movement to an interest group. Intrafactional war continued into the 1980s, as seen in heated exchanges over feminism and pornography. Debates continued over bisexualism and lesbianism.[68]

This disappointment on the part of many feminists followed a similar pattern of previous social activists who sought radical social transformation only to find the established political order watering down and absorbing parts of their agenda. Such was the case with second-wave feminism. Revolutionary demands gave way to reform. Yet, whatever the disappointment, feminism as a social movement achieved much. By the twenty-first century, women were earning the majority of bachelor's, master's, and doctoral degrees in the social sciences. A higher proportion of Hispanic women were attending college than white males. The majority of pharmacists and accountants were women. A third of physicians, lawyers, and judges were women. Nearly 140,000 women in the sixty leading corporations had made it into middle management. Trends suggest that in the twenty-first century, women will be wealthier, more powerful, and more competitive than men.[69] Of course, these social trends were not the result of the feminist movement exclusively, but grassroots pressure forced private and public organizations to open doors.

Grassroots activism bolstered feminists involved in traditional politics by presenting feminism as a large social movement. Established politicians within both the Republican and Democratic Parties assumed the women's vote was up for grabs, so they wanted to court this vote by presenting themselves as pro-woman. This was evident in the bipartisan support given to the Equal Rights Amendment when it passed Congress in 1972. The female vote, always important, became a deciding vote on the national and state levels. The widening "gender gap" presented an exceptional problem for Republicans, who discovered that more female voters described themselves as and voted Democratic than Republican. In the Democratic Party in particular, women emerged as powerful players. In 2016, the Democratic Party nominated the first woman, Hillary Rodham Clinton, to head its ticket, and the speaker of the House in 2020 was a woman, Nancy Pelosi. In 2018, 102 women were elected to the House, many of them women of color. This set a record for women winning congressional races.

Legal and legislative gains were made in this period despite the defeat of the ERA. Most notable was the inclusion of women in the Civil Rights Act of 1964. In 1967, President Johnson signed Executive Order 11375 banning discrimination on the basis of sex in hiring and employment in the federal workforce and among government contractors. The Equal Employment Opportunity Commission eliminated segregated job advertising. In 1972, Title IX of the U.S. Education Amendment outlawed discrimination in any educational program or activity involving women. Social Security benefits for women were extended in 1972. In 1974, the Equal Credit Opportunity Act was enacted. Congress outlawed in 1978 pregnancy discrimination in the workplace. Throughout this period, an array of court decisions expanded the rights of women.

Arguably the more important changes fostered by grassroots activism occurred on the cultural level. Ascertaining a direct connection between grassroots activism and cultural change is difficult to measure, but attitudes toward women's equality became more acceptable. For example, a Roper opinion poll conducted in 1974 showed a remarkable shift in attitudes toward women from 1970 to 1974. In 1970, a majority of men and women opposed efforts to strengthen or change women's status in society. By 1974, strong majorities supported strengthening women's social status. Surprisingly, a higher percentage of men (63 percent) than women (57 percent) declared they were in favor of strengthening women's status in society.[70]

This positive feeling toward the women's liberation movement continued into the twenty-first century, as two-thirds to three-quarters of men and

women reported "very" or "mostly favorable" opinions of the women's movement in the late 1980s and 1990s. These favorable attitudes were especially
apparent among younger men and women.[71] Ironically, while the majority of
American men and women supported the "women's movement," they were
less favorable to "feminists." The majority of men and women described their
feeling for feminists as unfavorable. Furthermore, an increasing number of
Americans found the term *feminist* an insult. Only about a fourth of women
describe themselves as feminists, with little difference between older and
younger women. In short, Americans appeared to support the goals of the
movement and the movement itself but not those who called themselves feminists. The label *feminist* might carry a negative connotation, but overall attitu-
dinal changes in the status of women had changed significantly in the postwar
period. At the same time, the success of the movement seemed to undermine
the importance many Americans placed on women's rights. Most men and
women see women's rights as personally important, but only a small percentage rate the issue as "very important." Most of those surveyed in various polls
revealed that they did not pay a lot of attention to the women's movement.

While the term *feminism* continued to have negative connotations in the
general public, feminist influence was apparent in popular culture itself. Television sit-coms, once focused in the 1950s on traditional families, gave way
to such shows as *The Mary Tyler Show* (1970–1977), *Maude* (1972–1978),
One Day at a Time (1975–1984), and *Alice* (1970–1985). *Wonder Woman*
premiered in 1975. Television watchers were introduced to tough women on
such shows as *The Avengers*, premiering on American television in 1965, and
Police Woman. Female rock stars, such as Pat Benatar, Joan Jett, Patti Smith,
and Nancy and Ann Wilson broke through in the late 1960s and 1970s,
often singing overtly feminist songs. Australian pop singer Helen Reddy had
a smash hit, "I Am Woman," in 1971, while Nancy Sinatra released "These
Boots Are Made for Walking" in 1966.

Science fiction writer Ursula K. Le Guin explored androgyny in her best-
seller novel *The Left Hand of Darkness,* published in 1969, in which her main
characters are ambisexual, able to change gender at will. Older feminist novels, such as Charlotte Perkins Gilman's *Herland* (1915) and Kate Chopin's
The Awakening (1899), were republished to wide readerships. Mary Griffith's
Three Hundred Years Hence, published in 1836, was rediscovered. The power
of this literature was found in its popular readership, classroom assignments,
and academic discourse.[72] Indeed, many feminists noted that one of the
greatest gains feminism made was inside the academy, as women's studies

programs took root. Within the humanities and social sciences, as well as in many science courses, the inclusion of gender became required. Radical feminist categories informed much feminist theory in these courses.[73]

Second-wave feminism accomplished much from its perspective in the 1970s. These gains came through social protest and grassroots organizing. Feminism became institutionalized, in its liberal form in employment law and practices and in more radical articulation within universities and colleges through women's and gender studies programs. Responding to social protest and anxious to secure the woman's vote, the Democratic and Republican Parties proclaimed themselves defenders of women's and gay rights. State ERA constitutional amendments became the legal foundation in *Obergefell v. Hodges* in 2015, the Supreme Court case that recognized same-sex marriage. Second-wave feminism sought at times revolutionary transformation. Gains were made, but feminists failed in creating a completely new social egalitarian order.[74] Instead, the political order, resting on a powerful administrative state created in the twentieth century, was maintained. The struggle for female equality was turned over to the experts—bureaucrats, human resource officers, and lawyers. In this world, feminist activists became another interest group competing among many others.

5 | The Populist Right: Anti-Statism and Anti-Elitism

Following World War II, a right-wing grassroots movement emerged that transformed modern American politics, just as had the black civil rights and second-wave feminist movements. Unlike previous social movements, though, right-wing protest appeared without a single dominant leader or organization but nonetheless attracted mass support. Like other protest movements it was anti-elitist in challenging party leaders, politics as usual, the administrative state, and the privileged order. More important, right-wing populists did not demand more government; they demanded less government. The grassroots right expressed a rebellion against the welfare-regulatory-administrative state that was a consequence of previous social protest movements. Right-wing populism sowed the seeds of distrust in government that by the end of the twentieth century were shared by the political left and right.

The grassroots right expressed a general suspicion of the ability of a massive governmental bureaucracy to solve the nation's problems.[1] This anti-statism expressed itself in multiple ways—an intense anti-communism, local protests against public education bureaucrats, and, later, opposition to radical feminism and high taxes. The populist right was a diverse movement, organizationally and in membership. These protests raised legitimate concerns, but often leaders and the rank and file broached, and indeed dove deep into, paranoia, conspiracy theories, and racial and religious bigotry. The Republican Party tapped into this suspicion of big government and generalized fear that things in America had gone awry. The challenge for the GOP was to channel the popular right into votes, without alienating the mainstream or taking on the baggage of trying to defend political extremism. Always swirling around the popular right was a centrifugal force of third-party politics.

Right-wing protest in post–World War II America—although taking different organizational forms and addressing a range of issues from anti-communism in the 1950s to cultural decay in the 1960s and 1970s—expressed a popular social protest movement against big government.[2] As one Republican declared after his party took control of Congress in 1946, "The results of last November's election showed a strong protest against Federal bureaucracy and its dictatorial tactics. They indicate that our people are at last coming to realize the growing menace to our liberties under the New Deal regime." Bureaucracy, conservatives believed, was the nemesis to American liberty. Representative Harold Knutson, representing Minnesota's Fifth District, spoke for many in 1943 when he declared, "For years we Republicans have been warning that short-haired women and long-haired men of alien minds in the administrative branch of government were trying to corrupt the American way of life and install a hybrid oligarchy in Washington."[3] Knutson's sexual innuendo joined with anti-bureaucratic rhetoric was not uncommon.

The populist right can be divided into two phases: popular anti-communism from 1946 to 1959; and a cultural and economic backlash that began in the late 1960s. The first period was characterized by deep denominational and factional divisions within the anti-communist right. In the second phase, the right unified in opposition to abortion, radical feminism, and high taxes. In both phases the grassroots right expressed its fear that the federal government had become an instrument subverting American liberty—and traditional culture itself.

Those writing about the far right at the time along with later scholars tended to lump all right-wing groups in both periods together. However, right-wing leaders, organizations, and membership should be distinguished ideologically and demographically. The ultra-extremist and overtly racist organizations, such as the Ku Klux Klan, and paramilitary organizations that emerged in the 1960s and 1970s, such as the Minutemen and Aryan Nation, undertook violent, illegal, and unconstitutional actions in pursuit of its goals. Ultra-extremist formations employed violence—from cross burnings to terrorism—to achieve their ends. They believed that government, established political parties, and major institutions were controlled by a global Jewish cabal. These ultra-extremist groups attracted lower-income, poorly educated whites, often from rural areas.

The popular grassroots right—as distinguished from the ultra-extremists—saw themselves as restoring constitutional order and traditional culture and preventing what they perceived as the threat to political liberty. They worked within the legal confines of the system. The popular grassroots right, as surveys showed at the time, attracted middle-class, college-educated suburban whites.

They believed communism and secularism represented the nation's drift away from the founding principles that had made America an exceptional nation, but their mission was to awaken average Americans to this threat through education and political mobilization. This is not to say that leaders and their followers were not given at times to political paranoia or to conspiracy theories, but they were not violent revolutionaries. The populist right shared a distrust of elites in politics, the media, education, and entertainment, even while disagreeing often as to the underlying forces subverting the American republic and traditional culture. At the same time, right-wing leaders often spent more time attacking one another than they did the alleged enemy.

Within the popular grassroots right, there was not agreement on partisan alignment.[4] Many of the anti-communist organizations viewed themselves as nonpartisan. For example, evangelist Reverend Bob Jones in the 1950s aligned his religious anti-communist crusade with the Republican Party; yet other popular anti-communist organizations welcomed Democrats. For example, Senator Thomas Dodd, a Democrat from Connecticut, and Senator Paul Douglas, a Democrat from Illinois, were featured at anti-communist rallies.

Channeling right-wing populist sentiment into traditional partisan politics proved formidable. The larger mainstream conservative movement, led by William F. Buckley, founding editor of the *National Review* in 1955, sought to distance itself from anti-Semites and conspiracy theorists who talked about global conspiracies involving Communists directed by Moscow, corporate globalists seeking a "one world government," a Jewish cabal, and even Masons operating through the Bavarian Illuminati. Buckley understood that such theories and their proponents provided easy targets for opponents. In the early 1960s, Buckley sought to distance the mainstream conservative movement from what he considered extremists in the John Birch Society, who provided easy targets for liberals trying to link the Goldwater presidential campaign with right-wing nuts.

Republicans found bringing Catholics, Protestants, and Mormons together into a coherent voting block equally difficult. Important in this regard was Phyllis Schlafly's crusade against feminism in the 1970s. In her STOP ERA movement, she discovered that traditional Catholic, evangelical Protestant, and Mormon women shared a common enemy in feminism. Republican strategists, seeing what Schlafly accomplished in her anti-ERA fight, took a cue from her in the 1978 midterm elections. These strategists used social issues—abortion and anti-feminism—as wedge issues to attract former Democratic voters to cast ballots for Republican candidates. Led by such ministers as Pat Robertson and Jerry Falwell, the religious right engaged 50 million evangelical Christians, who constituted a radical form of grassroots activism.[5] The mobilization of evangelical Protestants proved critical in winning the South for the Republican Party.

This coincided with a pro-growth economic agenda put forward by the GOP. Republican critics charged that the GOP southern strategy then and later was merely rhetoric to attract racist voters. No doubt, race remained an important issue in American politics then as it does today, but the channeling of the grassroots right into the Republican Party had been brewing since the end of World War II. The movement tapped into the patriotism, deep religiosity, and anti-statist impulse within the electorate. In this respect, the grassroots populism of the right expressed a reaction against the liberal state that had emerged as a consequence of earlier popular protest movements.

Stage 1: Popular Anti-Communism and the Enemy Within

Anti-communism became the primary focus of the postwar right. Widespread anti-communist sentiment within the American public existed before and throughout World War II, but intensified in the early Cold War years with revelations of Soviet spy activity inside the United States during World War II. The Soviet Union's expansion into Eastern Europe only heightened distrust of the Soviet Union and communist domestic activity. The outbreak of the Korean War in June 1950 further accelerated anti-communist feelings throughout the American public. Anti-communism expressed genuine concern among average Americans and right-wing activists of the threat posed by the Soviet Union (and later China) and domestic communist activity. Grassroots anti-communist activists and leaders differed among themselves about the threats posed by domestic communists, but all agreed on the external threat posed by the Soviet Union.

The popular anti-communism movement reached its height in the 1950s and began to decline in the early 1960s under direct attack from the John F. Kennedy administration and liberal critics. Popular anti-communism gained momentum in the early Cold War through a religious revival that swept across America in the 1950s.[6] Anti-communism found expression in national right-wing organizations, religious bodies, local groups that came together over specific issues, and right-wing media outlets. Anti-communist radio programs could be heard across the country. Tens of thousands of radio listeners tuned in every week to hear fervid denunciations of the communist threat.[7]

Although many leading anti-communist organizations and leaders received support from big donors and conservative foundations, the anti-communist crusade struck a chord within the larger public. Many average Americans did not need advertisers or corporations to convince them to be anti-communist or Christian. Communist hatred of religion helped fuel anti-communism during the religious upsurge in 1950s America.

Two points are important to note in understanding the Cold War anti-communist crusade. First, in the beginning liberals took the lead in confronting communism at home. Anxious to address Communist Party factions in the Democratic Party, labor unions, student organizations, religious organizations, civil liberties and civil rights organizations, and various liberal groups purged Communist Party members from their ranks. The Truman administration enthusiastically rooted communists out of government and unions and indicted party leaders. Communist factions controlled nine unions and had sizable factions in other unions, including the United Auto Workers. Communist leaders were ousted in some unions, and in some cases, Communist Party–controlled unions were expelled from the American Federation of Labor (AFL) and the Congress for Industrial Unions (CIO). Communists were banned in the American Civil Liberties Union and the National Association for the Advancement of Colored People. Within the Democratic Party large-scale and bitter purges of Communist Party members occurred, usually led by liberals, such as Hubert Humphrey in the Minnesota Democratic Farmer-Labor Party. The Americans for Democratic Action, a liberal organization, recruited young organizers such as George McGovern, later a Democratic Party presidential nominee, to help in these purges.

The second point worth making about Cold War anti-communism is that the popular right was not unified. At the height of the Red Scare, the visibility of Senator Joseph McCarthy, the House Un-American Activities Committee hearings, and such visible anti-communist personalities as Monsignor Fulton Sheen, former party member Ben Mandel, J. B. Matthews, and others, suggested a cohesive and coherent movement existed. Historians looking back on this period reached similar conclusions about a well-organized network of right-wing anti-communists. As one historian writes, these key members of the anti-communist movement represented "a surprisingly self-conscious and effective network that helped shape the anti-communist crusade of the 1940s and 1950s."[8] A more accurate description of popular anti-communism is to describe it as anti-communist "movements." Various organizations, local movements, political leaders, and popular figures shared obvious hostility toward

Soviet Communism and fears of domestic communism. At times there was shared cooperation between leaders and organization. But anti-communist activity sprang up from a variety of sources, including religious groups, local activists, politicians, self-identified patriots, and opportunists. They differed sharply as to strategy, tactics, and the extent of the communist domestic threat. Popular anti-communist organizations and leaders often seemed to be more at war with one another than with communists.

Given the involvement of religious organizations and leaders—Roman Catholics, evangelical Protestants, and fundamentalist Christians—inevitably differences emerged in the anti-communist crusade that precluded a unified front. Deep anti-Catholic prejudices among Protestant anti-communists prevented easy alliance with Roman Catholics. At the same time, anti-communist Protestants divided between fundamentalists and evangelicals theologically and politically. For example, fundamentalist Carl McIntire, a fervent anti-communist with a national following, publicly denounced evangelist Billy Graham for his support of the Republican Party. Furthermore, McIntire was as anti-Catholic as he was anti-communist. He denounced the Vatican as the whore of Babylon. He refused to cooperate with Protestant evangelicals, even though they shared anti-communist views and agreed that secularism was a threat to a Christian republic. McIntire did not spare mainstream Protestants from his attacks. He enlisted well-known anti-communist and Senator Joseph McCarthy staffer J. B. Matthews to produce a widely circulated pamphlet, *How Red Is the National Council of Churches?* a twelve-page polemic accusing communists or party supporters (fellow travelers) of having infiltrated denominations, especially Methodists.

Divisions within the Protestant anti-communist right went beyond just fundamentalism versus evangelicalism. Fundamentalist Reverend Bob Jones, whose father had founded a university, made anti-communism a principal focus of his revivalist project. Initially, he worked on and promoted Billy Graham's revival efforts. However, in the late 1950s he broke with Graham, publicly denouncing him for cooperating with mainline Protestant churches. The rise of the black civil rights movement in the 1950s also aggravated differences in the religious right. Billy Graham, the nation's leading evangelist, denounced segregation as anti-Christian and sought cooperation with black civil rights leader Martin Luther King Jr., a fellow Baptist. Fundamentalists, such as McIntire and Jones, denounced King as an "apostate" and a tool of the communists, if not a communist himself. In their opposition to black civil rights, they sided with the segregationists and racists in the South.

Noel Smith, editor of the fundamentalist newspaper *Baptist Bible Tribune*, made repeated charges that that civil rights activists who supported legalization of racial intermarriage were communists out to subvert the nation. He declared, "To make intermarriage between Whites and Negroes as commonplace as black tomcats squalling in back alleys is the supreme goal of this integration campaign."[9] In Texas, Reverend Carey Daniel invoked the Bible in defense of racial segregation with the publication *God, the Original Segregationist* (1955), which sold a million copies and was abridged in the *Dallas Morning News.*[10] The fundamentalist defense of racial segregation and racist statements alienated evangelical Protestants and Roman Catholics. More important, fundamentalists through their racism isolated themselves politically, especially among Republicans, both in the North and the South.

If organizational disagreements were apparent on the anti-communist right, even greater differences were apparent between leaders and the rank and file. Surveys of grassroots anti-communist activists in this period are few and far between, but those that were taken reveal a far different story about how contemporary observers and later scholars depicted followers of anti-communists Fred Schwarz and his Christian Anti-Communist Crusade or Robert Welch and his John Birch Society. Surveys showed that rank-and-file activists differed significantly from their leaders on key issues.[11] Those who attended Schwarz's Christian Anti-Communist Crusade seminars and rallies identified themselves as Christian, but they were not Protestant fundamentalists. Nor were they racists. In fact, they overwhelmingly opposed southern segregation (92 percent), favored medical care for the aged and federal aid to education, and were divided as to the extent of communist infiltration into government. Sixty-five percent believed that there was some communist infiltration in the State Department but not in other government agencies, and the majority of respondents did not believe there was widespread communist infiltration in government at all.[12]

Those involved in the Christian Anti-Communist Crusade were more favorably disposed to universal suffrage and opposed voter restrictions based on education or property than other college-educated Americans.[13] The social scientists who conducted this survey attributed this high support for universal suffrage to Crusaders' faith in "democratic procedures." This belief in the democratic process belies caricatures of the extreme right at the time and later as anti-democratic racists.

Surveys of the John Birch Society rank and file (known as Birchers) are equally scarce, but those few that were conducted also reveal a different profile than what we think of as a typical Bircher.[14] Birchers were overwhelmingly Protestant, more highly educated than the national average, and generally white-collar professionals. Most identified as Republicans. Most favored weakening the presidency while strengthening Congress. Birchers expressed anti-statist sentiment by opposing the welfare state and supporting low taxes. This sentiment expressed distrust of a centralized federal government, not explicit racism. Only 14 of the 650 Bircher respondents in one survey believed the civil rights movement was a major problem.[15] Most interestingly, their opposition to communism was oriented to foreign policy: they feared the Soviet Union. *Overall, rank-and-file Birchers did not believe communism in government to be of great importance and only a small percentage of Birchers believed that there were communist traitors in government.*[16] Indeed, only 10 percent of the Birchers believed domestic communism was a threat. Instead, members focused their anti-communism on the external threat posed by the Soviet Union. This attitude was in direct opposition to the official Birch leadership position that the major threat was domestic ("insider") communist infiltration into government. Furthermore, the official Birch opposition to the war in Vietnam was also not supported by the rank and file. Indeed, official Bircher opposition to the war in Vietnam hurt membership recruitment and marked the decline of the John Birch Society in American politics by the 1960s.

These surveys belie facile depictions of popular anti-communist activists of being anti-democratic, protofascist, and racist. Furthermore, they show that distinctions between the anti-communist leaders and rank and file should be made when discussing the popular anti-communist movement. Leadership is critical in social protest movements, but a less ideological rank-and-file base makes it easy for established political parties to redirect activists into mainstream politics.

The Religious Foundations of Popular Anti-Communism

Religion played a pivotal role in popular anti-communism in its heyday of the 1950s. Catholics, evangelical Protestants, and fundamentalist Protestants gave impetus to popular anti-communism, but it made for disunited and organizational incoherence.

The Catholic Church had a long tradition dating back to the nineteenth century of opposing communism.[17] Catholic social teaching was pro-worker and supported unions and "a living wage" for the working class. In the 1920s and 1930s, the European Catholic Church supported moderate anti-communist political parties and expressed vociferous opposition to the Republican government involved in a brutal civil war against Francisco Franco's Nationalist forces. The American Catholic Church joined in this opposition to the Spanish republican government by calling for American nonintervention in the civil war. Anti-communism intensified during the Cold War with the Soviet takeover of Poland, Hungary, Czech Republic (Czechoslovakia at that time), and other Eastern European countries. New York bishop Fulton Sheen personified the church's stance on anti-communism. His weekly television show, *Life Worth Living,* appeared every Tuesday night from 1951 to 1957 and drew 30 million viewers at its height. His previous radio show, *The Catholic Hour,* which began in 1930 and lasted until he became a television celebrity, had focused primarily on religious matters until the outbreak of World War II. He denounced Hitler as the "anti-Christ." In his television program, he turned increasingly to anti-communism. Bishop Sheen's message appealed especially to ethnic Roman Catholics. On the far right, Father Arthur Terminiello, a priest from Mobile, Alabama, joined Gerald L. K. Smith on a two-month speaking tour in 1946, bringing their message that combined anti-communism and anti-Semitism to various Christian nationalist groups.[18]

Throughout the country, Catholic masses often ended with a prayer for the freedom of people behind the Iron Curtain. Parochial schools and Catholic universities offered courses and programs on anti-communism. The power of the anti-communist message was evident in major cities with large ethnic communities. For example, in Detroit on May 1, 1947, more than 5,000 men knelt in driving rain in downtown Detroit, clutching their rosaries praying to return Russia to Christianity. This tradition continued to draw 3,000 to 10,000 participants until 1958. At this same period, a spontaneous grassroots prayer movement began in 1952 in which tens of thousands of people gathered each week in Detroit homes to pray, invoking the Virgin Mary to vanquish the modern-day anti-Christ—the Soviet Communists. The *Michigan Catholic* and other diocese newspapers regularly published articles on Soviet oppression in Poland.[19] This anti-communist devotional culture was found in most large American cities with sizable ethnic communities. The Catholic Church institutionalized, in effect, anti-communism.

Anti-communism had sunk deep roots also in some evangelical Protestant groups during the 1920s, as seen by the activities of William Dudley Pelley, publisher of the *New Liberator,* which claimed a circulation of 10,000. He became a pronounced anti-Semite and advocated for the pro-Hitler Silver Shirts, organized in 1933. Huey Long's self-proclaimed heir, Gerald L. K.

Smith, also combined militant Protestantism and anti-Semitism. He worked closely with Gerald B. Winrod, who built the Defenders of the Christian Faith and who railed against modernism, Jews, communism, and fascism. He warned that the next anti-Christ would be a Jew.[20]

Protestant Christians were more diverse institutionally. As a result, specific anti-communist organizations emerged, proclaiming the mantle of Christian crusaders. These organizations often found themselves at odds with one another as they competed for members and funds. Three of these Christian-proclaiming organizations stand out for reaching tens of thousands of Americans with intense anti-communist messages that drew wide denunciation from critics for their extremism: Carl McIntire's *Twentieth Century Reformation Hour,* Billy James Hargis's Christian Crusade, and Fred Schwarz's Christian Anti-Communism Crusade. Schwarz tried to carefully distance himself without offending other Christian anti-communists, such as Hargis and McIntire. Schwarz shared an anti-communist message with Hargis and McIntire, but he thought they lacked restraint, moderation, and propriety. Neither McIntire nor Hargis ever tired of attacking mainline Protestant denominations as tools of communists. Both Hargis and McIntire coupled their anti-communism to their support for racial segregation in the South.

McIntire revealed the sectarian side to the popular anti-communist movement.[21] McIntire was a religious and racial bigot who declared himself a Christian Nationalist. For him, opposition to communism was about opposing modernism and the subversion of moral order in America. He feared communistic ideas had infiltrated mainstream Protestant churches and theology. His organization, the American Council of Christian Churches, claimed 1.2 million members, and his newspaper, the *Christian Beacon*, reached 150,000 subscribers. His anti-communist message was clear, however: "Communism Is the Devil." He broadcast this message on a thirty-minute radio program, Monday through Friday, that reached tens of thousands of listeners.

McIntire worked with other far-right groups, including the Church League of America headed by Edgar Bundy, who took up the charge of investigating alleged communist infiltration into the Methodist Church; Billy Hargis's Christian Crusade; and the American Council of Christian Laymen led by anti-communist Verne Paul Kaub. McIntire was as fiercely anti-Catholic as he was anti-communist. He declared in 1945 that "without doubt the greatest enemy of freedom and liberty that the world has to face today is the Roman Catholic system." Roman Catholicism, he believed, was worse than Soviet Communism. "Yes, we have communism in Russia and all that is involved there, but if one had to choose between the two, one would be much better off in a Communist society than in a Roman Catholic fascist society."[22]

McIntire's ultrafundamentalist, anti-Catholic, anti-communist message reached tens of thousands of people. By 1960, *Twentieth Century Reformation Hour* had revenues of $3.8 million. McIntire, like Hargis, saw the civil rights movement as having been infiltrated by communists. Both denied they were racist, however, and schools that identified with the Twentieth Century Reformation admitted blacks. Both Hargis and McIntire threw their support behind Barry Goldwater in the presidential 1964 race, but by 1968, McIntire had become a George Wallace supporter.

Billy Hargis was a poor boy who made good through religion.[23] His Christian Crusade, operated through his Christian Echoes National Ministry based in Tulsa, Oklahoma, reached tens of thousands of Americans with a zealous anti-communist message. His radio broadcasts reached an audience of 75,000 people, from Pennsylvania through Texas on 400 stations. His newsletter, the *Weekly Crusader*, reached a circulation of 120,000 at its height. Hargis aimed at the uneducated. He believed a university education often distracted from God's message found in the Bible. He declared, "I think it is ignorant people who are going to save this country."[24]

His style was fire and brimstone, beginning his speeches (sermons) with a quiet voice to build to a crescendo with a thundering voice. The battle, he told audiences, is "essentially a religious battle. It's Christ versus anti-Christ, God versus Satan, light versus darkness." The Christian Crusade's fight against communism was "Christ's fight." He declared, "I am convinced that this is the time for God's conservatives across the nation to step up their attacks against liberalism and/or Communism." He warned that "Communists are very close to grasping control of America." Unlike Schwarz, Hargis felt communism was a domestic problem. He declared, "Clean up Communism INTERNALLY and America's problems with Communism INTERNATIONALLY will be solved."[25]

From the outset, Hargis associated with the extreme right. He denied he was an anti-Semite. Nonetheless, he was involved with such figures as Ed Hill, a trustee of the Christian Crusade and a financial contributor to Gerald L. K. Smith; Pedro A. del Valle, an anti-Semite on Hargis's national advisory board; Allen Zoll, a notorious anti-Semite in the 1940s; and Willis Carto, founder of the anti-Semite Liberty Lobby and a speaker at Hargis's rallies. Other frequent speakers at Hargis's rallies were Kent and Phoebe Courtney, who declared themselves "constitutionalists" and attempted to form a pro-segregation third party, the Constitutional Party. It failed.

Hargis supported segregation and denounced Martin Luther King Jr. as being "communist-educated." Hargis's projection of communism as part of an apocalyptic struggle between Satan and Christ led him into conspiracy theories. In 1965, his associate David Noebel published one of the most bizarre conspiracy pamphlets, "Communism, Hypnotism, and the Beatles," accusing the rock band of being part of a Soviet conspiracy to "brainwash" American youth through well-developed hypnotic techniques.[26]

In 1963, Hargis launched Operation Midnight Ride, a seventeen-state, twenty-seven-city speaking tour. As a drawing card, Hargis invited Major General Edwin A. Walker to join him. Walker had gained public attention for having been relieved of command of an infantry division in Germany in 1961 for extolling the John Birch Society philosophy and attacking Harry S. Truman, Eleanor Roosevelt, and Dean Acheson as "definitely pink." Through his crusade, Hargis gained ground, largely through his radio broadcasts heard on 400 U.S. stations daily and another 110 stations in Latin America.

As late as November 1963, Hargis was telling his audiences, "The healthiest thing would be to get these conservatives out of both parties and start a conservative party!"[27] This was a general sentiment on much of the far Christian right. They did not see a difference between Republicans and Democrats. Once Goldwater, the conservative Republican senator from Arizona, announced his candidacy for the presidency, however, Hargis tried to tie his crusade to the Goldwater campaign. Following Goldwater's defeat, Hargis returned to calling for a New Christian Right political party.

Fred Schwarz's Christian Anti-Communist Crusade emerged as one of the most effective anti-communist organizations. He drew thousands of people to his rallies and anti-communist schools. Although popular anti-communism as a movement was beginning to lose momentum by 1961, Schwarz was able to fill the Hollywood Bowl in October 1961, drawing tens of thousands to his anti-communist rally. The rally was televised across the state. The audience was drawn by headliners, including actors Ronald Reagan, John Wayne, and Rock Hudson (among other stars); studio head Walt Disney; singers Nat King Cole and Pat Boone; and television stars Ozzie and Harriet Nelson.[28] Aging actor George Murphy hosted the event and eventually parlayed his fame into a term in the U.S. Senate.

As an evangelical Christian, Schwarz saw the world as a Manichean struggle between the forces of light and the forces of darkness, the Christian West versus Atheistic Communism.[29] He came to America from Australia in 1952 at the invitation of Carl McIntire to preach. In his first years in the

United States, he worked with McIntire and Billy Hargis, but soon broke off on his own to launch the Anti-Communist Christian Crusade. He focused more on the ideology of Marxism—its philosophy, morality, organization, techniques.[30] Schwarz's popular *You Can Trust the Communists (to Be Communists)* sold over a million copies.

In 1958, Schwarz launched his first School of Anti-Communism. The schools brought in an array of "faculty" speakers, including Fred Schlafly, an Illinois attorney married to another anti-communist activist Phyllis Schlafly, who spoke on law and anti-communism; Herbert Philbrick, on his experiences as a former FBI informant in the Communist Party; and George Schuyler, an African American journalist and author who had moved from socialism to fierce anti-communism. The schools proved immensely popular, enrolling hundreds who participated in five-day programs in Los Angeles, New York, Chicago, Houston, Dallas, Miami, San Diego, San Francisco, Seattle, and Portland. Schwarz's success was due to his charismatic presence as an anti-communist speaker and financial support from major conservative donors, such as Patrick Frawley, who owned the Schick Safety Razor Company.[31] Schwarz's message that Christianity was under threat from communism, with its basis in dialectical materialism, resonated with average Americans.

Schwarz understood that even with financial support from major corporate donors and widespread advertising that he needed to have a product to sell, and this product was anti-communism, which was already deeply rooted in the American public. Even Schwarz's most ardent critics, Arnold Forster and Benjamin Epstein, authors of *Danger on the Right* (1964), observed that those attending Schwarz's schools are "not crackpots and malcontents, nor are they lonely frustrated individuals looking to join about anything that meets and screams." Instead, the authors concluded, "Because of their high educational and income status, most of them are active members of all kinds of church, civic, and veterans' organizations."[32]

No other organization embodied anti-communism more than the John Birch Society (JBS), founded in 1958 by Massachusetts candy manufacturer Robert Welch. The JBS was not overtly religious but attracted many churchgoing folks. Welch proclaimed that Soviet Communism was winning the Cold War through steady advances through domestic subversion. He warned that "a patient gradualism has been the key to the Communists' overwhelming success." The communist advance, he declared, was through domestic subversion, not military conquest. In his two-day seminar on communism, later reprinted as *The John Birch Society Blue Book,* he traced the steady advance of communism through Eastern Europe, China, and North Vietnam. He warned that Syria, Lebanon, Egypt, Libya, Tunisia, Algeria, and Morocco were already under the control of communists or about to become communist nations. He believed that Finland, Iceland, and Norway were already in the hands of the communists. In the Western Hemisphere, British Guyana, Bolivia, and Venezuela were already under the control of communists. Castro's rise to power in Cuba only escalated fears of communist victory.

In each of these case studies of communist takeover, Welch believed domestic subversion—not military takeovers—were how communists gained power. He dismissed the Soviet military threat, convinced that communism was such an inefficient economic system that Russians would be unable to produce an effective military. Indeed, Welch was convinced that Sputnik, Russia's first satellite, was a hoax.

Welch brought organizing skills to the John Birch Society, which attracted notable businessmen to his cause. Well financed and tightly organized, the JBS formed chapters throughout the country by attracting mostly average, white, middle-class Americans.[33] The Birch Society was tightly run from above by Welch. Membership was kept secret. At its height, membership reached an estimated 100,000. Its influence on the grassroots right extended beyond its numbers, however. Bircher meetings were educational—and Welch stayed clear of direct involvement in partisan politics, especially given that he accused Dwight D. Eisenhower of being a communist agent. He later retracted this accusation but not before political damage to his organization had been done. While the Birch Society was educational, and its chapter meetings revolved around reading the organizational bulletins and watching anti-communist films, individual members became involved in partisan politics, especially in some local Republican parties in the North. In the Deep South, Birchers worked as conservative Democrats. Bircher involvement in the Republican Party presented a real problem for GOP officials. Birchers were seen as nuts by most American voters, and being associated with the John Birch Society usually was not a path to winning elections. Two members of the John Birch Society from California, it should be noted, did win election to Congress, but they were exceptions. JBS membership in California and Texas was strong and exerted political influence in these states.

The emergence of the John Birch Society aggravated tensions within the popular anti-communist movement. Welsh's obsession with domestic communist infiltration and his accusations that Dwight D. Eisenhower was a Soviet agent, went a step too far for crusaders such as Schwarz. Troubles began in

1960 when Welch heard that Schwarz had been deriding him in private for his hyperbolic claims of widespread communist infiltration into the federal government. Schwarz tried to mollify Welch by declaring that he might have misspoken when he used the word *fascist* to describe the John Birch Society. He added, "You and I stand together in an awareness of the vastness and the imminence of the Communist danger."[34] The Schwarz-Welch dispute, though, reflected deeper divisions within the popular anti-communist movement. Discussing Soviet spy activity in the Roosevelt government during World War II was a horse of a completely different color than accusing Roosevelt himself of being a communist or claiming, as author George Racey Jordan did, that FDR's principal foreign relations adviser, Harry Hopkins, had given Stalin atomic secrets and arranged a secret transportation of enriched uranium to Russia in 1943.[35]

The John Birch Society became an easy target for charges of extremism. By 1960 a full-scale attack on the "far-right" was under way, evidenced in dozens of books and magazine articles warning of the extremist threat within the Republican Party. For example, Alan Barth, an academic writing in the *New York Times Magazine* in 1961, declared that right-wing groups shared a "deep distrust of democratic institutions and of the democratic process," and that Barry Goldwater, "the darling" of the right, would have to "choose between the support of the Right and support of real Republicans who will not care to forsake the traditions of their party for a forlorn kind of fascism."[36] This theme that the far right, Goldwater's supporters, were racist, xenophobic, and easily manipulated by would-be Hitlers found expression in major magazines and in such books as Forster and Epstein's *Danger on the Right.*

In 1961, President John F. Kennedy had seen enough of these anti-communist crusaders. Kennedy feared that the influence of the popular anti-communist right was influencing American public opinion to oppose any accommodation with the Soviet Union on matters of trade or arms control. He directed the Internal Revenue Service to gather data on tax-exempt anti-communist organizations. In November 1961, Kennedy ventured to Southern California, a hotbed of right-wing activism, to deliver a major speech at the Hollywood Palladium. There he denounced those who counseled "fear and suspicion" by viewing recent history as that of conspiracies and sellouts. Three months before Kennedy's death in November 1963, presidential aide Myer Feldman warned that "the radical right-wing constitutes a formidable force in American life today" and urged a federal investigation into the John Birch Society and other extremist groups.[37]

Goldwater had sought to head off attacks on him by associating him with the John Birch Society. This lead him to arrange a secret summit at the Breakers Hotel in Miami Beach with William F. Buckley and others in October 1962. Goldwater wanted to devise a strategy on how to isolate Birchers from the conservative movement without directly tying him to any attack on Welch and his organization. Buckley's *National Review* had already tangled with Robert Welch over his suggestion that Dwight D. Eisenhower was a communist agent, his call for Supreme Court Justice Earl Warren's impeachment, and his accusation that China fell to Mao because elements in the U.S. government planned it. At the Miami meeting with Goldwater and his staff, Buckley agree to launch a full-scale offensive against Welch. In the editorial "The Question of Robert Welch," the *National Review* tried to excommunicate, in effect, Robert Welch from the conservative movement and the Republican Party.[38] The excommunication of the John Birch Society from the mainstream conservative movement failed to prevent attacks on the Goldwater movement as filled with extremists. In the 1964 presidential campaign, the Goldwater movement was assailed by opponents within the Republican Party and the Democratic Party as an "extremist." Channeling the passions of far-right anti-communists into the Republican Party while appealing to mainstream voters remained a continuous problem for GOP strategists.

The attacks on the extreme right, however, took its toll. The decline of popular anti-communism can be charted. Fred Schwarz noted that attendance to his anti-communist schools began to decline in 1961 and then dropped significantly in 1962. Popular anti-communist speaker Herbert Philbrick, author of *I Led Three Lives,* which became a short-run television program in early 1951, observed that by 1962 he was receiving fewer invitations to speak. He found himself in serious financial straits. He spent the rest of his career on the fringes of conservative politics.[39]

By the early 1960s, the popular anti-communist movement was clearly fading as a political influence. Although Schwarz, Hargis, McIntire, and Welch remained on the scene, membership in their organizations declined. Welch lived until 1985, but his organization had drifted into the realms of attacking the New World Order, a Masonic conspiracy.[40] The Cuban revolution kept popular anti-communism going a bit, but the threat of an imminent communist takeover of America seemed extremely remote to most

Americans. In this changing environment, anti-communists increasingly focused on the strategic threat posed by the Soviet Union.

Stage 2: Reviving the Grassroots Right

When Barry Goldwater received the Republican Party's presidential nomination, the grassroots right appeared to have triumphed. Goldwater's *Conscience of a Conservative* (1960), which became a best seller, convinced the grassroots right that they stood on the edge of triumph. Lyndon Johnson's landslide victory in 1964 did not persuade grassroots activists that theirs was a lost cause. They saw Goldwater's popular vote of 27 million (39 percent) as a kind of triumph. Yet behind the rhetoric of victory the grassroots right was marred by division and discord. The Republican Party was already divided between its eastern moderate-liberal and Sunbelt conservative wings when Goldwater won the nomination. Grassroots activist Phyllis Schlafly's self-published pro-Goldwater campaign book, *A Choice Not an Echo* (1964), spent more time attacking what she called the "kingmakers"—the eastern wing of the party—than she did liberals. For her, the kingmakers were those financial interests (mostly white, Anglo-Saxon Protestants) who had controlled the GOP for too long. These eastern liberals within the party were Republicans in Name Only (RINOs) who had sold conservative GOP down the river by not offering voters true conservatives such as Barry Goldwater. Goldwater's defeat in 1964 only deepened this divide within the Republican Party.

In the 1960s deep divisions arose in the popular right over a range of issues, including the Vietnam War. Although most of the right supported the troops in Vietnam, many activists such as Phyllis Schlafly thought American intervention in Vietnam was a mistake and a distraction from the Soviet strategic buildup.[41] Richard Nixon's election to the White House and his subsequent administration only heightened a sense of isolation within the grassroots right. By the 1970s, grassroots conservatism seemed to have become a lost cause. What revived grassroots populism was a cultural backlash and an economy hit by combined inflation and economic stagnation. The first signs of renewal for the grassroots right came in the fight over abortion.

Before the Supreme Court's ruling in *Roe v. Wade* in 1973, the fight over abortion was already under way in the states.[42] A movement to liberalize state abortion laws arose in the early 1960s. In early state battles, Catholic anti-abortion activists were pitted against Protestant proponents, with Republican legislators often siding with the Protestants.[43]

The political fight over abortion came earlier in California when Anthony Beilenson, a young Democratic state legislator, introduced a liberalized abortion bill in the state legislature in late 1963. The bill was opposed by Bay Area Missouri Synod Lutheran pastor Arnim Polster, who established himself as a leader in the emerging anti-abortion movement. Opponents of the Beilenson bill failed in defeating it, however. Despite the lobbying efforts by the Catholic Church hierarchy, newly elected Governor Ronald Reagan signed the bill into law. Too many Republican legislators had put themselves on the line in support of the bill, and Reagan did not want to leave them hanging.

The abortion issue came at a time when the American Catholic Church found itself in deep division over oral contraception. In the summer of 1968, the Vatican under Pope Paul VI issued the encyclical *Humanae Vitae*, condemning oral contraception as a threat to the traditional family and an expression of a hedonistic sexual revolution. The proclamation divided Catholic bishops and priests. Furthermore, the church's combined opposition to oral contraception and abortion intertwined the two issues. Public acceptance of oral contraception, including the majority of self-identified Roman Catholics, provided a climate for growing support for abortion reform. Polls at the time showed that the majority of Roman Catholics opposed the church's position on abortion. The Catholic Church hierarchy realized that an educational effort needed to be undertaken on the issue.

Bishops appointed a thirty-five-year-old priest, Father James McHugh, to undertake a campaign to educate parishioners on abortion. McHugh understood that key to building a right-to-life effort was separating the oral contraception issue from abortion. Abortion, he declared, was a separate matter and "a more serious threat to human life."[44] Moreover, McHugh believed that critical to the future success of the right-to-life movement was the need to foster independent pro-life organizations that reached beyond the church. He found a model for independent, grassroots pro-life groups in New York and California, where such groups had already emerged among Protestant congregations. Critical to the groups' success was the reaching out to Protestant church members by church clergy and leaders, who had enlisted their support in the fledgling anti-abortion movement. These clergy came from mainline Protestant denominations, not evangelical churches. For example, in California, the leading Protestant right-to-life clergyman was Charles Carroll, an Episcopalian priest who had been active in the civil rights movement in Mississippi and was also an anti–Vietnam War activist. He brought the credentials of a liberal opposed to abortion.

McHugh and other activists welcomed Paul Ramsey, a Methodist theologian at Princeton University, who declared that abortion was a violation of the "sanctity of life."[45]

From 1968 to 1971, liberalized abortion laws were enacted in North Carolina, Georgia, Arkansas, South Carolina, Virginia, Maryland, Delaware, Oregon, New Mexico, and Kansas. In 1973, the anti-abortion movement suffered what it considered its greatest blow when the Supreme Court ruled in *Roe v. Wade* that abortion was a constitutional right for women, although the public interest should be considered integral in the third trimester of a pregnancy. This qualification allowed state legislators, acting in the public interest, to regulate abortion. As a consequence, issues of regulation were thrown into state politics, and it is on the state level that pro-life organizations began to flourish. Pro-life activists began to emphasize the importance of aiding the poor rather than curbing population growth and the need for adoption of "unwanted" children. Opposition to "abortion on demand" and late-term abortion resonated with many voters who generally supported *Roe* but saw the need for reasonable regulation. By 1970, polls began to shift against "legalizing abortion for almost any reason."[46]

State activists declaring themselves "pro-life feminists" added momentum to grassroots efforts. In Pennsylvania, a Catholic homemaker, Mary Winter, formed an alternative group to the Catholic Church–sponsored Pennsylvanians for Human Life. Beginning with just twelve women convened in her living room in Pittsburgh in 1970, Winter organized Women Concerned for the Unborn Child, which became a leading anti-abortion organization in the state. Within two years, Winter's organization had more than 7,000 active women. Winter declared herself a pro-life feminist who saw abortion as sexual exploitation of women. Especially important to promoting pro-life was the feminist Sidney Callahan, an Ivy League–educated, licensed psychologist and wife a pro-choice husband, Daniel. She provided the intellectual foundation for her position in many books and articles promoting anti-abortion. She declared forcefully, "In my feminist view, every abortion represents an abandonment of women and children."[47] In Arizona, Minnesota, Michigan, and other states, grassroots pro-life groups sprang up that were led by Protestant women who considered themselves political liberals on matters of social welfare, feminism, and anti-abortion. These organizations became critical in legislative lobbying in their states and pushed Republican candidates to take pro-life positions. By 1980, most Republicans running for office—whether on the local, state, or national level—had to declare themselves as "pro-life." This was a seismic shift for the Republican Party and American politics.

The Battle over the Equal Rights Amendment

Even as the anti-abortion movement emerged, the left still looked ascendant. Richard Nixon had been forced from the White House; his successor, Gerald Ford, was defeated in the next election; Democrats controlled Congress and many elected were clearly on the left. Women had won the constitutional right for abortion, and although anti-abortion movements had appeared, polls showed that the majority of Americans supported abortion. Feminism looked like it was on the rise culturally and politically. Second-wave feminism had made cultural inroads. Polls showed that radical feminists turned off many Americans, but feminists' goals of equal treatment and opportunity were widely accepted. The final ratification of the Equal Rights Amendment was just a step away.

The only hang-up with the ERA, it seemed, was one woman: Phyllis Schlafly. Her crusade against the amendment had mobilized tens of thousands of anti-feminist women across the country to join STOP ERA. In the end, Schlafly and her allies did stop ratification of the ERA. It was a stunning and demoralizing defeat for feminists. Schlafly's movement had thwarted the political establishment in the Democratic and Republican Parties through grassroots organizing. Her movement astounded contemporary pundits and scholars later who were perplexed by "why ERA lost." Often overlooked, however, is how decisive Schlafly's movement was in transforming the Republican Party by integrating the grassroots right and right-wing populist sentiment into the party. Schlafly, a decided right-winger herself, carefully threaded the grassroots right and the Republican Party establishment. For the party establishment, she was often a pain in the neck; for the grassroots right, she was a heroine. Her importance, though, lay in opening the doors and providing a strategy for the GOP to expand its base and bring social activists into the party.

Schlafly brought to the ERA battle great intelligence, political experience, and skills as a debater. She had been a longtime activist in the Republican Party and the National Federation of Republican Women. She came to the ERA issue only by circumstance, after being invited to speak on the subject by a Republican women's group. Until the invitation, Schlafly shared with other Republicans a pro-ERA perspective. At the urging of her followers, she studied the issue and came out against it. In the February 1972 *Phyllis*

Schlafly Report she issued "What's Wrong with 'Equal Rights' for Women," which became the manifesto of the anti-feminist crusade. It provided a critique of Betty Friedan's *Feminist Mystique* by maintaining the importance of the family and the mother's role in what she described as "the basic unit of society." She maintained in her essay and future speeches that American women had made great legal strides through the legislative process. If other inequalities remained, they should be addressed through further legislation and not a sweeping, loosely worded constitutional amendment that would be interpreted by the courts. In promoting the family and the homemaker, she was accused of being opposed to women having careers and of seeking to keep women at home. She was not anti-career for women but maintained that a mother should place children over careers.

In July 1972 she launched the STOP ERA movement. She decided not to align the movement directly with any other political group and to bring women together in a single-issue group with one goal—defeating the amendment. It was a clever strategy. Instead of opening the anti-feminist movement to heated debates on differences, her organization united anti-feminists and the right into a single cause and a single lobbying strategy. This strategy focused on persuading state legislators to vote no on ratification. Anti-ERA women used the art of persuasion—old-time techniques of lobbying—in their efforts. Pro-amendment activists were divided organizationally and in strategy on how to win state legislations. NOW refused to join with the principal umbrella group, ERAmerica, representing 120 groups. The highly centralized ERAmerica advised state coalitions on techniques of legislative lobbying and public education campaigns, while the loosely knit NOW chapters sought to link legalized abortion and gay rights to the ERA. Local NOW activists often took to the politics of the street by organizing demonstrations, local sit-ins, and confrontations with state legislators.

Within a half-year, STOP ERA had organizations in twenty-six states. The STOP ERA movement swept through the grassroots right. By the end of the battle, membership in Schlafly's Eagle Forum, formed before the ERA fight, had swelled to 60,000. Although this paled next to the National Organization for Women with its membership of 220,000, Eagle Forum and STOP ERA members were active.

STOP ERA chapters were especially strong in states critical to final ratification. She kept tight control of the organization by appointing state directors, allowing each state to devise its own tactics raising their own funds. STOP ERA activists mirrored pro-ERA activists in that they were mostly white, middle class, and well educated. The fundamental distinction was that most anti-ERA activists, a remarkable 98 percent, had religious affiliations, while less than half of pro-ERA supporters claimed such an affiliation. Schlafly, a devout Roman Catholic, showed a great ability to draw evangelical Protestant and Mormon women into her cause. This proved decisive in critical states needed for ratification.

Schlafly and her followers challenged the entire political, media, entertainment, and mainstream cultural establishment in their anti-feminist crusade. Her campaign took on Republicans and Democrats alike. Nixon had endorsed the ERA, followed by Gerald Ford, who directed his administration to support ratification. Ford's wife, Betty, who supported the amendment, abortion rights, and women's liberation, appeared at pro-ERA events, including the International Women's Year Houston conference. When the ratification deadline set initially by Congress expired, Carter successfully persuaded a Democratic-controlled Congress to extend the ratification deadline to June 30, 1982. His wife, Rosalynn, joined the ERA campaign, traveling to states to support the amendment. Carter hosted a White House reception for five hundred people in conjunction with a NOW fundraiser. After his firing of Bella Abzug from the President's Advisory Committee for Women because of her open criticism of his economic policies and his ambivalent stance on abortion rights, feminists turned on him with a vengeance. NOW refused to endorse him for reelection in 1980. This division within the Democratic Party aided Schlafly's grassroots anti-ERA campaign.

The anti-ERA fight helped revive the right. Conservative operatives saw what Schlafly had accomplished in her anti-ERA campaign by introducing social issues into politics. In the 1978 midterms, Republicans used social issues to separate socially conservative voters from Democratic candidates. When election results came in, Democratic seats had declined from 292 to 277 in the House and from 61 to 59 in the Senate. Even more significantly, returns showed that Democrats had lost white evangelical voters in the South and the North.

Tax Revolt: California and Beyond

While the anti-abortion movement took shape and a fight over ratification of the Equal Rights Amendment was occurring in the states, a tax revolt in California erupted in 1978 over a proposed ballot proposition to reduce property taxes. Arguably, the United States was founded on anti-tax protest, and tax revolts have been common throughout American history.[48] In the early 1930s, six states limited property taxes by means of initiatives. By the late 1930s, national resistance to high taxes had become apparent. Anti-tax sentiment took on particular poignancy in California in 1978, when an anti–property tax measure was placed on the state ballot. With taxes soaring because of increasing property values in California, a revolt had been brewing before two conservative activists Howard Jarvis and Paul Gann rocked the state with Proposition 13. In such counties as Orange and San Bernardino, tax assessments had increased 30 percent in the period from 1973 to 1976. The stage was set for a tax revolt. From 1970 to 1978 dozens of direct leg-islative propositions had been proposed but all failed. Meanwhile, Governor Jerry Brown had piled up a huge state surplus. When Jarvis asked how lower property taxes could still support services, he pointed to the surplus.

The proposal, placed on the ballot with 1.2 million signatures, set the value of property at its 1975–76 market value and limited property tax to 1 percent of that value with almost no increases in the future.[49] What began in California spread to other states. Proposition 13 and similar proposals in other states meant fierce opposition from established politicians, the business community, and unions. As a result, the battle over lowering property taxes appeared to pit "the people" against "the elites." This anti-government, anti-elitist view was captured in a pro–Proposition 13 spot, which declared, "Give the politicians a budget instead of a blank check. Vote Yes." Pat Caddell, President Carter's pollster, concluded, "This is not just a tax revolt. It's a revolution against government."[50]

If anti-elitist rhetoric defines populism, broadly defined, these move-ments were populist. More important, the Jarvis-Gann anti-tax crusade was a grassroots movement that appealed to anti-tax sentiment, as well as strong anti-bureaucratic and anti-government feelings across the political and ideo-logical spectrum.[51] Sociologist Clarence Lo, who interviewed over a hundred community activists involved in Proposition 13, concluded the movement was "a revolt of communities against big government and bureaucratic in-terest groups associated with it," as hundreds of community associations were formed out of countless small meetings and neighborhood discussion groups.[52] This movement gathered more than 1,263,000 signatures to place Proposition 13 on the ballot. This was the highest number of signatures gathered for an legislative initiative and the first time that the number of signatures (81 percent) was valid. The campaign in the general election for Proposition 13 proved equally effective in mobilizing voters.

Opposition came from business interests, public employees' unions, leading liberal Democrat politicians, and Governor Jerry Brown. A well-funded anti–Proposition 13 campaign warned of cataclysmic consequences if the proposition passed. Police, fire, and other services would be shut down. Paramedical services would be virtually nonexistent. Massive layoffs in government would occur. Bond ratings for the state would crash. In a last-ditch effort to head off Proposition 13, the state legislature passed the Property Tax Relief Act of 1978, placed on the ballot as Proposition 8, which provided approximately $1.2 million in tax relief for 1978–79 through a 30 percent reduction in homeowner's property taxes (as compared to the 50 percent reduction of Proposition 13). The legislative bill came too late to head off the taxpayers' revolt.

Jarvis and Gann brought to the Proposition 13 campaign deep experience in grassroots organizing. Gann's political experience dated back to the 1950s. In 1974, he created People's Advocate, Inc., that focused on the problem of rising crime rates in the state. He became involved in tax reform later in the decade. Jarvis cut a different figure. He was a firebrand who had run for various political offices, but his true cause was tax reform. He became chair of the United Taxpayers Organization, a grassroots group in the San Fernando Valley intent on lowering property taxes. Before making his sole cause property taxes, he had been involved in local anti-union right-to-work efforts, served on the national board of the Liberty Amendment Committee that called for the repeal of the federal income tax, and formed an unauthorized "Businessmen for Goldwater Committee" in 1964, which was accused of raising money that never went to the Goldwater presidential campaign.[53] Although Gann and Jarvis cowrote Proposition 13, they did not especially like one another. After writing the proposition, they established separate organizations to promote it through voluntary organization.

This tax revolt attracted property owners across class, partisan, and ethnic lines, including whites, Hispanics, and Asian Americans. A Field Poll before the vote showed that strong conservatives (82 percent), moderate conservatives (71 percent), middle-of-the-road voters (61 percent), and nearly the majority of moderate liberals (48 percent) of identified voters supported Proposition 13. Similar support showed across income lines: those making an annual income of less than $10,000 supported it (53 percent); those making $20,000 to $30,000 gave even higher support (58 percent); and stronger support grew with higher incomes. White, Asian, and Hispanic support stood at 60 percent or higher. The only groups that opposed Proposition 13 were strong liberals and African Americans.[54]

Proposition 13 proved to be just the beginning of the revolt. In 1979, Gann rallied support for a new proposition to limit state and local funding based on population growth and the consumer price index. Liberal Democratic politicians swung on board to support the campaign. Business, too, provided support. It won easily with 74 percent of the vote in a low voter turnout election. Not to be outdone, Jarvis the following year proposed a more draconian measure to reduce personal income tax and repeal the business inventory tax. His proposal called for reducing personal income tax rates based on 1978 taxes. The measure failed. Never one to be easily discouraged, he came back in 1982 with Proposition 7, which provided a full indexing of state income taxes beginning in the 1982 tax year. Once again an alliance of powerful interest groups aligned with state government warned in a massive ad campaign about the danger to the state of declining revenues. Nonetheless, Proposition 7 passed with 54 percent of the vote.[55]

The tax revolt spread to other states—Michigan, Idaho, Nevada, and Arizona—but in most cases, power business lobbyists and established politicians carefully channeled voter anger to more moderate legislation.[56] As a result the tax revolt appeared to have fizzled out in the states within a matter of a few years. The tax revolt on the state level, however, set the stage for a national tax revolt in 1981 during the Reagan administration. This revolt was part of a larger public sentiment that big money and special interests were benefiting from big government, and the revolt against government corruption expressed itself with the emergence of the public interest group—viewed as on the left—Common Cause and Ralph Nader's campaign finance reform efforts.

Observers at the time, and later, described the tax revolt as a conservative, manipulated political campaign, and therefore as a kind of "faux" populist movement.[57] Such a description misses the anger and hostility toward what the public saw as corruption, misuse of public funds, and gained privileges within the public sphere. The tax revolt captured a deepening anti-elitist and anti-government sentiment that had been gestating since the late 1960s. The real problem in the 1970s was that the cost of living and property taxes were rising faster than wages. The tax revolt that began in California marked a political watershed in American politics—a revolt against the New Deal and Great Society spending programs. The revolt expressed a genuine political upheaval and genuine popular grievance captured by the populist right.[58] The movement did not destroy the liberal welfare or regulatory state but drew on a deeply American impulse to distrust elites and centralized government.

Republicans Capture the Grassroots Right

The Republican response to grassroots activism came gradually. Even as late as 1976, public opinion polls showed that Republicans on average were more pro-choice than their Democratic counterparts.[59] Fewer than 40 percent of the delegates to the Republican Party National Convention considered themselves pro-life. Republican strategists believed, however, that the key to winning a majority for their party was cultivating Roman Catholic voters, traditionally aligned with Democrats. Party strategists began to see that there was a shift in the public in opposition to feminism and the sexual revolution. Even more important, evangelical Protestants had shifted from pro-choice to anti-choice in the 1970s with the emergence of the religious right. Seeing this shift, Reagan sought to rally pro-life voters to his primary challenge to incumbent President Gerald Ford in 1976 by coming out in favor of a human life amendment. In response to Reagan's declaration, Ford tried to moderate his position on abortion, although few pro-life activists thought Ford was really on their side.

By the time Ronald Reagan won the 1980 Republican presidential nomination, the GOP had become the voice of conservatism. The GOP was the party of low taxes, anti-abortion, and anti-ERA, and it declared itself "pro-family." Grassroots activism shifted the Republican Party to the right on social issues. In the end, the ERA failed to be ratified. At the same time, Congress failed in Reagan's first term to pass a pro-life amendment, even with Reagan lobbying for the measure. In this respect, the Reagan revolution failed to be a complete revolution, as critics pointed out. Nonetheless, social conservatives—evangelical Christians—became a core constituency within the party, and their values were evident in Republican politics and policy. By 2010, the majority of Catholics who attended church weekly voted Republican in presidential elections. More than 70 percent of evangelical Protestants voted Republican. The emergence of the evangelical Protestant vote proved critical in shifting the South from Democratic country to Republican country. In the industrial Midwest, traditional Catholic voters turned Republican. No single factor led to this realignment. But essential were grassroots activists who challenged the party establishment and demanded candidates who represented their values on taxes, small government, abortion, traditional family values, and the threat of the Soviet Union. Reagan, both as a presidential candidate and as president, articulated many voters' distrust of the bureaucrats in Washington, D.C.

Reagan won election no doubt because incumbent president Jimmy Carter had become so unpopular among the electorate; Reagan, though, articulated voters' belief that government had become too big, too far removed, and run by bureaucrats too prone to do the bidding of special interests. The Reagan revolution was not entirely successful in fulfilling its many promises—although it accomplished much. After eight years in the White House, Reagan concluded that one of the major obstacles in fulfilling his agenda lay in the administrative state.

In one of his final speeches, Reagan repeated the warnings he had made when he first entered the White House eight years before. He declared that the most important lesson he had learned is that "parts of Congress, the media, and special interest groups" are "transforming and placing out of focus our constitutional balance." He described this configuration as the power of the "iron triangle" that remained permanent even in the face of elections. This configuration—the bureaucracy, the media, and special interest groups—had become "a virtual permanent chamber, no longer truly responsive to the people."[60]

The regulatory-welfare-administrative state erected by progressive reformers withstood the conservative assault that had culminated in the Reagan presidency. It endured. And it came under direct assault again in 2016 with Donald Trump's election to the White House. Reagan imparted a populist message to his voters. Trump amplified that message. The political polarization during the Reagan years had intensified and deepened by 2016. Right and left shared little—except on a single point: government should not be trusted. And for grassroots activists, left and right, the only solution to government controlled by elites, special interests, and inside politicians lay in a popular insurgency—at the polls or in the streets.

6 Protest in a Polarized Age

Social protest continued into the twenty-first century: the Tea Party, Occupy Wall Street, Black Lives Matter, Antifa, and others. These organizations and groupings have failed, however, to coalesce. Current social protest differs from previous movements in fundamental ways, which suggests the limitations of current protest activism to become larger movements. First, many of these protest movements are less grassroots organizations than "astro-turf" groupings funded and sometimes created by special interests aligned with partisan factions within the Republican and Democratic parties. For example, the Tea Party movement, while emerging spontaneously in protest to Wall Street bailouts during the crash of 2008 and the enactment of the Affordable Care Act (Obamacare), received encouragement and funding from Freedom-Works, a libertarian organization funded by billionaire brothers Charles and David Koch. Similarly, on the left, billionaire George Soros and his Open Society Foundations are major funders of many left-wing activist groups. As a consequence, grassroots social protest takes on a different meaning in a world of wealthy benefactors with their own social and political agendas. Movements in the past often attracted wealthy benefactors, frequently local or state figures. Today, however, multibillionaires and well-endowed philanthropic foundations have poured unprecedented amounts into supporting grassroots activism as well as partisan political campaigns. Indeed, today's politics of the street appears closer to that of the late Roman Republic when oligarchs, such as Caesar, Sulla, and Catiline, organized mobs to serve their factional interests.

Unlike activists in past social movements, today's activists on both the right and the left tend toward pessimism. For them government is so utterly corrupt and so controlled by special interests, they place little confidence in meaningful social change through policy reform. Farmers in the nineteenth century demanded monetary reforms; Progressives at the turn of the century demanded corporate regulation; New Deal grassroots campaigns demanded social programs such as Social Security; civil rights activists after World War II called for federal legislation and involvement to end racial segregation and voter suppression; feminists in the 1970s organized for an Equal Rights Amendment and legislation to protect reproductive rights and address discrimination in the workplace. Today's activists on the left and right share, ironically perhaps, as deep a distrust of government as right-wing populists expressed toward government at the height of Cold War anti-communism.

Past social movements called for fulfilling the promise of the American Dream, although it is an ambiguous term open to interpretation. Many activists today hold that that dream is merely a figment conjured by privileged elites as a means to distract the masses from an oppressive system of governance that favors interests other than their own. Both the left and the right—and many middle-of-the-road Americans—believe democracy simply is not working. There is a belief that politics is too rancorous, too partisan, and too deadlocked, that the system is corrupt and beneficial only to a few insiders. Paralleling this suspicion is a fear that powerful, unseen forces are controlling events and that the people, average Americans, are not in control of their fate. Look at the internet: it is full of conspiracies (virtually an American industry), coming from the left and the right. Movies, television, and books reinforce this conspiratorial view of unseen forces at work. If the system is rigged and always has been, and no progress is ever made in reforming the system for the better, why struggle for a better world at all? Pessimism and cynicism are not good organizing tools.

Many Americans have become disenchanted with politics as usual. Many Americans do not bother to register to vote, and even fewer actually do vote. Survey after survey shows that Americans distrust their political institutions and representatives, the office of the president, Congress, and the courts. They do not trust their ministers or priests, their lawyers or doctors, the teachers of their children, business leaders or labor leaders. Americans believe that the news media are biased and slanted. These surveys show that Americans do not trust the courts to dispense fair and equal justice. Such cynicism does not inspire social change.

Within the context of this decreased trust in institutions and the global economic crisis in 2008, the environment was conducive to a populist explosion.[1]

The Koch Brothers and Grassroots Activism on the Right

The global economic crash in 2008 deepened fissures already existing in European and American politics. Across Europe and the United States large segments of the electorate expressed their frustrations with the political establishment. The collapse of financial institutions in New York spread to international markets. Voter anger increased when it was learned that Wall Street had sold investment-fund managers, cities, states, and countries supposedly recession-proof bonds based on derivative rates determined through complex computer modeling. When the housing market collapsed, these oversold, overhyped bonds went with them.[2] Without warning, pension funds collapsed; small businesses went belly up; corporations and government agencies downsized. Fearing another 1930s global depression, the George W. Bush administration undertook to bail out some Wall Street firms and allowed others, such as Lehman Brothers, to fail. When Democrat Barack Obama entered the White House in 2009, after defeating a weak rival, John McCain, a moderate Republican senator from Arizona, the new administration arranged to bail out America's largest automobile industry, General Motors, to the detriment of bond holders and to the benefit of unions. With Democrats in control of Congress, the Obama administration pushed through an economic stimulus package and a major health care reform act, the Patient Protection and Affordable Care Act. The Great Recession of 2008 exacerbated conditions already ripe for political explosion in the United States and in Europe. The explosion came from the left and the right, as grassroots protest groups sprang up spontaneously. Political actors with their own agendas sought to channel this grassroots protest to fulfill those agendas, creating an unusual intersection of grassroots activism, millionaire donors, and established politicians all vying for control.[3]

The Tea Party movement expressed built-up anger that the conservative base of the Republican Party had been feeling long before the government bailouts, the Affordable Care Act, and the Obama stimulus package were undertaken. Many on the right were already frustrated with what appeared to be the never-ending war in Afghanistan and Iraq. The nomination of John McCain—who was seen as a media hound and Washington insider by many within the party—and his disastrous presidential campaign against the charismatic Barack Obama dismayed conservative Republicans. The rationale for bailouts of Wall Street firms seen as "too big to fail," followed by health care reform that especially burdened small businesses during hard times, added flammable material to the combustion that burst forth with the Tea Party movement.

The spark that lit the fire came on February 19, 2009, when CNBC television reporter Rick Santelli, not known for expressing political views, vented on air about Obama's proposed foreclosure relief plan. He declared, "The government is rewarding bad behavior."[4] He invited people to a "Chicago Tea Party" to protest the measures. His comments were picked up by the libertarian internet site the *Drudge Report.* Across the country a spontaneous Tea Party movement sprang up through online social-networking sites. Rightwing radio announcers and bloggers promoted the Tea Party.

In March and April, hundreds of thousands came to rallies protesting perceived threats to liberty and the Constitution posed by the Obama administration. The polls taken at early rallies showed supporters were equally divided among Republicans, Democrats, and independents. They were united in their rage. On-the-ground organizing by local activists followed these rallies. At that point local Republicans took notice. Democrats were still largely caught up in enthusiasm for Obama. By the 2010 midterm elections, more than a thousand local Tea Party groups had emerged. In early September 2009, at least 70,000 Tea Party protesters, a low estimate, marched in Washington. These early local and state rallies and the march on Washington were picked up by Fox News and promoted by Glenn Beck, who had his own show on Fox.

The Tea Party movement was not a single organization, but various local and state groups identified with it. Indeed, the movement lacked even a coordinated network.[5] As such the movement did not have a single spokesperson, and in some states different organizations and leaders claimed to speak for the movement. By the fall of 2009 approximately 1,400 Tea Party organizations had been formed, with some states, such as California, Florida, and Texas, listing more than 50 groups each. Estimates placed about 46 million Americans, about one-fifth of voting-age adults, as strong Tea Party supporters.[6] Most Tea Party activists and those attending the rallies were middle aged and older. They were generally above average in education, with higher incomes, but most were not wealthy. They were furious that the banks got bailed out while they were forced to the brink of economic dislocation. Women played an especially important role in local organizing. Most were Republicans, although about a third disavowed allegiance to the GOP. Over 60 percent self-identified as conservatives. Many attended church regularly, especially evangelical Protestant churches. At the same time, nearly half of Tea Partyers had never heard of the religious right, and one in ten expressed disagreement with religious conservatism. Many of the early activists came out of libertarian Ron Paul's 2008 presidential campaign.

As the Tea Party movement emerged, libertarians through Koch brother–funded organizations, such as FreedomWorks and Americans for Prosperity, sought to direct the movement toward small-government and ultra–free market policies. Within the Tea Party, activists shared a common belief that constitutional principles were under threat, and thereby the foundations of the nation were being subverted. Most Tea Partyers abhorred "big government" and saw America headed toward socialism. Yet many of those involved in the Tea Party movement were Christian social conservatives and as such did not share the libertarian philosophy of open borders, decriminalization of marijuana, gay rights, and abortion rights. Ideological tensions within the Tea Party movement were subsumed for the time being in anti–big government and anti-Obama messages, but these divisions reappeared in 2016 when Donald Trump entered the Republican primaries.

FreedomWorks was a Koch-funded advocacy organization based in Washington, D.C. The organization emerged from an earlier group, Citizens for a Sound Economy, founded in 1984, with major funding from the arch-conservative petrochemical billionaires Charles and David Koch. David Koch had run on the Libertarian Party presidential ticket in 1980. After receiving only 1 percent of the vote, David joined his brother in viewing the Republican Party as a conduit for libertarian ideas.[7] FreedomWorks had been founded in 2004 as a professionally staffed advocacy organization headed by Dick Armey, a former congressperson from Texas who had joined Representative Newt Gingrich in winning the House for Republicans in 1994. FreedomWorks on the national level and Koch-funded Americans for Prosperity on state and local levels sought to align themselves with the Tea Party movement. FreedomWorks promoted and funded the September 2009 Tea Party rally in Washington, and Americans for Prosperity state organizers joined local Tea Party groups. The goal was to push for a libertarian philosophy of small government and economic deregulation.

Behind the scenes inevitable tensions arose in this relationship. Koch organizations, following the libertarian philosophy of their founders, called for open borders and free trade. Within the Tea Party, open borders—and even free trade—were nearly as abhorrent as Obamacare. The Koch agenda for drug legalization and criminal justice reform also did not fly well with many Tea Party organizations. State organizers for Americans for Prosperity warned Koch headquarters in Arlington, Virginia, that these policies should not be pushed in Tea Party meetings. It was bad politics. For the Kochs, however, these were matters of principle. The differences between Koch libertarianism and Tea Party conservatism signaled the first signs of fissure between the Koch brothers and Republican conservatism, which ruptured when Donald Trump won the White House in 2016. By then, many conservatives in the Republican base were attacking the Kochs as globalists out for their own interests.

Although the Tea Party was not launched by the Republican Party, Republicans sought to take advantage of the movement, especially those outside the state party establishments who sought to turn the GOP further to the right. But the Tea Party movement proved to be a double-edged sword for the Republican Party. Tea Party activists on the local and state levels helped rally the Republican base in the 2010 midterm elections but at the same time threatened the party establishment and many incumbent office holders. Even candidates who aligned themselves with the Tea Party during the election later found themselves at odds with Tea Party activists. For example, Congressman Paul Ryan, a Republican from Wisconsin, traveled the country in 2010 promoting Tea Party–endorsed candidates. As speaker of the House, a position he assumed in October 2015, he discovered that many in the base of the party saw him as a RINO (Republican in Name Only). Similarly, Marco Rubio, who won a U.S. Senate seat from Florida with Tea Party support in 2010, came to be seen as part of the Republican establishment. From the outset, Tea Party activists despised the party establishment, especially on the national level, and refused to accept the chair of the Republican National Committee, Michael Steele, when he tried to get involved. Political strategist Karl Rove, who had played a key role in George W. Bush's election and re-election to the White House in 2000 and 2004, was distrusted by movement activists as a Washington insider. In 2009, a Sacramento political consulting firm headed by Sal Russo, a longtime Republican operator, formed the Tea Party Express, a political action committee, to funnel money to Tea Party candidates in 2010, challenging the GOP establishment. In Delaware, funding was directed to Christine O'Donnell's challenge to establishment Republican Mike Castle for the GOP nomination for the U.S. Senate. In Alaska, Joe Miller was backed in the primary to defeat incumbent Lisa Murkowski. O'Donnell won the primary, while Murkowski survived with a write-in campaign in November.

In the 2010 midterms, Republicans swept into office on the national and state levels. Republican candidates gained sixty-three seats to win a majority in the House and gained six additional seats in the U.S. Senate. On the state level, Republicans gained 720 legislative seats, and twenty-two states switched majority control to Republicans. Tea Party–endorsed candidates often won, but the exact influence of the Tea Party was difficult to measure because 2010 proved to be a Republican wave in a year of prolonged economic recession. Furthermore, some Tea Party–backed candidates proved to be a disaster. In Delaware, Christine O'Donnell lost to her Democratic opponent by seventeen points. Similarly, the Tea Party also failed to elect Sharron Angle in Nevada, Ken Buck in Colorado, and Jim Miller in Alaska. Faced with this mixed success, Tea Party organizations on the local and state levels were more circumspect in choosing candidates for the 2012 elections. Following those elections most of the Tea Party movement had been absorbed into the Republican Party.

Though relatively short-lived, the Tea Party challenged the Republican Party. In doing so, the movement showed the potential of grassroots activists to affect an established political party. The Tea Party started as a grassroots movement, yet to describe it solely as a grassroots movement neglects the role played by billionaire donors, the Koch brothers, and big media, Fox News, in channeling the energies of the Tea Party to achieve their own agenda. Thus characterizations of the Tea Party as either "grassroots" or "astro-turf" do not capture how social movements in the early twenty-first century are both. The politics of social protest in twenty-first-century America has become more and more about big money funding activism. This is as apparent on the left as it is on the right.

George Soros and Grassroots Activism on the Left

While the Tea Party took shape, left-wing activists showed they were equally upset with the status quo. In September 2011, the Occupy Wall Street movement gained national attention when thousands of demonstrators converged in New York City's financial district to protest what they saw as the ills of corporate America. The call to occupy Wall Street began when a Canadian anti-capitalist magazine, *Adbusters,* called for a march on Wall Street and Washington, D.C. Small anarchist collectives began promoting the demonstration. They envisioned a kind of decentralized Arab Spring movement that had swept across the Middle East the year before and overturned governments in the region. The first day of the protest, only a few thousand people showed up at Zuccotti Park to camp out in protest of the "one percent" of ultrarich Americans who were profiting at the expense of the other "99 percent" of

Americans. For the next two months, Occupy Wall Street protesters disrupted corporate board meetings, corporate offices, and university campuses across the country. Occupy demonstrations broke out in Boston, Chicago, Los Angeles, Portland, Atlanta, San Diego, and dozens of other cities. The movement caught the media and political pundits by surprise.

Activists in the movement envisioned people's assemblies across America being formed to arrive at collective solutions for a nation perceived to be benefiting the ultrarich. As such, the Occupy movement offered a list of grievances rather than a specific program. The Declaration of the Occupation of New York City, issued on September 29, became a model for other occupy groups. The declaration accused the "one percenters" of placing "profit over people," "self-interest over justice," and "oppression over equality." The ultrarich were the ones who "run our governments." The accusations continued, "They have taken bailouts from taxpayers with impunity, and continue to give executives exorbitant bonuses." "They," the protesters claimed, have "taken our houses through an illegal foreclosure process," and "they" have perpetuated "inequality and discrimination in the workplace based on age, the color of one's skin, sex, gender identity, and sexual orientation." The declaration maintained, "They have profited off the torture, confinement, and cruel treatment of countless animals and actively hide these practices."[8] It was a grab bag of grievances without a prescription for curing the ills of society.

For a brief moment, a couple of months, the Occupy movement gained national attention. Hollywood celebrities arrived to support it. The left-wing Transportation Workers Union gave its support to the protesters. More than $700,000 was collected to help the protesters with food, the camp site, and printed materials. The average donation came from those making between $50,000 to $100,000, though former New York Mercantile Exchange vice chair Robert Halper became Occupy's largest donor.

Hungarian-born multibillionaire George Soros and his philanthropic foundation, the Open Society Foundations, present a good example of how funding of grassroots activism on the left operates in today's polarized world of politics. Soros funds a vast array of organizations that give new meaning to grassroots social mobilization. His network extends from the United States to Europe, the Middle East, and Africa. In the United States, Soros-supported organizations include Black Lives Matter, MoveOn.org, the Center for American Progress, America Coming Together, the Drug Policy Alliance, various immigration organizations, Israel divestment groups, criminal law reform groups, and environmental justice organizations, among others. In total, Open Society supports more than five hundred organizations worldwide and has donated in the last two decades an estimated $11 billion to progressive causes and some charitable groups.

Soros told an interviewer for the *Independent* in 1993 that he sometimes thinks of himself as "some kind of god, the creator of everything." He expanded on this theme in his 1991 book *Underwriting Democracy*, in which he confessed, "If truth be known, I carried some rather potent messianic fantasies with me since childhood."[9] He compared himself to the God of the Old Testament.

Soros was born to a nonpracticing Jewish family in Budapest, Hungary, in August 1931. When the Nazis occupied the city in 1944, his father saved the family from the Holocaust by working with the government delivering deportation notices to Hungarian Jews.[10] In 1947, the Soros family relocated to England, where George attended the London School of Economics. He fell under the sway of Viennese-born philosopher Karl Popper, who became his spiritual mentor. Popper was best known for his 1945 book *The Open Society and Its Enemies,* an attack on Plato and others who maintained a "block view" of the universe. Following graduation in 1952, Soros eventually joined the London brokerage firm of Singer and Friedlander, where he became a trader in international securities. He relocated to New York four years later to work on Wall Street. He lived in the Greenwich Village area of Manhattan, a center of the 1960s counterculture. In 1969, Soros founded a private partnership called the Soros Fund, later renamed the Quantum Fund, which by 1985 was worth more than a billion dollars. By the late 1980s, Soros had become a dominant figure in international currency and investment trading. In 1992, Soros made a fortune shorting the British pound. On September 16, 1992, the Soros fund sold short more than $10 billion in pounds, forcing the European Exchange Rate Mechanism to devalue the pound. Soros became known as the man who broke the Bank of England.

In 1979 Soros founded his Open Society Foundations. Its mission was to build "vibrant and tolerant democracies." From the outset, Soros relied on the advice of Aryeh Neier, who became the president of the entire Soros foundations network. Neier came directly out of a New Left group, Students for a Democratic Society (SDS), which he had helped found as a young man. After the SDS, Neier went to work for the next fifteen years for the American Civil Liberties Union. Following his work for the ACLU, Neier founded Human Rights Watch in 1978. In the 1990s, Human Rights Watch became a major critic of the war on terror, charging the U.S. government of routinely using torture and engaging in inhumane treatment of captured jihadists in Afghanistan and Iraq. Between 2000 and 2008, the Open Society Foundations awarded over $6 million to Human Rights Watch.

Soros's political activism grew after President George W. Bush's declaration of war on terror after the 9/11 attacks.[11] He poured money into the Center for American Progress ($2.5 million) and into MoveOn.org and America Coming Together ($20 million), both of which were partisan groups working to defeat Bush in 2004. In addition, the Center for Responsive Politics estimates that Soros donated more than $23 million to various tax-exempt groups aimed at defeating Bush. Soros joined other donors in creating a new group, Democracy Alliance, a fundraising organization whose mission is to support progressive causes and an infrastructure for left-wing activism. By 2018, the network of Soros-funded groups was vast.[12] His empire promoting grassroots activism includes support for 187 known activist groups in America.[13] This funding has been directed to supporting community activism through Black Lives Matter, the Center for Community Change, the Gamaliel Foundations, the Ruckus Society, People for the American Way, and Democracy for America.

The Soros network also provides support for an array of think tanks, including the Center for Economic and Policy Research, the Center on Budget and Policy Priorities, and the Ella Baker Center for Human Rights. At the same time, funding is provided for voter mobilization and registration through such groups as Project Vote and the Progressive States Network. Soros's funding for left-wing media includes support for the left-wing intellectual journal the *American Prospect*, the Independent Media Institute, the Nation Institute, Media Matters for America, and the Sundance Institute, which gets money through the Soros Documentary Fund to produce "social justice" and "social change" documentaries.

Like the Koch brothers on the right, Soros provides an example of the thin line separating grassroots politics and partisan politics. Soros was a major funder of Hillary Clinton's presidential campaign in 2016. Aside from being one of Clinton's top donors, Soros mobilized his media, community organizing groups, and voter mobilization organizations on behalf of the Clinton campaign. The nonpartisan Center for Responsive Politics listed Soros as the sixth largest donor in the 2016 political cycle, giving millions of dollars to Clinton and other Democratic Party candidates.

This funding pattern was repeated in the 2018 midterm elections. In California, for example, Soros and other progressives, including Cari Tuna, wife of Facebook cofounder Dustin Moskovitz, poured millions of dollars into four key district attorney races.[14] Only one of these candidates won—in this case in Oakland—but these campaigns show how big money can support grassroots insurgency.

The races for the Sacramento County and San Diego prosecutors are especially revealing as to how thin these lines have become in practice. In the race for Sacramento County prosecutor, incumbent Anne Marie Schubert fended off an insurgent campaign by Noah Phillips, who had served as Schubert's deputy prosecutor. Phillips attacked his boss for failing to indict a police officer who mistakenly shot an unarmed black man during a call. Phillips credited the Soros team with scripting and paying for his television ad. Behind Phillips's fundraising campaign was a political action committee known as Real Justice, underwritten by Cari Tuna. Other national philanthropists provided writing services and media coaching for the Phillips campaign. Only the revelations of earlier racist and sexist emails from Phillips turned the tide. Each candidate in the race raised about $1.1 million. Most of Schubert's contributions came from other prosecutors, the business community, and police unions. More than half of Phillips's million came from Soros.

Soros's campaign to defeat Summer Stephan for San Diego's district attorney also went south. Challenger Geneviéve Jones-Wright received only about 34 percent of the vote but not for lack of money. The Soros political action committee contributed a whopping $2.2 million in support of Jones-Wright. Her platform called for releasing low-level offenders from prosecution, reforming the bail system, and creating a police misconduct unit, but the heart of the campaign was about how blacks and other racial minorities were being persecuted through a racist criminal justice system. Jones-Wright decried what she described as "criminalizing poverty."[15]

Campaign money is just one avenue for Soros. His network supports activism concerning criminal justice reform, immigration, climate change, health care reform, and voter registration.

Black Lives Matter: A Case Study of Funding Grassroots Activism

Black Lives Matter, an activist group involved in many demonstrations for racial justice, offers another case study in the proximity of mega-funding and grassroots activism today.[16] The group emerged in response to the Trayvon Martin shooting in 2012. The incident, which led to a national protest movement, occurred on the evening of February 25, 2012, in Sanford, Florida, when George Zimmerman, a twenty-eight-year-old man of Hispanic, white, and black ancestry, fatally shot seventeen-year-old African American high school student Trayvon Martin during an altercation. Zimmerman was acting as his neighborhood watch coordinator when he encountered Martin. Zimmerman's release caused thousands of protesters to call for his arrest. Six weeks after the shooting, amid extensive media coverage and protests across the country, Zimmerman was charged with murder by a special prosecutor appointed by the governor. On July 13, 2013, Zimmerman was acquitted by a jury. In February 2015, the Obama administration's Department of Justice announced there was not enough evidence to prosecute the case as a "federal hate crime."[17]

Stepping into the widespread outrage over Zimmerman's acquittal was Alicia Garza, a thirty-four-year-old activist from Oakland, California. Following the July 2013 acquittal, Garza posted on Facebook, "Black people. I love you. I love us. Our lives matter, Black Lives Matter." Patrisse Cullors, a longtime Los Angeles activist, shared the posting under the hashtag #BlackLivesMatter. Joining the two was Opal Tometi, a Nigerian immigrant involved in the Black Alliance for Just Immigration. The three activists shared a belief in grassroots organizing to transform America, a nation they believed was racist, xenophobic, imperialist, misogynist, and homophobic. The backgrounds of these three women illuminate the commitment of Black Lives Matter to grassroots protest as a mode of social change.

Alicia Garza brought to the movement a long record as an activist. She is gay, married to a biracial transgender spouse. Before becoming involved in Black Lives Matter, she was an activist for health care reform, a union organizer for domestic workers, and an organizer against violence toward "transgender and gender people of color." She served as director of People Organized to Win Employment Rights in the San Francisco Bay Area, which won the right for youth to use public transportation for free in San Francisco. She mobilized community groups against gentrification in San Francisco and police brutality in the city. She was appointed to the board of directors of Forward Together, an organization that trains people of color as community organizers. She won community and national awards from gay activist groups. She appeared often in the left-wing publications the *Guardian* and the *Nation*, proclaiming gay black women as the vanguard of social change.[18]

Patrisse Cullors emerged as an activist early in life. At age fifteen she left her home in Los Angeles at the request of her parents when she revealed she was gay. She rejected her religious upbringing as a Jehovah's Witness and became interested in the religious tradition of Ifá, a African divination religion. Following college, she became the executive director of the Coalition to End Sheriff Violence in Los Angeles jails and played a critical but unsuccessful role in the campaign to elect a new Los Angeles sheriff in 2014.[19]

Opal Tometi, a New York–based activist, is the daughter of Nigerian immigrants.[20] She grew up in Phoenix and completed a BA in history and an MA degree in communications and advocacy at the University of Arizona. While in college she began working for the ACLU. Her activism led her to become the executive director for the Black Alliance for Just Immigration, an organization that collaborates with immigration activists in Los Angeles, Phoenix, New York, Oakland, and Washington, D.C. She proclaims herself a follower of liberation theology, a Marxist-informed worldview.

Black Lives Matter has received funding from multiple Soros-backed groups, including at least $33 million in one year that supported on-the-ground activists during the 2015 Ferguson, Missouri, protests.[21] The organizations involved in Black Lives Matter in Ferguson included the Samuel Dewitt Proctor Conference, Drug Policy Alliance, Make the Road New York, and Equal Justice USA. On-the-ground troops deployed to support Black Lives Matter in Ferguson included Sojourners, the Advance Project, the Center for Community Change, and networks from the Gamaliel Foundation, all funded in part by Soros. Colorlines, an online news site, which received $200,000 from Soros's foundation to its sponsoring organization Race Forward, published tirelessly on Ferguson. In 2015, Soros gave a total of $5.4 million to grassroots efforts in Ferguson and in Staten Island, where activists protested Eric Garner's death at the hands of police.

Following the Ferguson protests, Black Lives Matter organized more than a thousand demonstrations across the country. Organizers have been involved in protests in Brooklyn, Newark, Boston, Chicago, Columbus, Miami, Detroit, Houston, Oakland, San Francisco, Los Angeles, Nashville, Portland, Tucson, and Washington, D.C. The movement spread to Toronto, Canada. At the same time, this activism drew considerable support from major donors. In 2019, the Borealis Philanthropy partnered with Black Lives Matter to found the Black-Led Movement Fund.[22] The Borealis Philanthropy was founded in 2014 in Minneapolis to serve as an intermediary between philanthropic foundations and social activist organizations. Led by Margarita "Magui" Rubalcava, a longtime activist involved in immigration reform, Borealis Philanthropy played a critical role in securing a six-year commitment from the Ford Foundation to Black Lives Matter. Prior to the Ford Foundation commitment, the Black-Led Movement Fund had received funding from Hill-Snowden Foundation, Solidaire, the NoVo Foundation, the Association of Black Foundation Executives, the Neighborhood Funders Group–Funders for Justice, and Anonymous Donors fund. In announcing this multimillion-dollar commitment, the Ford Foundation grant officers Brook Kelly-Green and Luna Yasui stated in a press release, "We are living in anxious, often frightening times," characterized by a "toxic blend of racism, hypermasculinity, and state violence that has taken the lives of too many black men and women and people of color in the US." The purpose of the grant was to "engage with and learn from the movement." "We want," they declared, "to nurture bold experiments and help the movement build the solid infrastructure that will enable it to flourish. As we do so, we believe it's essential that our funding not dictate or distort the work underway."[23]

The foundations supporting Black Lives Matter express genuine concerns about justice in America, and their support of activists involved in a movement for racial justice is intended to strengthen participation within American democracy. In a polarized political environment, however, funding support from foundations and private donors with deep pockets reinforces the belief among right-wing voters that an insidious axis of elites has been created.

Populism: Its Future

Do the lessons of past populist movements provide a template for the revival of reform movements today? The verdict is still out on this question because the factors necessary for successful reform appear to be mostly missing today. Narrow identity politics tends to preclude reaching beyond a core activist base. These protest movements reflect, however, a profound sense of discontent that prevails in American politics today. This discontent portends the potential for larger social protest in the future. Political opinion has become polarized; partisanship has prevented necessary enactment of reform legislation to address problems concerning national defense, the financial health of society, income inequality, a deteriorating infrastructure, and social ills from crime, drug addiction, children in poverty, and immigration. Moreover, the influence of the ultrarich on today's grassroots social movements casts a shadow over the ability of these movements to reflect the interests of the people they claim to represent.

Anti-elitist rhetoric has found expression in American politics from its earliest beginnings. American politicians found early that claiming to represent common folks against the powerful elites made for good politics. In the early nineteenth century, translating elites to mean international financiers, especially London bankers, was an easy step to make in American politics, especially given British investment in the United States and pervasive anti-British sentiment in American society. In the 1830s, Andrew Jackson railed against British bankers and their connection with the Second U.S. Bank. In vetoing the charter for the bank on July 14, 1832, he declared, "More than eight millions of the stock of this bank are held by foreigners. By this act the American Republic proposes virtually to make them a present of some millions of dollars. For these gratuities to foreigners and to some of our own opulent citizens the act secures no equivalent whatever."[24]

Such rhetoric became commonplace in American politics throughout the late nineteenth century. Agrarian agitators were not unique in accusing international financiers of controlling the world gold supply and manipulating the gold market to the detriment of American farmers and the common people. Such language appealed to a shared patriotism among nineteenth-century populists. Outright appeals to nationalism, however, took a more insidious turn with the rise of fascism in Europe. In America, such populists as Father Charles Coughlin conflated his attacks on the New Deal and international finance with his isolationist foreign policy. As such, populism, nationalism, and fascism became nearly synonymous. Populism became associated with demagogic appeals to the base passions of the masses. This association was especially evident in the aftermath of World War II. Later assessments of populism, focused on nineteenth-century agrarian populism, emphasized the anti-elitist character of the movement, while critics of agrarian populism took note of its anti-Semitism and xenophobia. This debate, waged in academic and pundit circles, spilled over into the popular anti-communism of the 1950s and the Goldwater presidential campaign in 1964. Liberal newspaper columnist Drew Pearson revealed the anxieties of many on the left witnessing the rise of Barry Goldwater when he warned of the "smell of fascism" in the air. Roy Wilkins, of the NAACP, told readers of the *New York Times* that "a man came out of the beer halls of Munich" and "all the same elements are there in San Francisco now," where the Republican convention that nominated Goldwater was meeting. Writing in *Esquire*, author Norman Mailer, always talented in capturing fashionable left-wing opinion, compared the Republican National Convention to a Nazi rally.[25]

The recent resurgence of populist-nationalist parties in Europe, the popular vote in the United Kingdom to exit the European Union, and Donald Trump's election to the White House in 2016 set up renewed fears of the phoenix-like revival of fascism associated with populism and nationalism.[26] The 2008–2009 economic crisis, followed by mass immigration from the Middle East and Africa into Europe, created conditions for political upheaval as populist-nationalist parties rose and made significant gains throughout central and western Europe. These parties—the Alternative for Germany, France's National Rally, the Netherlands' Freedom Party, Hungary's Fidesz Party, Poland's Law and Justice Party, Italy's Lega Party, Finland's Finns Party, and Austria's Freedom Party—made significant gains in their respective countries and in the recent E.U. parliamentary elections. At the same time, Tories in the United Kingdom replaced a moderate pro-Brexit prime minister, Theresa May, with hardline Brexiter Boris Johnson. In December 2019, Johnson and the Conservative Party swept parliamentary elections in a landslide victory running on a populist message of getting the United Kingdom out of the European Union. Three years earlier in 2016, Donald Trump, running as an anti-elitist and against illegal immigration ("Build the Wall"), won election to the White House.

The rise of the populist-nationalist right sent shock waves through established political circles. The world appeared to have been turned upside down for them and was not about to be turned right-side up anytime soon. In this environment, progressives began to make gains, especially among Green parties in western Europe, in the continued move left under Jeremy Corbyn's Labour Party, and in the United States as the Democratic Party swung further to the left under the influence of populist-progressive candidates Bernie Sanders and Elizabeth Warren, both of whom made a point of shunning big-money donations from the ultrarich.

In this polarized environment, great consternation manifested itself among established political leaders and the media about the rise of populist nationalism. Fears of the rise of fascism expressed itself in political rhetoric and in the media, as racism, xenophobia, anti-Semitism, nativism, and homophobia were denounced—often with just cause. There is no question that some of the parties on the far right in Europe have historical and current associations with neofascism.

Populist-nationalist parties—as well as the Greens in certain countries—are on the rise, attracting large numbers of voters. The losers in this polarized political climate have been, in general, centrist parties, in particular social democratic parties. To make sense of these events, we must begin with an understanding that, following the global crash of 2008 and the emergence of the immigration problem, many voters across central and western Europe, the United Kingdom, and the United States expressed deep anger at their respective established parties. Expressions of political discontent took different forms and occurred at different times. These populist movements revealed strong anti-establishment feelings. Although populist-nationalist parties shared opposition to immigration and multiculturalism, populism was first and foremost about the perceived degeneration of representative democracy.[27] An "us" versus "them" mentality was expressed in these movements, found in opposition to global elites, globalization, and international institutions, such as the European Union, the European Bank, and the International Monetary Fund. Anti-immigration sentiment prevails in these populist-nationalist parties. Yet aside from general similarities, most of these parties in Europe are characterized by internal tensions, often over winning elections, which would mean pragmatic compromise on ideological principle.[28]

These populist-nationalist political formations in Europe today suggest three major conclusions before there is panic that Europe is about to become fascist. First, all of these parties face internal tensions within their own parties. Second, these parties, while falling into the category of populist-nationalist, differ significantly ideologically. Some are more liberal economically; others are more protectionist and social welfare oriented. While all bewail the E.U. hegemony, they vary in opposition to Brussels. France's National Rally party is opposed to ending the euro, and Poland's Law and Justice Party does not want the dismantling of the European Union. Third, these differences—and many others—reveal that these parties, as might be expected, represent national differences and the unique politics and histories of their own countries. Nationalism is a two-edged sword, rallying voters in their own countries but making close cooperation among the parties in the E.U. parliament or European politics in general difficult. Of course, a global economic or major political crisis in Europe might change this.

Within the context of the rise of populist-nationalist parties in Europe, the election of Donald Trump to the White House in 2016 raised inevitable questions about the role of populism and nationalism in American politics.[29] Although Trump did not win a majority of primary state voters until late in his nomination campaign, and while he did not win the popular vote in his election to the White House, Trump tapped into a sizable segment within the electorate who were discontented with politics as usual within the Republican and Democratic Parties. Bernie Sanders capitalized on similar resentments; one-third of Sanders's primary voters went for Trump in November. Arguably Trump won election to the White House in large part because of an anti–Hillary Clinton sentiment within the electorate, but his election cannot be dismissed as a fluke. Trump's election came at an inflection point in American politics when many voters had become distrustful of government itself, disdained politicians who seemed more self-interested than genuine representatives of the people, and observed that powerful special interests and corporate lobbyists exerted what was perceived as undue influence on government. For many Trump supporters, the whole political system seemed corrupt.

Trump brought to his primary and general campaign a populist message intent on capturing voter discontent. Often vituperative, always quotable, and most often divisive, Trump rallied his supporters by calling for border control and denouncing his opponents. He drew huge crowds who cheered his denunciation of corporate elites, Washington insiders, and establishment politicians, including those within his own party. He accused them of having betrayed the interests of the American people and those left behind—American workers—in trade deals that benefited the rich and powerful. His call for an "America First" foreign policy, issued during the campaign and reiterated once he was in the White House, struck a chord among many voters who felt that America had become a kind of world police force.

The Democratic Party presidential nominee, Hillary Clinton, came under special attack by Trump for her alleged corruption. Trump supporters responded with wild enthusiasm, chanting "Build That Wall" and "Lock Her Up." He assailed his critics in the press as "Fake Media." He accused Washington elites as being out of touch. Typical was an address he gave in Phoenix, Arizona, a border state, in which he told an enthusiastic crowd, "Only the out of touch media elites think the biggest problems facing America—you know this, this is what they talk about facing American society today. . . . It's not nuclear, and it's not ISIS, it's not Russia, it's not China, it's global warming." He concluded his speech, "Let's stop the drugs and the crime from pouring into our country. Let's protect our social security and Medicare. Let's get unemployed Americans off the welfare and back to work in this country. . . . Together we can save American lives, American jobs, and American futures. Together we can save America itself. Join me in this mission; we're going to make America great again."[30] His appeals to populist resentment proved as divisive as William Jennings Bryan's rhetoric in 1896. Unlike populism of the late nineteenth century, Trump added to this modern populist brew a volatile nationalist ingredient. Trump's election to the White House sent shock waves through American politics.

Essential to Trump's election were white voters, especially in key battle-ground states in the Midwest. He won the white vote across every category, lower income to high income, non–college educated and college educated. His margin among whites without a college degree was the largest among any candidate in exit polls since the 1980s. Two-thirds of non–college educated whites voted for Trump. This resulted in a whopping 30 percent margin for Trump over Clinton in that group. He won college-educated whites as well (49 percent to 45 percent), which should be a warning to the Democrats and belies many pundits who describe Trump voters as angry, non-college edu-cated, white males. The only exception were college-educated women, among whom he won only 48 percent. Exit polls showed that white working-class voters with no college degrees went overwhelmingly for him, 71 percent to 23 percent. Trump's appeal to the white working class was striking: of the 660 counties that are 85 percent white earning a median income, Trump won all of them with the exception of two, which went for Clinton. Trump won the white working-class vote because of economic dislocation, fears of profes-sional managerial elites, and social and racial anxieties, as well as opposition to Hillary Clinton for various reasons.[31]

White non-Hispanic voters went for Trump by a margin of 21 percentage points (58 percent to 37 percent), according to the Pew Research Institute. He fared about a percentage point better among Hispanic voters than did Mitt Romney in 2012, by winning about 30 percent of these voters. Within the black vote, Trump actually received two points over what Romney re-ceived. The real difference in the black vote for Clinton was that blacks just did not turn out in the numbers for her that they had for Obama. She was a white woman from a political dynasty offering the status quo.[32]

Trump entered the White House pledged to an agenda that benefited the national interest over global elite interests. As president, Trump continued to use rhetoric that he had used as a candidate by denouncing global elites, fake media, political insiders, and corruption within the "deep state." This rhetoric tapped into a wellspring of anger within the Republican base and a segment of the American public who believed, rightly or wrongly, that they had been betrayed by promises of economic prosperity in the new global economy, trade with China, and the North American Free Trade Agreement of 1994. This anger within the Republican base had been brewing long before Trump declared himself a presidential candidate. The Tea Party movement expressed this anger, which lay festering in the 2012 presidential race, when Republicans rallied behind their party's presidential nominee, Mitt Romney, who proved articulate, intelligent, and quite polite. He lost to incumbent president Barack Obama, whose campaign portrayed Romney as an elitist, a Wall Street insider, a man who did not care about average people, and a candidate out of touch with current realities of the world. The media seized on the image of Romney strapping his dog in a crate on top of the family's station wagon while on a summer vacation; Romney's wife was portrayed as a rich woman who loved riding thoroughbred horses; and Romney's warning that Russia was America's number-one threat was dismissed as early Cold War thinking. Romney's seeming refusal to counterpunch left many within the Republican base angry. They were reminded of George W. Bush, who refused to counter accusations of being a warmonger. Thus, when Trump stepped on the stage and hit his opponents hard—whether Bush's brother, Jeb Bush, who was seeking the nomination, or Hillary Clinton—they cheered, even as some cringed and others were repulsed by his rhetoric.

Below the volcano of emotion lie deeper layers of discontent: a woke culture that criticized white privilege and systematic racism and intolerant and bigoted Christians; continued political setbacks for the GOP; and failure of Republican Party leaders to respond to the concerns of the base. Trumpism captured voter discontent, but with or without Trump as the leader of the Republican Party, this populist sentiment within the electorate is not going to disappear.[33] Trump became a conduit for a populist revolt within American politics. He appealed to a sense of patriotism within the electorate, although his critics denounced it as racist and xenophobic, echoing fascist dictators of the 1930s.

Much like "populism," descriptions relying on "nationalism" and "anti-globalism" lack precise definition. The standard dictionary definition of *nationalism* is placing one's nation first, spirit and aspirations to the nation as a whole, and devotion and loyalty to one's nation. Nationalism is closely associated with patriotism. The nation-state arose late in European history as a socially constructed political organization to bring diverse people and regions together into a political entity. Nationalism per se should be distinguished from ethnic nationalism (white or Aryan supremacy), xenophobia, nativism, or imperialism. These tendencies can be found within nationalism, just as patriotism can be translated into a hyperpatriotism that does not allow dissent.

One way of thinking about a healthy nationalism and patriotism is to look at Abraham Lincoln's nationalism and patriotism. As a young Whig in Congress, Lincoln opposed the Mexican-American War as a war of aggression. In his opposition, he continued to proclaim his nationalism and patriotism. The Whig Party, under Henry Clay and the American System, stood above all else as a nationalist party. Lincoln's nationalism continued into the Civil War. The war was fought, as Lincoln declared, over preserving the nation. In this sense, he stood as a nationalist. How else can Lincoln's opening lines of the Gettysburg Address in 1863 be read other than as a healthy nationalism: "Fourscore and seven years ago our fathers brought forth, on this continent, a new nation, conceived in liberty, and dedicated to the proposition that all men are created equal. Now we are engaged in a great civil war, testing whether that nation, or any nation so conceived, and so dedicated, can long endure."

Lincoln understood that a healthy nation—a healthy nationalism, if you will—needed to rest on higher principles, universal principles. For this nation, the American nation, it was that "all men are created equal." The American Civil War was fought to preserve the Union and to uphold the belief that all men were created equal. Seen from this perspective, Lincoln's was a healthy nationalism.

When nationalism is used to promote racial or ethnic superiority at the exclusion of citizens of the nation, it subverts the nation itself. When populism—a distrust of elites—degenerates into anti-Semitic, racist conspiracy—it misdirects a healthy suspicion of centralized power. When patriotism is used to suppress legitimate dissent or to rally people for wars of aggression, national values are translated into dictatorships. Yet nationalism should be seen as a double-edged sword, depending on who wields it.

However nationalism is used, the outburst of populism and nationalist expression is not going away in European and American politics until voters believe that established parties have addressed their legitimate concerns. The forms that populism and nationalism take will vary in time and place. In the United States, partisan divide within Congress and a polarized electorate have prevented the translation of populist social protest into meaningful reform legislation, at this point, on a wide range of issues, including health care, immigration, entitlements, and the public debt. If elected representatives and party establishments fail to respond to an angry electorate, found in both parties, the politics of the street can be expected. Violence has been seen already. Political protest, however, does not inevitably translate into viable or coherent social movements necessary for political reform. Instead, the politics of the street can easily escalate into mob violence and inevitable reaction from a citizenry insistent on order. The result is greater partisan divide and greater political volatility.

In such tumultuous times, the voice of the prophet Isaiah is heard: "And thorns shall come up in her palaces, nettles and brambles in the fortresses thereof: and it shall be an habitation of dragons, and a court for owls [in desolate ruins]."[34]

Notes

Introduction

1. Cas Mudde, "Voices of the Peoples: Populism in Europe and Latin America Compared," Kellogg Institute for Foreign Policy, Notre Dame, IN, Working Paper 20110378, 201; especially useful is Paul Wilkinson, *Social Movements* (New York, 1971). In his influential study of populism, historian Michael Kazin focuses on the rhetoric of populist leaders, which he maintains can be used by vested interests to further their own privilege. As a result he distinguishes between the real populism of a genuine populist movement and the faux populism of recent right-wing movements. Kazin, *The Populist Persuasion: An American History* (New York, 1995).

2. Jan-Werner Müller, *What Is Populism?* (Philadelphia, 2016). A counter argument to Müller is Michael Lind, *The New Class War: Saving Democracy from the Managerial Elite* (New York, 2020).

3. Rudolf Heberle, *Social Movements: An Introduction to Political Sociology* (New York, 1951); Theodore Lowi, *The Politics of Disorder* (New York, 1971); and Harmon Zeigler, *Interest Groups in American Society* (Englewood Cliffs, NJ, 1964). This observation is drawn from Jo Freeman in her pioneering study *The Politics of Women's Liberation: A Case Study of an Emerging Social Movement and Its Relation to the Policy Process* (New York, 1975).

4. Jeffrey Ostler, *Prairie Populism: The Fate of Agrarian Radicalism in Kansas, Nebraska, and Iowa, 1880–1892* (Lawrence, KS, 1993), 7. Some excellent studies of social mobilization are found in J. Craig Jenkins, "Resource Mobilization Theory and the Study of Social Movements," *Annual Review of Sociology* 9 (1983): 527–53: John D. McCarthy and Mayer N. Zald, "Resource Mobilization and Social Movements: A Partial Theory," in *Social Movements in an Organization Society,* ed. McCarthy and Zald (New Brunswick, NJ, 1977): 1212–41; Anthony Obersall, "Theories of Social Conflict," *Annual Review of Sociology* 4 (1978): 291–315; and Charles Tilly, *From Mobilization to Revolution* (New York, 1978). Especially useful for this study are Luther P. Gerlach and Virginia H. Hine, *People, Power, Change: Movements and Social Transformation* (Indianapolis, 1970); Jerome Skolnick, *The Politics of Protest* (New York, 1969); Lewis S. Feuer, *The Conflict of Generations: The Character and Significance of Student Movements* (New York, 1969); and Freeman, *Politics of Women's Liberation.* Although the latter study focuses on second-wave

feminism, Freeman offers an important study of the relationship between a social movement and political change.

5. Language for this observation is drawn from Scott G. McNall, *The Road to Rebellion: Class Formation and Kansas Populism, 1865–1900* (Chicago, 1988), 14–16. McNall, following the lead of Lawrence Goodwyn's *The Populist Moment* (New York, 1978), offers a Marxist interpretation of the Populist movement, although most recent scholarship on the Populists shows the category of class is not a useful instrument in understanding their movement.

6. McNall, *Road to Rebellion*.

7. These factors for a successful social movement are drawn from a reading of a sizable literature on collective action. Especially informative were David Reisman, *Theories of Collective Action: Downs, Olson, and Hirsch* (New York, 1990); Anthony Smith, *Social Change* (London, 1978); J. Craig Jenkins and Bert Klandermans, ed., *The Politics of Social Protest: Comparative Perspectives on States and Social Movements* (Minneapolis, 1995); Neil J. Smelser, *Theory of Collective Behavior* (New York, 1962); and Sara Diamond, *Roads to Dominion: Right Wing Movements and Political Power in the United States* (New York, 1995).

Chapter 1

1. Lawrence Goodwyn, *Democratic Promise: The Populist Moment in America* (New York, 1976); and Robert F. Durden, *The Climax of Populism: The Election of 1896* (Lexington, KY, 1965), 165–67.

2. Michael Lind, *Land of Promise: An Economic History of the United States* (New York, 2012).

3. For the most recent discussion of inequality in America in the late nineteenth century, see Jeffrey Gale Williamson, *Unequal Gains: American Growth and Inequality Since 1700* (Princeton, NJ, 2016). Of particular use on the question of inequality, see Clayne Pope, "Inequality in the Nineteenth Century," in *The Cambridge History of the United States,* vol. 2, ed. Stanley L. Engerman and Robert E. Gallman (New York, 2000), 109–42. Pope maintains that the distribution of wealth was probably influenced by urbanization and immigration. He concludes, "Households who were foreign-born or headed by a woman, or a black or individuals with disadvantaged family backgrounds were much more likely to be poor. All these characteristics created significant disadvantages for an individual to overcome, though the disadvantages of foreign birth were ameliorated with time in the United States" (137). Other chapters of importance in understanding economic inequality in this period are found in the same volume: Robert A. Margo, "The Labor Force in the Nineteenth Century," 207–44; Stanley L. Engerman and Kenneth L. Sokoloff, "Technology and Industrialization, 1790–1914," 367–402; and Robert E. Gallman, "Economic Growth and Structural Change in the Long Nineteenth Century," 1–56.

4. Allan G. Bogue, *Money at Interest: The Farm Mortgage on the Middle Border* (New York, 1955); and Douglass North, *Growth and Welfare in the American Past* (Englewood Cliffs, NJ, 1966).

5. For a revisionist perspective of the trial, contrary to the narrative, see Timothy Messer-Kruse, *The Trial of the Haymarket Anarchists: Terrorism and Justice in the Gilded Age* (New York, 2011).

6. Caro Lloyd, *Henry Demarest Lloyd, 1847–1903: A Biography* (New York, 1912), 96.

7. Charles Hoffman, *The Depression of the Nineties: An Economic History* (Westport, CT, 1970).

8. "William Jennings Bryan: Henry George One of the World's Foremost Thinkers," *New York Times,* October 30, 1897.

9. John Peter Altgeld, *Live Questions* (Chicago, 1890), 776.

10. Henry George's son wrote a laudatory but detailed biography of his father, Henry George Jr., titled *The Life of Henry George* (New York, 1900). The most thorough biography of George remains Charles Albro Barker, *Henry George* (New York, 1955). A more recent book is Henry T. O'Donnell, *Henry George and the Crisis of Inequality* (New York, 2015). Insightful is John L. Thomas, *Alternative America: Henry George, Edward Bellamy, Henry Demarest Lloyd and the Adversary Tradition* (Cambridge, MA, 1983). A more recent study of the Single Tax movement is found in Christopher William England, "Land and Liberty: Henry George, the Single Tax Movement, and the Origins of Twentieth Century Liberalism," PhD dissertation, Georgetown University, 2015; and for a more specific study of the influence of Single Taxers in Portland, Oregon, at the turn of the nineteenth century, see Robert D. Johnston, *The Radical Middle Class: Populist Democracy and the Question of Capitalism in Progressive Era Portland, Oregon* (Princeton, NJ, 2003).

11. Quoted in England, "Land and Liberty," 56–57.

12. Spencer G. Olin Jr. *California's Prodigal Sons: Hiram Johnson and the Progressives, 1911–17* (Berkeley, CA, 1968), 27.

13. Discussion of *Progress and Poverty* relies on the Appleton and Sons 1886 edition.

14. George, *Progress and Poverty*, x–xi and 241.

15. Although later economists rejected George's solution to overheated land speculation, Carmen M. Reinhart and Kenneth S. Rogoff in *The Time Is Different: Eight Centuries of Financial Folly* (Princeton, NJ, 2009) maintain that property speculation explains much of the boom-bust cycle. For a sweeping understanding of capitalist development, see David Landes, *Wealth and Poverty of Nations: Why Some Are So Rich and Some So Poor* (New York, 1998).

16. Members of the Socialist Labor Party, the first large socialist party in the United States, initially aligned themselves with the Single Tax movement, but broke with it when George's followers hesitated to adopt nationalization of railroads. For a full critique of socialism and a defense of the single tax remedy and the importance of individualism, see Max Hirsch, *Democracy Versus Socialism: A Critical Examination of Socialism as a Remedy for Social Injustice and an Exposition of the Single Tax Doctrine* (New York, 1901, 4th ed., 1966).

17. The relationship between George and his followers and the Knights of Labor in the end proved fragile. Terence Powderly, leader of the Knights, later broke with George. See Robert E. Weir, "A Fragile Alliance: Henry George and the Knights of Labor," *American Journal of Economics and Sociology* (October 1997): 421–39.

18. An excellent discussion of George's mayoral race is found in England, "Land and Liberty," 109–19; and Stephen Bell, *Rebel, Priest, and Prophet: A Biography of Dr. Edward McGlynn* (New York, 1937).

19. Quoted in Fred E. Haynes, *Social Politics in the United States* (New York, 1924), 125.

20. Thomas, *Alternative America*, 262.

21. The best biography of Bellamy remains Arthur E. Morgan, *The Philosophy of Edward Bellamy* (New York, 1945); but see also Sylvia E. Bowman, *The Year 2000: A Critical Biography of Edward Bellamy* (New York, 1958).

22. Fred E. Haynes, *Social Politics in the United States* (Boston, 1924; repr. 1970), 138–51; and Arthur Lipow, *Authoritarian Socialism in America: Edward Bellamy and the Nationalist Movement* (Berkeley, CA, 1982).

23. Critical to this shift were leaders such as Thomas Cator, whose career as an activist illustrates the churning of reform sentiment in these years. Cator began as a Prohibitionist, later an Anti-Monopolist, a Nationalist, a Reform Democrat, a nominee of the nativist American Party, and finally a Republican. John T. McGreevy, "Farmers, Nationalists, and the Origins of California Populism," *Pacific Historical Review* (November 1989).

24. Quoted in Thomas, *Alternative America*, 276.

25. Thomas, *Alternative America*, 279–80. The personal differences within the Fabian intellectuals largely revolved around H. G. Wells's sexual exploits, captured in David Lodge's fictional *Man of Parts* (New York, 2011).

26. H. Wayne Morgan, *From Hayes to McKinley: National Party Politics, 1877–1896* (Syracuse, NY, 1969), 355.

27. Jeffrey Ostler, *Prairie Populism: The Fate of Agrarian Radicalism in Kansas, Nebraska, and Iowa, 1880–1892* (Lawrence, KS, 1993), 35; and Scott G. McNall, *The Road to Rebellion: Class Formation and Kansas Populism, 1865–1900* (Chicago, 1988), 48–49. See also Brooks Speer Ore, "Mary Elizabeth Lease: Nineteenth-Century Populist and Twentieth-Century Progressive," PhD dissertation, George Washington University, 2002; and Ostler, *Prairie Populism*.

28. McNall, *Road to Rebellion*.

29. Morgan, *From Hayes to McKinley*, 366.

30. Thomas, *Alternative America*, 320; Charles Postel, *The Populist Vision* (New York, 2007), 20.

31. Postel, *Populist Vision*, 36. For a full history of the Southern Alliance, see Robert C. McMath Jr., *Populist Vanguard: A History of the Southern Farmers' Alliance* (Chapel Hill, NC, 1975).

32. Postel, *Populist Vision*, 61.

33. Postel, *Populist Vision*, 177–78.

34. Postel, *Populist Vision*, 183.

35. E. A. Allen, *The Life and Public Services of James Baird Weaver* (Chicago, 1892), 515.

36. Allen, *Life and Public Services of James Baird Weaver*, 521.

37. Ostler, *Prairie Populism*, is especially good on the political limitations of the Populist insurgency, 11–13.

38. For a balanced and well-informed synthetic account of Populists as a forward-looking movement, see Postel, *Populist Vision*.

39. For a contemporary understanding of the monetary issue, see the often overlooked *Great Debate on the Financial Question Between Hon. Roswell G. Horr of New York and William H. Harvey of Illinois* (Chicago, 1895).

40. The literature on populism is immense. The first major scholarly argument for populism as progressive began with John D. Hicks, *The Populist Revolt* (Minneapolis, 1931). Richard Hofstadter's dismissal of populism as reactionary in *The Age of Reform: From Bryan to F.D.R.* (New York, 1955) and *The Paranoid Style in American Politics* (New York, 1964) set off a wave of scholarship on populism. For the intellectual context of Hofstadter's changing views of populism and mass democracy, see David S. Brown's superb biography *Richard Hofstadter: An Intellectual Biography* (Chicago, 2006). For a defense of populists as tolerant, see Walter Nugent, *The Tolerant Populists: Kansas Populism and Nativism* (Chicago, 1964). For a more nuanced examination of Kansas populism, see O. Gene Clanton, *Kansas Populism: Ideas and Men* (Lawrence, KS, 1970). Exceptionally useful on the Midwest is Ostler's *Prairie Populism*; Peter H. Argersinger, *Populism and Politics: William Alfred Peffer and the People's Party* (Lawrence, KS, 1974); and Argersinger's study of populism in the Mountain states, *The Limits of Agrarian Radicalism: Western Populism and American Politics* (Lawrence, KS, 1996). Some scholars posit a stronger progressivism to populism: e.g., Goodwyn, *Democratic Promise,* and to a lesser extent, Michael Kazin, *The Populist Persuasion, An American History* (New York, 1995); and Kazin, *A Godly Hero: The Life of William Jennings Bryan* (New York, 2007).

41. Brooks Speer Ore, "Mary Elizabeth Lease: Nineteenth-Century Populist and Twentieth-Century Progressive" PhD dissertation, George Washington University, 2002; McNall, *Road to Rebellion*; and Ostler, *Prairie Populism*, especially pp. 127–31. For Ignatius Donnelly, see Martin Ridge, *Ignatius Donnelly: The Portrait of a Politician* (Chicago, 1963).

42. Betty Gay, "The Object of the Alliance," in Gary Noy, *Distant Horizons: Documents from the Nineteenth-Century American West* (Lincoln, 1999), 300.

43. Arguments for voting along ethnic-religious lines are developed by Paul Kleppner, *The Cross of Culture: A Social Analysis of Midwestern Politics, 1850–1900* (New York, 1970); Kleppner, *The Third Electoral System, 1853–1892* (Chapel Hill, NC, 1979); and Richard J. Jensen, *The Winning of the Midwest: Social and Political Conflict, 1888–1896* (Chicago, 1972). Jeffrey C. Williams argues that farmer voting behavior was more complex than just cultural, religious, or ethnic factors, in "Economics and Politics: Voting Behavior in Kansas During the Populist Decade," *Explorations in Economic History* (1981): 233–55.

44. Chester McArthur Destler, *American Radicalism, 1865–1901*, (Chicago, 1966): 162.

45. Destler, *American Radicalism*, 169–72.

46. Ridge's *Ignatius Donnelly* captures Donnelly the man and politician. Useful on Donnelly's success as a best-selling author of such books as *Atlantis* and his utopian novel, *Caesar's Column*, is David D. Anderson, *Ignatius Donnelly* (Boston, 1980).

47. Peffer offers his own account of the movement in a series of essays published in the *Chicago Tribune* in 1899 and later published as a book, *Populism: Its Rise and Fall* (1899), which was still later ably edited and annotated by Peter Argersinger under the same title in 1991. For a further understanding of Kansas populism, see Argersinger, *Populism and Politics*; Clanton, *Kansas Populism*; and McNall, *Road to Rebellion*.

48. Quoted in Morgan, *From Hayes to McKinley,* 380.

49. Morgan, *From Hayes to McKinley,* 383.

50. Quoted in R. Hal Williams, *Realigning America: McKinley, Bryan, and the Remarkable Election of 1896* (Lawrence, KS, 2010), 23.

51. Clanton, *Kansas Populism*, 136–50.

52. Legislative chaos in Kansas is discussed by McNall, *Road to Rebellion*; and the general failure of the People's Party is discussed fully in Argersinger, *Populism and Politics*.

53. Williams, *Realigning America*, 31–34.

54. Donald L. McMurry, *Coxey's Army: A Study of the Industrial Army Movement of 1894* (Seattle, 1929); and Carlos Arnaldo Schwantes, *Coxey's Army: An American Odyssey* (Lincoln, NE, 1985).

55. Postel, *Populist Vision*, 229.

56. Postel, *Populist Vision*, 197–203.

57. Morgan, *From Hayes to McKinley*, 477–79.

58. Peffer, *Populism: Its Rise and Fall*, ed. Argersinger, 145.

59. Lloyd, *Henry Demarest Lloyd*, 259.

60. Lloyd, *Henry Demarest Lloyd*, 261–63.

61. Allan Nevins, *Grover Cleveland: A Study in Courage* (New York, 1933), 700; and Durden, *Climax of Populism*, 19.

62. Quoted in Ridge, *Ignatius Donnelly*, 351.

63. Quoted in H. Wayne Morgan, *William McKinley and His America* (Syracuse, NY, 1963), 514.

64. Morgan, *William McKinley and His America*, 159.

65. Quoted in Gilbert C. Fite, "Republican Strategy and the Farm Vote in the Presidential Campaign of 1896," *American Historical Review* (July 1960): 790.

66. Fite, "Republican Strategy and the Farm Vote."

67. Morgan, *William McKinley and His America*, 209–48.

68. An extensive literature on the 1896 realignment exists, but early interest in explaining the urban-rural divide is found in William Diamond, "Urban and Rural Voting in 1896," *American Historical Review* (January 1941): 281–305.

69. Morgan, *William McKinley and His America*, 481.

70. Roger L. Hart, *Redeemers, Bourbons and Populists: Tennessee, 1870–1896* (Baton Rouge, 1975), 72–73.

71. Postel, *Populist Vision*, 278–79.

72. "Address by D. H. Talbot in Proceedings of the National Farmers Alliance," Allen, *Life and Public Services of James Baird Weaver*, 526.

73. Olin, *California's Prodigal Sons*, 128–44.

74. Peffer, *Populism: Its Rise and Fall*, ed. Argersinger, 21; Clanton, *Kansas Populism*, 216–17 and 224–25.

75. Quoted in George E. Mowry, *The California Progressives* (Chicago, 1951), 299.

76. Frederic C. Howe, *The Confessions of a Reformer* (New York, 1925), 343.

77. Howe, *Confessions of a Reformer*, 343.

Chapter 2

1. Woodrow Wilson: "Democracy and Efficiency," *Atlantic Monthly* (March 1901), in *Selected Literary and Political Papers and Addresses of Woodrow Wilson*, vol. 1 (New York, 1926), 112.

2. The two most readable studies of Townsend, Coughlin, and Long are Alan Brinkley, *Voices of Protest: Huey Long, Father Coughlin, and the Great Depression* (New York, 1983); and David H. Bennett, *Demagogues in the Depression: American Radicals and the Union Party, 1932–1936* (New Brunswick, NJ, 1969).

3. See, for example, Robert Cohen, *When the Old Left Was Young: Student Radicals and America's First Student Movement, 1929–1941* (New York, 1993); Hal Draper, "The Student Movement of the Thirties," in *As We Saw the Thirties: Essays on Social and Political Movements of the Decade,* ed. Rita James Simon (Urbana, IL, 1967), 151–89; and Glen Jeansonne, *Women of the Far Right: The Mothers' Movement and World War II* (Chicago, 1996).

4. The formation of the Minnesota Farmer-Labor Party following World War I paralleled the emergence of state radicalism, albeit sparse and sporadic, evident in the North Dakota Nonpartisan League, the Idaho Progressive Party (1920–1926), and the Farmer-Labor Reconstruction League (1922). Richard M. Valelly, *Radicalism in the States: The Minnesota Farmer-Labor Party and the American Economy* (Chicago, 1989), 1–3.

5. Valelly, *Radicalism in the States*, 17–32.

6. The spirited organizing efforts of the Nonpartisan League are richly captured by Michael J. Lansing, *Insurgent Democracy: The Nonpartisan League in North American Politics* (Chicago, 2015).

7. Robert Morlan, *Political Prairie Fire: The Nonpartisan League, 1915–22* (Minneapolis, 1955).

8. This discussion of the Minnesota Farmer-Labor Party relies on Millard L. Gieske, *Minnesota Farmer-Laborism: The Third-Party Alternative* (Minneapolis, 1979); and excellent studies by John Earl Haynes, *Dubious Alliance: The Making of Minnesota's DFL Party* (Minneapolis, 1984); and Valelly, *Radicalism in the States.* Supplementing these books are "Arthur C. Townley," State Historical Society of North Dakota (website), https://www.ndstudies.gov/gr8/content/unit-iii-waves-development-1861-1920/lesson-4-alliances-and-conflicts/topic-7-nonpartisan-league-and-iva/section-2-origins-nonpartisan-league; Frederick L. Johnson, "The 'Mother of the Farmer-Labor Party' Did Not Really Want to Add the 'D' to the Beginning," MinnPost, MNopedia, March 20, 2017, https://www.minnpost.com/mnopedia/2017/03/mother-farmer-labor-party-didn-t-really-want-add-d-beginning/; William Millikan, "Defenders of Business: The Minneapolis Civic and Commerce Association Versus Labor During World War I," *Minnesota History* (Spring 1986): 3–17; and Steven J. Keillor, "A Country Editor in Politics: Hjalmar Petersen, Minnesota Governor," *Minnesota History* (Fall 1983): 283–94.

9. Paul S. Holbo, "The Farmer-Labor Association: Minnesota's Party Within a Party," *Minnesota History* (September 1963): 421–39.

10. Gieske, *Minnesota Farmer-Laborism*, 69; and Lansing, *Insurgent Democracy*, 197.

11. Nancy C. Unger, *Fighting Bob La Follette* (Chapel Hill, NC, 2000), especially 263–304 on the 1924 campaign; David P. Thelen, *Robert M. La Follette and the Insurgent Spirit* (Boston, 1976); and Edward N. Doan, *The La Follettes and the Wisconsin Idea* (New York, 1947).

12. Valelly, *Radicalism in the States*, 46–47.

13. Unger, *Fighting Bob La Follette*, 297.

14. Gieske, *Minnesota Farmer-Laborism*, 175.

15. There is a sizable scholarly and popular literature on A. J. Muste, including Leilah Danielson, *American Gandhi: A. J. Muste and the History of Radicalism in the Twentieth Century* (Philadelphia, 2014); Jo Ann Ooiman Robinson, *Abraham Went Out: A Biography of A. J. Muste* (Philadelphia, 1981); Nat Hentoff, *Peace Agitator: The Story of A. J. Muste* (New York, 1963); and A. J. Muste's own writings found in Nat Hentoff, ed., *The Essays of A. J. Muste* (Indianapolis, 1967), especially Muste's "Sketches for an Autobiography," 1–175, and his 1935 declaration for revolutionary violence, "Trade Unions and the Revolution," 186–94.

16. Roy Rosenzweig, "Radicals and the Jobless: The Musteites and the Unemployment Leagues 1932–1936," *Labor History* (Winter 1975): 52–77.

17. An especially useful contemporary study of the Seattle League is Arthur Hillman, *The Unemployed Citizens' League of Seattle* (Seattle, 1933).

18. Quoted in Rosenzweig, "Radicals and the Jobless," 56.

19. Harvey Klehr, *The Heyday of American Communism: The Depression Decade* (New York, 1984), 51–64.

20. This point is made by the best historian on Minneapolis grassroots organizing in the 1930s: Elizabeth Faue, *Community of Suffering and Struggle: Women, Men, and the Labor Movement in Minneapolis, 1915–1945* (Chapel Hill, NC, 1991), 67. Glimpses of party activities are found in the Meridel Le Sueur Papers at the Minneapolis Historical Society: e.g., see Ellen Blake to Meridel Le Sueur, June 6, 1937; and Louis Budenz to Sam Darcy, January 5, 1938, Loc. 152.K.18, Box 1. See also Meridel Le Sueur, "What Happens in a Strike," *American Mercury* (November 1934): 329–35.

21. John L. Shover, *Cornbelt Rebellion: The Farmers' Holiday Association* (Champaign, IL, 1965), 11. The following discussion of the Farmers' Holiday movement relies heavily on this work.

22. A good source for understanding farmer sentiment at this time is found in a lengthy report by Minnesota activists, "Transcript Farmer Holiday Reunion," Minnesota Radicalism Project files, Minnesota Historical Society, Loc. 148.F.12.2F.

23. "Transcript Farmer Holiday Reunion," 41–56.

24. Quoted in Arthur M. Schlesinger Jr., *The Age of Roosevelt: The Crisis of the Old Order* (Boston, 1957), 7.

25. This discussion of the EPIC campaign relies on Greg Mitchell, *The Campaign of the Century: Upton Sinclair's Race for Governor of California and the Birth of Media Politics* (New York, 1992), which details the anti-Sinclair part of the campaign, as well as Sinclair's extensive collection of papers located at the Lilly Library, Bloomington, Indiana.

26. Mitchell, *Campaign of the Century*, 11.

27. For example, Mitchell in *Campaign of the Century* consistently portrays Merriam as a reactionary buffoon.

28. Jackson K. Putnam, *Modern California Politics* (San Francisco, 1984), 21–22.

29. A brief account of the strike is found in Sidney Fine, *The Automobile Under the Blue Eagle: Labor, Management, and the Automobile Manufacturing Code* (Ann Arbor, MI, 1963), 274.

30. Gieske, *Minnesota Farmer-Laborism*, 191.

31. Barry Eidlin, "'Upon This (Foundering) Rock': Minneapolis Teamsters and the Transformation of U.S. Business Unionism, 1935–1941," *Labor History* (August 2009): 249–67; Constance Ashton Myers, "American Trotskyists: The First Years," *Studies in Comparative Communism* (Spring/Summer 1977); William Millikan, *A Union Against Unions: The Minneapolis Citizens Alliance and Its Fight Against Organized Labor, 1903–1947* (Minneapolis, 2001); Thomas E. Blantz, *A Priest in Public Service: Fr. Haas and the New Deal* (South Bend, IN, 1982); Farrell Dobbs, *Teamster Power* (New York, 1973); James Thomas Burnett, "American Trotskyism and the Russian Question," PhD dissertation, University of California, Berkeley, 1968, especially 111–14.

32. Insight into the stridency of both sides is from Employers' Advisory Board to National Labor Relations Board, November 17, 1934; and Francis J. Hass to National Labor Relations Board, November 27, 1934; both in Minnesota Radicalism Project, Minneapolis Historical Society, 148.F.11.9B.

33. Edwin Amenta, *When Movements Matter: The Townsend Plan and the Rise of Social Security* (Princeton, NJ, 2006). Also useful in understanding the Townsend movement is a contemporary account: Richard L. Neuberger and Kelley Loe, *An Army of the Aged: A History and Analysis of the Townsend Old Age Pension Plan* (Caldwell, ID, 1936). Edwin Amenta uses regression analysis to assess the specific political effects of the movement in a number of articles, including Edwin Amenta and Yvonne Zylan, "It Happened Here: Political Opportunity, the New Institutionalism, and the Townsend Movement," *American Sociological Review* (April 1991): 250–65; Edwin Amenta, Neal Caren, and Sheer Joy Olasky, "Age for Leisure: Political Mediation and the Impact of the Pension Movement on U.S. Old Age Policy," *American Sociological Review* (June 2005): 250–65; Edwin Amenta, Bruce G. Carruthers, and Yvonne Zylan, "A Hero for the Aged? The Townsend Movement, the Political Mediation Model, and U.S. Old-Age Policy, 1934–1950," *American Journal of Sociology* (September 1992): 308–39; and Edwin Amenta, Drew Halfmann, and Michael P. Young, "The Strategies and Contexts of Social Protest: Political Mediation and the Impact of the Townsend Movement in California," *Mobilization* (1999): 1–23. Also of importance for understanding the movement are Daniel J. B. Mitchell, "Townsend and Roosevelt: Lessons from the Struggle for Elderly Support," *Labor History* (August 2001): 255–76; J. D. Gaydowski, "Eight Letters to the Editor: The Genesis of the Townsend National Recovery Plan," *Southern California Quarterly* (December 1970): 365 c81; and Peter B. Bulkley, "Townsendism as an Eastern and Urban Phenomenon, Chautauqua County, New York, as a Case Study," *New York History* (April 1974): 179–98.

34. This concept of a "revolving" sales tax was strikingly similar to a proposal made for a "social credit" tax by Major C. H. Douglas in England. Douglas's social credit scheme gave rise to the Social Credit Party, which promoted the plan in western Canada. Douglas's social credit plan embodied an odd mixture of Catholic social thought, monetary radicalism, and egalitarianism. See Janet Martin-Nielsen, "An Engineer's View of an Ideal Society: The Economic Reforms of C. H. Douglas, 1916–1920," *Spontaneous Generations* (2007): 95–109; and C. H. Douglas, "The Delusion of Super-Production," *English Review* (December 1918): 1–6. Townsend described the origins of his plan in a series of letters to the Long Beach *Press Telegram* in late September 1933, reprinted in J. D. Gaydowski,

"The Genesis of the Townsend National Recovery Plan," *Southern California Quarterly* (December 1970).

35. Edwin Amenta, *When Movements Matter: The Townsend Plan and the Rise of Social Security* (Princeton, NJ, 2006), 170–71.

36. Amenta, *When Movements Mattered,* 76; and Bulkley, "Townsendism as an Eastern and Urban Phenomenon."

37. Donald T. Critchlow, *When Hollywood Was Right* (New York, 2015).

38. Critchlow, *When Hollywood Was Right,* 84–85.

39. "Father Coughlin Speaks," Universal Newsreel, https://www.youtube.com/watch?v=c96mDsgRwbc.

40. Donald Warren, *Radio Priest: Charles Coughlin, the Father of Hate Radio* (New York, 1996). Written after the Oklahoma City bombing, Warren's book places Coughlin within the tradition of right-wing radio. A more careful study of Coughlin placing him within an anti-capitalist Catholic social justice tradition is found in Charles J. Tull, *Father Coughlin and the New Deal* (Syracuse, NY, 1965).

41. Charles E. Coughlin, *Am I an Anti-Semite? 9 Addresses on Various "Isms," Answering the Question* (Detroit, 1939).

42. Reprinted in Warren, *Radio Priest,* 62–63.

43. Brinkley, *Voices of Protest,* 166. Coughlin's faith in parishes as instruments for the fulfillment of social justice and his insistence on democratic control of money—however incoherent in policy—suggests control on the local level.

44. Brinkley, *Voices of Protest,* 189.

45. Amenta, *When Movements Matter.*

46. Under questioning, Townsend admitted that millionaires, such as Morgan and Rockefeller, were eligible for pensions. The worst came when it was shown that Townsend had profited monetarily from the movement. Congressional investigators found that Townsend and Clements had earned $35,000 alone from their newspaper and had paid a team of Washington lobbyists $20,000 for a couple months of work in Washington. Bennett, *Demagogues of the Depression,* 179.

47. Glen Jeansonne, *Gerald L. K. Smith: Minister of Hate* (Baton Rouge, 1988).

48. Warren, *Radio Priest,* 87.

49. William Lemke, a congressman from North Dakota, got his start as a supporter of the Nonpartisan League in North Dakota. Initially a New Deal supporter, Lemke turned against Roosevelt after his refusal to support the demonetization of silver. Lemke became an agrarian hero for pushing legislation in 1934 that placed a five-year moratorium on mortgage payments for farmers threatened with foreclosure. Lemke spoke as a Jeffersonian Democrat, but his support for the Townsend Plan, Share Our Wealth, and government ownership of railroads, regulation of interstate commerce, and farm refinance bills assumed massive government intervention. Edward C. Blackorby, *Prairie Rebel: The Public Life of William Lemke* (Lincoln, NE, 1963); Bennett, *Demagogues in the Depression,* especially 85–102 and 215–60; and Jeansonne, *Gerald L. K. Smith,* 57–63.

50. Tull, *Father Coughlin and the New Deal,* 144.

51. Especially useful in understanding Coughlin's turn to anti-Semitism and the influence of Irish theologian Denis Fahey are Mary Christine Athans, "A New Perspective

on Father Charles E. Coughlin," *Church History* (June 1987): 224–35; and Ronald Mo-
dras, "Father Coughlin and Anti-Semitism: Fifty Years Later," *Journal of Church and State*
(1989): 231–47. For a new perspective on the Gallagher-Coughlin relationship, see Earl
Boyea, "The Reverend Charles Coughlin and the Church: The Gallagher Years, 1930–
1937," *Catholic Historical Review* (April 1995): 221–25.

52. For contemporary insight into the movement for a third party, see Charles R.
Walter, "The Farmer-Labor Party of Minnesota," *Nation,* March 13, 1937; and Joseph
Starr, "Labor and Farmer Groups and the Three-Party System," *Southwest Social Science
Quarterly* (June 1936): 7–19.

53. Opposition to Benson's nomination came from Hjalmar Peterson, who assumed
the governorship when Olson died of stomach cancer a few months before the election. In
office, Benson proved to fulfill Peterson's worst nightmares of a party too aligned with
Communist Party Popular Front policies. Steven J. Keillor, "A Country Editor in Politics:
Hjalmar Peterson, Minnesota Governor," *Minnesota History* (Fall 1983).

54. Haynes, *Dubious Alliance,* 18–19; and Hugh T. Lovin, "The Fall of Farmer-Labor
Parties, 1936–1938," *Pacific Northwest Quarterly* (January 1971): 16–26.

55. Haynes, *Dubious Alliance,* 19.

56. Warren Creel, "The Minneapolis Farmer-Labor Party," *Fourth International*
(March 1946): 77.

57. Creel, "Minneapolis Farmer-Labor Party," 245–49.

58. Gieske, *Minnesota Farmer-Laborism,* 240–42.

59. The Communist faction knew that Benson's turn right was only strategic. Meridel
Le Sueur wrote in the Communist Party's *New Masses* that "the Communist Party of
Minnesota, without selfish political aims, fights the pro-fascist Stassen, the tory in liberal
disguise, and stands solidly and powerfully behind Elmer Benson." Quoted in Gieske,
Minnesota Farmer-Laborism, 271.

60. Gieske, *Minnesota Farmer-Laborism,* 272.

61. "Meeting of the Hennepin County Farmer-Labor Association," transcript, March
22, 1939, Susie Stageberg Papers, Minnesota Historical Society, Box 2.

62. Later analysis showed that the backlash was a restoration of political equilibrium
in the two-party system. Jamie L. Carson, "Electoral and Partisan Forces in the Roosevelt
Era: The U.S. Congressional Election of 1938," *Congress and the Presidency* (September
2001): 161–83; Milton Plesur, "The Republican Congressional Comeback of 1938," *Review of Politics* (October 1962): 525–62; and Charles Price and Joseph Boskin, "The Roosevelt 'Purge': A Reappraisal," *Journal of Politics* (August 1966): 660–70.

63. Quoted in Barry Eiden, "'Upon this (Foundering) Rock': Minneapolis Teamsters and
the Transformation of U.S. Business Unionism, 1934–1941," *Labor History* 50.3 (2009): 255.

64. Michael Smith, "The Smith Act Trials, 1949," *Encyclopedia of the American Left,*
ed. Mari Jo Buhle and Paul Buhle (New York, 1990), 758.

65. Millikan, *A Union Against Unions,* 323–62.

66. Difficulties for the Farmer-Labor Party's isolationist position are explored in
George W. Garlid, "The Antiwar Dilemma of the Farmer-Labor Party," *Minnesota His-
tory* (Winter 1967): 365–76; and Barbara Stuhler, "The One Man Who Voted 'Nay,'"
Minnesota History (Fall 1972): 82–92.

67. Especially insightful on changes within the Farmer-Labor Party is Haynes, *Dubious Alliance*; and for a hostile view of Humphrey's role in assimilating the Farmer-Labor Party and expulsion of communists, see Elmer A. Benson, "Politics in My Lifetime," *Minnesota History* (Winter 1980): 154–60.

Chapter 3

1. Especially important in understanding how civil rights protest was translated politically into the Democratic Party is Christopher Baylor, *First to the Party: The Group Origins of Political Transformation* (Philadelphia, 2018), 86–100.

2. Useful for understanding the early NAACP are Beth Tompkins Bates, "A New Crowd Challenges the Agenda of the Old Guard in the NAACP, 1933–1941," *American Historical Review* (April 1997): 340–77; and the highly informative "'We Live's in a Free House Such as It Is': Class and the Creation of Modern Civil Rights," *University of Pennsylvania Law Review* (June 2003): 1977–2018; For a brief overview of the civil rights struggle, see Harvard Sitkoff, *The Struggle for Black Equality, 1954–1980* (New York, 1981).

3. Mary L. Dudziak, *Cold War Civil Rights: Race and the Image of American Democracy* (Princeton, NJ, 2000).

4. Generational conflict within social movements is insightfully explored by sociologist Lewis S. Feuer, *The Conflict of Generations: The Character and Significance of Student Movements* (New York, 1969).

5. Peter J. Ling, *Martin Luther King, Jr.,* (New York, 2002), 145.

6. Ling, *Martin Luther King, Jr.,* 190.

7. Job, 30:1, 12.

8. Ling, *Martin Luther King, Jr.,* 241.

9. Lewis Baldwin, *To Make the Wounded Whole: The Cultural Legacy of Martin Luther King, Jr.* (Minneapolis, 1991); and Albert J. Raboteau, *A Fire in the Bones: Reflections on African-American Religious History* (Boston, 1995).

10. This biographical sketch of King relies heavily on Taylor Branch, *Parting the Waters: America in the King Years, 1954–63* (New York, 1988); and the brief, insightful book by Ling, *Martin Luther King, Jr.*

11. David L. Chappell, *A Stone of Hope: Prophetic Religion and the Death of Jim Crow* (Chapel Hill, NC, 2004), 51–53. A terse summary of the history of black Baptists can be found in C. Eric Lincoln and Lawrence H. Mamiya, *The Black Church in the African American Experience* (Durham, NC, 1990), 20–46.

12. Joanne Grant, *Ella Baker: Freedom Bound* (New York, 1998), 101. See also Ella Baker, "Developing Community Leadership," in *Black Women in White America,* ed. Gerda Lerner (New York, 1970), 352.

13. Quoted in Branch, *Parting the Waters*, 140 and 141.

14. Ling, *Martin Luther King, Jr.*, 47.

15. Quoted in Branch, *Parting the Waters*.

16. For the 1957 legislative history, see David A. Nichols, *A Matter of Justice: Eisenhower and the Beginning of the Civil Rights Era* (New York, 2007).

17. Adam Fairclough, *To Redeem the Soul of America: The Southern Christian Leadership Conference and Martin Luther King, Jr.* (Athens, GA, 1987), 20; and David Garrow,

Bearing the Cross: Martin Luther King, Jr. and the Southern Christian Leadership Conference (New York, 1986), 644.

18. A detailed, sympathetic biography of Rustin can be found in John D'Emilio, *Lost Prophet: The Life and Times of Bayard Rustin* (New York, 2003); Daniel Levine, *Bayard Rustin and the Civil Rights Movement* (New Brunswick, NJ, 2000); and Garrow, *Bearing the Cross.*

19. Branch, *Parting the Waters*, 206–72, especially 225 for speaking engagements.

20. A superb account of the Greensboro sit-in is found in William H. Chafe, *Civilities and Civil Rights: Greensboro, North Carolina and the Black Struggle for Freedom* (New York, 1980); and Ling, *Martin Luther King, Jr.,* 65.

21. Ella Baker's importance to SNCC in its formation and development is found in Grant, *Ella Baker.* Useful examinations of Baker can be found in Marilyn Bordwell De-Laure, "Planting the Seeds of Change: Ella Baker's Radical Rhetoric," *Women's Studies in Communication* (Spring 2008): 1–28; Joy James, "'Black Women's Work' and Activist Intellectuals," *Black Scholar* (Fall 1994): 8–15; Aprele Elliott, "Ella Baker: Free Agent in the Civil Rights Movement," *Journal of Black Studies* (May 1996): 593–603; Joshua H. Miller, "Empowering Communities: Ella Baker's Decentralized Leadership Style and Conversational Eloquence," *Southern Communication Journal* (2016): 156–67; Charles Payne, "Ella Baker and Models of Social Change," *Signs* (Summer 1989): 885–99; Carol Mueller, "Ella Baker and the Origins of 'Participatory Democracy,'" in *Women in the Civil Rights Movement: Trailblazers and Torchbearers, 1941–1965*, ed. Vicki L. Crawford et al. (Brooklyn, NY, 1990), 51–70; and Robert P. Moses et al., "The Algebra Project: Organizing in the Spirit of Ella," *Harvard Educational Review* (November 1989): 423–43.

22. Lawson's ability to inspire students is recounted in John L. Lewis, *Walking with the Wind: A Memoir of the Movement* (New York, 1998), 80–117. The history of SNCC is found in the excellent Clayborne Carson, *In Struggle: SNCC and the Black Awakening of the 1960s* (Cambridge, MA, 1981); and the more recent Wesley C. Hogan, *Many Minds, One Heart: SNCC's Dream for a New America* (Chapel Hill, NC, 2007). Insight into the mindset of early SNCC activists is captured in Howard Zinn, *The New Abolitionists* (Boston, 1985).

23. Fairclough, *To Redeem the Soul of America*, 63.

24. Carson, *In Struggle*, 51. See also Francis Shor, "Utopian Aspirations in the Black Freedom Movement: SNCC and the Struggle for Civil Rights," *Utopian Studies* (Winter 2004): 173–89; and Emily Stoper, "The Student Nonviolent Coordinating Committee and the Fall of a Redemptive Organization," *Journal of Black Studies* (September 1977): 13–34.

25. Quoted in Carson, *In Struggle*, 69.

26. Carson, *In Struggle,* 3.

27. Carson, *In Struggle,* provides a good summary of the Freedom Rides, but for a dramatic insider account, see Lewis, *Walking with the Wind*, 121–76.

28. Lewis, *Walking with the Wind*, 170.

29. Within the sizable literature on the Freedom Rides, especially useful are Charles Payne, *I've Seen the Light of Freedom: The Organizing Tradition and the Mississippi Freedom Struggle* (Berkeley, CA, 1995); and Lewis, *Walking with the Wind*, especially 121–77.

30. Branch, *Parting the Waters*, 478; Ling, *Martin Luther King, Jr.,* 83; and Stephen B. Oates, *Let the Trumpet Sound: A Life of Martin Luther King, Jr.* (New York, 1982), 478.

31. Carson, *In Struggle.*

32. Ransby, *Ella Baker*, 287.

33. Branch, *Parting the Waters*, 556–57; Ling, *Martin Luther King, Jr.,* 93; and Hogan, *Many Minds, One Heart,* 66–70.

34. Garrow, *Bearing the Cross*; and Andrew M. Manis, *A Fire You Can't Put Out: The Civil Rights Life of Birmingham's Reverend Fred Shuttlesworth* (Tuscaloosa, AL, 1999). For a moving, very sympathetic account of the Birmingham struggle, see Diane McWhorter, *Carry Me Home: Birmingham, Alabama* (New York, 2001).

35. For the conclusion that "Birmingham could not easily be counted a victory in terms of its immediate, direct, local efforts," see Ling, *Martin Luther King, Jr.,* 133; and Manis, *A Fire You Can't Put Out*, 319–20.

36. Carson, *In Struggle*, 91.

37. Stephen Currier of the Taconic Foundation provided funds for the coordinating committee. Eventually Currier raised $800,000 for the march.

38. Quoted in Carson, *In Struggle,* 93; and Stoper, "Student Nonviolent Coordinating Committee," 45–46.

39. Quoted in Carson, *In Struggle,* 93.

40. Quoted in Ransby, *Ella Baker*, 269.

41. The following year, the Council of Federated Organizations, a coalition of civil rights groups, including SNCC, received a grant administered by the Southern Regional Council. Funds for the group came from New York philanthropic foundations, including the Taconic Foundation and Field Foundation.

42. Exact membership of these secret organizations cannot be determined. Membership estimates are from Sally Belfrage, *Freedom Summer* (New York, 1965), 105–6.

43. Lewis, *Walking with the Wind*, 267; John Dittmer, *Local People: The Struggle for Civil Rights in Mississippi* (Urbana, IL, 1994), 251; and Hogan, *Many Minds, One Heart,* 155–82.

44. Dittmer, *Local People*, 115; and Ransby, *Ella Baker*, 287. See also R. Edward Nordhaus, "SNCC and the Civil Rights Movement in Mississippi, 1963–64: A Time for Change," *History Teacher* (November 1983): 95–102; John R. Rachal, "'The Long, Hot Summer': The Mississippi Response to Freedom Summer, 1964," *Journal of Negro History* (Autumn 1999): 315–39; Daniel Perlstein, "Teaching Freedom: SNCC and the Creation of Mississippi Freedom Scholars," *History of Education Quarterly* (Autumn 1990): 297–324; Jon Hale, "'The Student as a Force for Social Change': The Mississippi Freedom Schools and Student Engagement," *Journal of African American History* (Summer 2011): 325–47; and Richard J. Jensen and John C. Hammerback, "Working in 'Quiet Places': The Community Organizing Rhetoric of Robert Parris Moses," *Howard Journal of Communications* (2000): 1–18.

45. Dittmer, *Local People*, 273.

46. Belfrage, *Freedom Summer*, 39. A well-researched overview of SNCC's strategy is Joseph A. Sinsheimer, "The Freedom Vote of 1963: New Strategies of Racial Protest in Mississippi," *Journal of Southern History* (May 1989): 217–44.

47. Carson, *In Struggle,* 111–28, especially 123 on northern mobilization. The Atlantic City Democratic National Convention is encapsulated in Hogan, *Many Minds, One Heart,* 185–96.

48. A list of these incidents is found in Grant, *Ella Baker,* 171–72.

49. Quoted in Ransby, *Ella Baker,* 338.

50. Stoper, "Student Nonviolent Coordinating Committee," 14 and 29.

51. For full insight into King's shifting views and strategy on nonviolence, see Garrow, *Bearing the Cross.*

52. In the excellent literature on the Selma march, see, among others, Taylor Branch, *Pillar of Fire: America in the King Years, 1963–1965* (New York, 1998); and David Garrow, *Protest at Selma* (New Haven, 1978).

53. An extensive literature on voting rights has developed, including Gary May, *Bending Toward Justice: The Voting Rights Act and the Transformation of American Democracy* (New York, 2013); and more recently, Ari Berman, *Give Us the Ballot: The Modern Struggle for Voting Rights in the United States* (New York, 2015). See also Chandler Davidson et al., eds., *Quiet Revolution: The Impact of the Voting Rights Act of 1965* (Princeton, NJ, 1994).

54. Carson, *In Struggle, 159.*

55. Steven White, "Civil Rights, World War II, and U.S. Public Opinion," *Studies in American Political Development* (April 2016), especially 49–50.

56. Gareth D. Pahowka, "Voices of Moderation: Southern Whites Respond to *Brown v. Board of Education,*" *Gettysburg Historical Journal* (2006), especially 51–52.

57. Daniel Stevens, "Public Opinion and Public Policy: The Case of Kennedy and Civil Rights," *Presidential Studies Quarterly* (March 2002), especially 123, 125, and 129.

58. Quoted in Robert F. Williams, *Negroes with Guns* (New York, 1962), 99.

59. Timothy B. Tyson, *Radio Free Dixie: Robert F. Williams and the Roots of Black Power* (Chapel Hill, NC, 1999).

60. Akinyele Umoja, "'It's Time for Black Men . . .': The Deacons for Defense and the Mississippi Movement," in *The Civil Rights Movement in Mississippi,* ed. Ted Ownby (Oxford, MS, 2013): 204–26; and Rickey Hill, "The Bogalusa Movement: Self-Defense and Black Power in the Civil Rights Struggle," *Black Scholar* (2011): 204–28.

61. Quoted in Hogan, *Many Minds, One Heart*, 36.

62. Stoper, "Student Nonviolent Coordinating Committee," 97–101, captures the resentment felt toward many white students during the Mississippi Freedom Summer. Tensions over sexism within SNCC is traced in Dennis J. Urban Jr., "The Women of SNCC: Struggle, Sexism, and the Emergence of Feminist Consciousness, 1966," *International Social Science Review* (2002): 185–90.

63. Stoper, "Student Nonviolent Coordinating Committee," 71–91.

64. Lewis, *Walking with the Wind,* 349–40, quotations 365 and 366.

65. Carmichael reflects on his political life in his memoir *Ready for Revolution: The Life and Struggles of Stokely Carmichael (Kwame Ture)* (New York, 2003), especially 22–136 for his early life before SNCC, and 520–728 for black power.

66. Carson, *In Struggle,* 226–28.

67. John Churchville, SNCC activists, quoted in Carson, *In Struggle,* 195.

68. Ransby, *Ella Baker,* 352; and Stoper, "Student Nonviolent Coordinating Committee," 171.

69. Quoted in Carson, *In Struggle,* 221.

70. Feuer, *Conflict of Generations,* 491.

71. Quoted in Manis, *A Fire You Can't Put Out,* 432.

72. Hugh Pearson, *The Shadow of the Panther: Huey Newton and the Price of Black Power in America* (Reading, MA, 1994). Pearson should be supplemented by a large memoir literature, varying in candor, listed in order of usefulness for this discussion: David Hilliard and Lewis Cole, *This Side of Glory: The Autobiography of David Hilliard and the Story of the Black Panther Party* (Boston, 1993); David Hilliard, with Keith and Kent Zimmerman, *Huey: The Spirit of the Panther* (New York, 2006); Flores A. Forbes, *Will You Die with Me: My Life and the Black Panther Party* (New York, 2006); Curtis J. Austin, *Up Against the Wall: Violence in the Making and Unmaking of the Black Panther Party* (Fayetteville, AR, 2006); Bobby Seale, *Seize the Time: The Story of the Black Panther Party and Huey Newton* (New York, 1968); Bobby Seale, *Lonely Rage: The Autobiography of Bobby Seale* (New York, 1978); and the somewhat bizarre Earl Anthony, *Spitting in the Wind: The True Story Behind the Violent Legacy of the Black Panther Party* (Malibu, CA, 1990). Especially self-serving are memoirs by Elaine Brown and Eldridge Cleaver. Michael Newton, *Bitter Grain: Huey Newton and the Black Panther Party* (Los Angeles, 1980) offers some nice informational details.

73. William L. Van Deburg, *New Day in Babylon: The Black Power Movement and American Culture, 1965–1975* (Chicago, 1993), 155.

74. Pearson, *Shadow of the Panther,* 139.

75. Van Deburg, *New Day in Babylon,* 4.

76. Pearson, *Shadow of the Panther,* 185.

77. For a summary of these confrontations, see Pearson, *Shadow of the Panther,* 206–9.

78. For insight into Panther community projects, see Ricky J. Pope and Shawn T. Flanigan, "Revolution for Breakfast: Intersections of Activism and Violence in the Black Panther Party's Community Service Programs," *Social Justice Research* (December 2013); and Mary Potori, "Feeding Revolution: The Black Panther Party and the Politics of Food," *Radical Teacher* (Winter 2014): 43–50.

79. "Newton-Cleaver Clash Puts Party Future in Doubt," *New York Times,* March 7, 1971.

80. Quoted in Hilliard and Cole, *This Side of Glory,* 323–24.

81. The story of the turn to terrorism in the New Left and liberation movements is told in Bryan Burrough, *Days of Rage: America's Radical Underground, the FBI, and the Forgotten Age of Revolutionary Violence* (New York, 2015).

82. Horowitz describes his political trajectory from the left to the right in *Radical Son: A Generational Odyssey* (New York, 1996).

83. For a compelling inside account of life as a Buddha Samurai, see Forbes, *Will You Die with Me?*.

84. For a background of blacks in southern politics, see Pat Watters and Reese Cleghorn, *Climbing Jacob's Ladder: The Arrival of Negroes in Southern Politics* (New York, 1967).

85. Lewis, *Walking with the Wind*, 415.

86. Juliet Eilperin, "What's Changed for African Americans Since 1963," *Washington Post*, April 22, 2013. Especially important for understanding demographic changes are William H. Frey, *Diversity Explosion: How New Racial Demographics Are Remaking America* (Washington, DC, 2015); and Richard Alba, *Blurring the Color Line: The New Chance for a More Integrated America* (Cambridge, MA, 2009).

87. Andrew Young provides important insight into King and the early civil rights movement in *An Easy Burden: The Civil Rights Movement and the Transformation of America* (New York, 1996).

88. This election is recounted in Lewis, *Walking with the Wind*, 437–53.

89. Listing a few indicates the extent of institutional commitment to civil rights—a movement that began on the streets and in the courts: Equal Employment Opportunity Commission (independent agency); Commission on Civil Rights (independent agency); Office of Equal Employment Opportunity and Office of Fair Housing and Equal Opportunity (Department of Housing and Urban Development); Office for Civil Rights (Department of Education) and under Office of Elementary and Secondary Education, multiple agencies. In the Department of Education can be found the Office of Civil Rights and Economic Impact and Diversity. The Department of Health includes the Office of Minority Health and Health Equity and the National Institute on Minority Health and Health Disparities. The Labor Department hosts the Civil Rights Center. The Department of Commerce includes an active Minority Small Business Development Agency. Within the Department of Agriculture is the Minority Farmers Advisory Committee. Most active on civil rights remains the Civil Rights Division within the Justice Department.

Chapter 4

1. Sara Evans, *Personal Politics: The Roots of Women's Liberation in the Civil Rights Movement and the New Left* (New York, 1980). See also Choonib Lee, "Women's Liberation and Sixties Armed Resistance," *Journal for the Study of Radicalism* (Spring 2017): 25–51, which explores radicalism and sexism within the Weathermen, a revolutionary New Left group. Dennis J. Urban Jr., "The Women of SNCC: Struggle, Sexism, and the Emergence of Feminism, 1960–66," *International Social Science Review* (2002): 185–90, contains interesting research on Casey Haden and the internal politics of SNCC not found in Evans.

2. Christine A. Kelly, "Whatever Happened to Women's Liberation? Feminist Legacies of '68," *New Political Science* (Winter 2000): 161–75.

3. This point is made by Anne N. Costain, "Representing Women: The Transition from Social Movement to Interest Group," *Western Political Quarterly* (March 1981): 100–113.

4. The best biography of Betty Friedan remains Daniel Horowitz, *Betty Friedan and the Making of the Feminine Mystique* (Amherst, MA, 2000); and his "Rethinking Betty Friedan and the Feminine Mystique: Labor Union Radicalism and Feminism in Cold War America," *American Quarterly* (March 1996); 673–88. See also Betty Friedan's memoir, *The Second Stage* (New York, 1981); Friedan, "Up From the Kitchen Floor," *New York Times*, March 4, 1973; and Dorothy Chansky, "Useable Performance Feminism for Our

Time: Reconsidering Betty Friedan," *Theatre Journal* (October 2008): 341–64, which is informative about Friedan's use of the media.

5. There is a sizable literature on female activism that cannot be captured in a single footnote, but useful overviews, listed alphabetically, are provided by Steven M. Buechler, *Women's Movements in the United States: Woman Suffrage, Equal Rights, and Beyond* (New Brunswick, NJ, 1990); Nancy F. Cott, *The Grounding of Modern Feminism* (New Haven, 1989); Cott, *No Small Courage: A History of Women in the United States* (New York, 2004); Ellen Carol Dubois, *Feminism and Suffrage: The Emergence of an Independent Women's Movement in America, 1848–1869* (Ithaca, NY, 1999); Sara Evans, *Born for Liberty: A History of Women in America* (New York, 1997); Eleanor Flexner and Ellen Fitzpatrick, *A Century of Struggle: The Women's Rights Movement in the United States* (New York, 1958); and Mary Jo Freeman, *A Room at a Time: How Women Entered Party Politics* (Lanham, MD, 2000). Flora Davis offers a popular account of feminism from an activist perspective in *Moving the Mountain: The Women's Movement in America Since 1960* (New York, 1991).

Especially useful for feminist struggles in the 1920s and 1930s, see J. Stanley Lemons, *The Woman Citizen: Social Feminism in the 1920s* (Urbana, IL, 1973); and Eileen Kraditor, *Ideas of the Woman Suffrage Movement* (New York, 1965). A short, useful examination of the feminist question within the Communist Party is found in Kate Weigand, *Red Feminism: American Communism and the Making of Women's Liberation* (Baltimore, 2001). Especially insightful on the Old Left and feminism is Amy Swerdlow, *Women Strike for Peace: Traditional Motherhood and Radical Politics in the 1960s* (Chicago, 1993).

For second-wave feminism, especially useful are Ruth Rosen, *The World Split Open: How the Modern Women's Movement Changed America* (New York, 2000); Alice Echols, *Daring to Be Bad: Radical Feminism in America, 1967–75* (Minneapolis, 1989); and Mary Jo Freeman, *The Politics of Women's Liberation* (New York, 1975). See also William O'Neill, *Everyone Was Brave: The Rise and Fall of Feminism in America* (Chicago, 1969). Robert V. Daniels places the feminist movement within a larger context in *The Fourth Revolution: Transformations in American Society from the Sixties to the Present* (New York, 2006), 119–46.

6. Freeman, *Politics of Women's Liberation*, 18–21. See also O'Neill, *Everyone Was Brave.*

7. This overview on women and feminism relies heavily on insights in Freeman, *Politics of Women's Liberation*. Particularly useful in understanding second-wave feminist goals at the time is Judith Hole and Ellen Levine, *Rebirth of Feminism* (New York, 1971).

8. Rosen, *World Split Open*, 65–68.

9. Abbott L. Ferriss, *Indicators of Trends in the Status of American Women* (New York, 1971).

10. Ferriss, *Indicators of Trends in the Status of American Women*, 67.

11. Cynthia Harrison, *On Account of Sex: The Politics of Women's Issues, 1945–1968* (Berkeley, CA, 1980), 69–109.

12. Hugh Davis Graham, *The Civil Rights Era: Origins and Development of National Policy, 1960–1972* (New York, 1990).

13. Freeman, *Politics of Women's Liberation*, 54.

14. Freeman, *Politics of Women's Liberation*, 55–56.

15. Susan Brownmiller, *In Our Time: A Memoir of a Revolution* (New York, 1999).

16. Karla Jay, *Tales of the Lavender Menace: A Memoir of Liberation* (New York, 1999), 142–43.

17. The resolution read, "Women's Liberation is a lesbian plot. . . . In all discussions of birth control, homosexuality must be included as a legitimate method of contraception. . . . All sex education curricula must include lesbianism as a valid, legitimate form of sexual expression and love." Quoted in Echols, *Daring to Be Bad,* 215. See also Victoria Hesford, *Feeling Women's Liberation* (Durham, NC, 2013), 1–24; Brownmiller, *In Our Time*, 97–101; Jay, *Tales of the Lavender Menace*; and "Congress to Unite Women: Report from the New York City Meeting of November 21, 22, 23, 1969," in *Radical Feminism*, ed. Anne Koedt (New York, 1973), 302–17.

18. Quoted in Deidre Carmody, "Feminists Shifting Emphasis from Persons to Politics," *New York Times,* August 21, 1972, 33.

19. "Goals Set Up by Women's Political Caucus," *New York Times,* July 13, 1971.

20. Gloria Steinem, *My Life on the Road* (New York, 2015), 152.

21. Betty Friedan, "Beyond Women's Liberation," *McCall's,* August 1972.

22. Deirdre Carmody, "Feminists Rebut Friedan Charge," *New York Times,* July 20, 1972. See also Robin Morgan, *Going Too Far: The Personal Chronicle of a Feminist* (New York, 1977), a collection of essays of which most useful for this study are those under the subheadings "Feminist Leanings" and "Radical Feminism," 113–213.

23. Friedan, "Up from the Kitchen Floor."

24. Betty Friedan, *It Changed My Life: Writing on the Women's Movement* (Location, Year), 179–80.

25. Sara Evans, "Women's Liberation: Seeing the Revolution Clearly," *Feminist Studies* (2015): 138–49; Judith Ezekiel, *Feminism in the Heartland* (Columbus, OH, 2002); and Anne M. Valk, *Radical Sisters: Second Wave Feminism and Black Liberation in Washington, D.C.* (Urbana, IL, 2008).

26. For a sense of the polemical tone of radical feminists, see, Ti-Grace Atkinson, *Amazon Odyssey* (New York, 1974), especially her "Resignation from NOW," 9–13, and "Declaration of War," 46–47.

27. Shulamith Firestone, *The Dialectic of Sex: The Case for Feminist Revolution* (New York, 1970), 11, 16, 36–40.

28. Aldous Huxley, *Brave New World* (New York, 1969 edition), 241.

29. James C. Mohr, *Abortion in America: The Origins of National Policy* (New York, 1978); Leslie Reagan, *When Abortion Was Against the Law: Women, Medicine and the Law, 1867–1973* (Berkeley, CA, 1996); Suzanne Staggenborg, *The Pro-Choice Movement: Organization and Activism in the Abortion Conflict* (New York, 1991); and David Garrow, *Liberty and Sexuality: The Right to Privacy and the Making of* Roe v. Wade (Berkeley, CA, 1998).

30. Quoted in Tasha N. Dubriwny, "Consciousness-Raising as Collective Rhetoric: The Articulation of Experience in the Redstockings's Abortion Speak-Out of 1969," *Quarterly Journal of Speech* (November 2005), 405 and 416. For the larger context of the speak-out, see Echols, *Daring to Be Bad,* 141–43.

31. Quotations are found in Dubriwny, "Consciousness-Raising as Collective Rhetoric, 404–6. Useful for a quick overview of radical feminism is Joshua Zeitz, "Rejecting the Center: Radical Grassroots Politics in the 1970s—Second Wave Feminism as a Case Study," *Journal of Contemporary History* (October 2008): 673–88.

32. Brownmiller, *In Our Time*, 79.

33. Quoted in Echols, *Daring to Be Bad*, 211, and 210–45.

34. There is an extensive popular and scholarly literature on the history of the gay liberation movement. Most informative for this study, see the recent encyclopedic account, Lillian Faderman, *The Gay Revolution: The Story of Struggle* (New York, 2016). For an insider account of the formation of the Daughters of Bilitis, see Del Martin and Phyllis Lyon, "Lesbian Liberation Begins," *Gay and Lesbian Review* (November–December 2012):19–22. For a perspective on gay and black legal civil rights and marriage within a historical perspective, see George Chauncey, *Why Marriage: The History Shaping Today's Debate over Gay Equality* (New York, 2004). A good beginning for understanding the use of history in legal interpretation sympathetic to same-sex marriage are Randall Kennedy, "Marriage and the Struggle for Gay, Lesbian, and Black Liberation," *Utah Law Review* (2005): 781–801; and Chandan Reddy, "Time for Rights? Loving, Gay Marriage and the Limits of Legal Justice," *Fordham Law Review* (2008): 2849–72.

35. Insight into the New York feminist movement is found in Kelly, "Whatever Happened to Women's Liberation?"

36. Quoted in Echols, *Daring to Be Bad,* 232, and 228–43.

37. This point is made by Brownmiller, *In Our Time,* 269.

38. Zeitz, "Rejecting the Center," 680–82.

39. Nancy Whittier, "Persistence and Transformation: Gloria Steinem, the Women's Action Alliance, and the Feminist Movement, 1971–1997," *Journal of Women's History* (Summer 2002): 148–50.

40. Zeitz, "Rejecting the Center," 682.

41. Brownmiller, *In Our Time*, 242.

42. An excellent essay on political accommodation to feminist social movements from an international perspective is found in Anne Marie Goetz and Rob Jenkins, "Feminist Activism and the Politics of Reform: When and Why Do States Respond to Demands of Gender Equality Politics?" *Development and Change* (Spring 2018): 714–34 See also M. Molyneux, "Analysing Women's Movements," in *Women's Movements in International Perspective: Latin America and Beyond*, ed. M. Molyneux (London, 2001), 140–62; and Scott Mainwaring, *Rethinking Party Systems in the Third Wave of Democratization: The Case of Brazil* (Stanford, CA, 1999).

43. Jane J. Mansbridge, *Why We Lost the ERA* (Chicago, 1986); and for the background of the ERA, see Cynthia Harrison, *On Account of Sex: The Politics of Women's Issues, 1945–1968* (Berkeley, CA, 1988). See also Donald G. Mathews and Jane Sherron De Hart, *Sex, Gender, and the Politics of ERA: A State and the Nation* (New York, 1990).

44. Donald T. Critchlow, *Phyllis Schlafly and Grassroots Conservatism: A Woman's Crusade* (Princeton, NJ, 2005).

45. Memo, Rothstein/Buckley to Jane Wells, May 19, 1956, ERAmerica Papers, Library of Congress (hereafter ERAmerica Papers).

46. Suone Cotner to William Glover Jr., December 14, 1979, Box 1, ERAmerica Papers.

47. Critchlow, *Phyllis Schlafly and Grassroots Conservatism,* 228–32. Division within the pro-ERA movement is fully explored in Mansbridge, *Why We Lost the ERA.*

48. Shelia Greenwald to Liz Carpenter, October 6, 1977, Box 18, Elly Peterson Papers, and Marie Bass to Stewart Mott, Box 1, ERAmerica Papers, Library of Congress. This section on divisions within the feminist movement draws heavily from the Eagle Forum Archives in Clayton, Missouri, which contains abundant newspaper clippings of the ERA state fights.

49. National Organization for Women, *Revolution: Tomorrow Is Now* (1972 mimeograph).

50. Patricia O'Brien, "Friedan Leads Rift in NOW," *Los Angeles Times,* November 27, 1975; Joan Zyda, "Internal Struggle Jeopardizes NOW," *Chicago Tribune,* November 20, 1975; and "Lesbian Rights Gets Top Billing," *Kansas City Times,* October 28, 1975.

51. Karen DeCrow, "Do It Now" (speech, mimeograph, March 1976).

52. Karen Potter, "Steinem Covers It All," *Daily Campus* [SMU], September 13, 1979; "Feminism Should Be Valued Above Nationalism," *Bloomington Herald,* July 15, 1979; and "Two Feminists Discount Some Women's Opposition," *St. Louis Dispatch,* May 9, 1973.

53. Quoted in "The Rightists Step In," *Homefront,* February 1973. *Homefront* was the official publication of the American Institute of Democracy, closely tied to the Methodist Federation for Social Action.

54. Paula Brookmire, "NOW Region Told to 'Seize the Power,'" *Rockford Journal,* June 12, 1973.

55. Bonnie Cowan to Jane Wells, March 19, 1976, Box 1, ERAmerica Papers.

56. Dorothy Haegele to ERAmerica National Office, January 19, 1980, Box 140, ERAmerica Papers.

57. Gloria Steinem, *Outrageous Acts and Everyday Rebellions* (New York, 1986), 328.

58. The best treatment of the IWY conference and its broader context is Marjorie J. Spruill, *Divided We Stand: The Battle over Women's Rights and Family Values That Polarized American Politics* (New York, 2017). Also of interest on state convention battles is Erin M. Kempker, "Battling 'Big Sister' Government: Hoosier Women and the Politics of International Women's Year," *Journal of Women's History* (Summer 2012): 144–70.

59. The following discussion of gay activism in the IWY relies on Doreen J. Mattingly and Jessica L. Nare, "'A Rainbow of Women': Diversity and Unity at the 1977 U.S. International Women's Conference," *Journal of Women's History* (Summer 2014), 88–112.

60. Mattingly and Nare, "'A Rainbow of Women.'"

61. Mattingly and Nare, "'A Rainbow of Women,'" 99.

62. Mattingly and Nare, "'A Rainbow of Women,'" 100.

63. Friedan's reflections on Houston are found in Betty Friedan, "Our Party," *New Republic* (October, 5, 1992), reprinted as "Betty Friedan Reflects on 1992, the Year of the Woman," *New Republic* (February 4, 2014).

64. Quoted in Critchlow, *Phyllis Schlafly and Grassroots Conservatism,* 248.

65. Critchlow, *Phyllis Schlafly and Grassroots Conservatism,* 253.

66. Sylvia Ann Hewlett, *A Less Life: The Myth of Women's Liberation in America* (New York, 1986), 211.

67. Jay, *The Lavender Menace,* 266.

68. Carolyn Bronstein, *Battling Pornography: The American Anti-Pornography Movement, 1976–1986* (New York, 2011); and the earlier but insightful Donald A. Downs, *The New Politics of Pornography* (Chicago, 1992). See also Jennifer Baumgardner, *Look Both Ways: Bisexual Politics* (New York, 2007).

69. U.S. Census Bureau, "Women in the Workforce" (Washington, D.C., 2010).

70. Costain, "Representing Women," 105.

71. An extensive analysis of attitudes toward the women's movement and feminism is found in Leonie Huddy, Francis Neely, and Marilyn R. Lafay, "Trends: Support for the Women's Movement," *American Association for Public Opinion Research* (Autumn 2000): 309–50. See also Jamie Ballard, "American Women Are More Likely to Identity as Feminist Now Than in 2016," YouGov, August 9, 2018, https://today.yougov.com/topics /lifestyle/articles-reports/2018/08/09/feminism-american-women-2018. Ballard points out that the majority of women and men do not describe themselves as feminists and of those non-feminist women, nearly half describe feminism as "too extreme."

72. Lillian M. Purdy, "Mary Griffith's *Three Hundred Years Hence*: Utopia, Women, and Marriage," *American Journal of Economics and Sociology* (November 2018): 1209–41; Susan Magarey, "Dreams and Desires: Four 1970s Feminist Visions of Utopia," *Australian Feminist Studies* (July 2007): 325–41; Evie Kendal, "Utopian Literature and Bioethics: Exploring Reproductive Difference and Gender Equality," *Literature and Medicine* (Spring 2018): 56–84; Alexandra W. Lough, "Editor's Introduction: Imagining a Better World: A Survey of Feminist Utopian Literature," *American Journal of Economics and Sociology* (November 2018): 1195–1208; and less insightful, Kirsten Imani Kasai, "Writing a Better Ending: How Feminist Utopian Literature Subverts Patriarchy," *American Journal of Economics and Sociology* (November 2018): 1377–1405.

73. Ellen Messer-David maintains that academic feminism and activist feminism developed separate paths to the detriment of each. See *Disciplining Feminism: From Social Activism to Academic Discourse* (Durham, NC, 2002).

74. The disappointment of the lesbian rights movement is conveyed in Arlene Stein, "Sisters and Queers: The Decentering of Lesbian Feminism," in *Cultural Politics and Social Movements*, ed. Marcy Darnovsky, Barbara Epstein, and Richard Flacks (Philadelphia, 1995), 161–67.

Chapter 5

1. Mark Hatfield, "Foreword," *The American Far Right* (Grand Rapids, MI, 1968), i.

2. J. Allen Broyles, "The John Birch Society: A Movement of Social Protest of the Radical Right," *Journal of Social Issues* (April 1963): 51–63.

3. *Congressional Record, 78th Congress, 1st Session* (1943), 717.

4. There is abundant popular and scholarly literature on anti-communism in the early Cold War. A good starting point is M. J. Heale, *American Anticommunism: Combatting the Enemy Within, 1830–1970* (Baltimore, 1970); and Ellen Schrecker, *Many Are the Crimes: McCarthyism in America* (New York, 1998). For effects on anti-communism in

universities, see Ellen Schrecker, *No Ivory Tower: McCarthyism and the Universities* (New York, 1986).

5. Joshua Zeitz, "Rejecting the Center: Radical Grassroots Politics in the 1970s—Second Wave Feminism as a Case Study," *Journal of Contemporary History* (October 2008): 673–88.

6. Historian Kevin M. Kruse attributes much of this religious revival in the 1950s to corporate America in his study *One Nation Under God: How Corporate America Invented Christian America* (New York, 2015).

7. The author would like to thank Paul Matzko who shared the page proofs of his forthcoming book *The Radio Right: How a Band of Broadcasters Took on the Federal Government and Built the Modern Conservative Movement* (Oxford University Press, 2020).

8. Schrecker, *Many Are the Crimes*, 42.

9. Quoted in Daniel K. Williams, *God's Own Party: The Making of the Christian Right* (New York, 2010), 64. This discussion of Christian fundamentalists draws heavily on Williams's superb book on the religious right and the Republican Party, especially 33–64.

10. Quoted in Edward H. Miller, *Nut Country: Right-Wing Dallas and the Birth of the Southern Strategy* (Chicago, 2015).

11. Raymond E. Wolfinger et al., "America's Radical Right: Politics and Ideology," and Fred W. Grupp Jr., "The Political Perspectives of Birch Society Members," in Robert A. Schoenberger, editor, *The American Right Wing: Readings in Political Behavior* (New York, 1960).

12. Wolfinger et al., "America's Radical Right," 65.

13. Wolfinger et al., "America's Radical Right," 67.

14. Grupp, "Political Perspectives of Birch Society Members," 83–118.

15. Grupp, "Political Perspectives of Birch Society Members," 106.

16. Grupp, "Political Perspectives of Birch Society Members," 107.

17. John Caiazza, "American Conservatism and the Catholic Church," *Modern Age* (2010): 14–24.

18. Leo P. Ribuffo, *The Old Christian Right: The Protestant Far Right from the Great Depression to the Cold War* (Philadelphia, 1983), 216–18.

19. Colleen Doody, *Detroit's Cold War: The Origins of Postwar Conservatism* (Urbana, IL, 2013), 1, 76, 81.

20. Ribuffo, *Old Christian Right*. For Gerald L. K. Smith, see Glen Jeansonne, *Gerald L. K. Smith: Minister of Hate* (Baton Rouge, LA, 1997).

21. Finnish historian Markku Ruotsila offers a circumspect and revisionist account of McIntire in "Carl McIntire and the Fundamentalist Origins of the Christian Right," *Church History* (June 2012): 378–407; and "'Russia's Most Effective Fifth Column'": Cold War Perceptions of Un-Americanism in U.S. Churches," *Journal of American Studies* 47 (2013): 1019–41; and in his book, *Fighting Fundamentalist: Carl McIntire and the Politicization of American Fundamentalism* (New York, 2015). Ruotsila challenges such authors as Darren Dochuk, *From Bible Belt to Sun Belt: Plain-Folk Religion, Grassroots Politics, and the Rise of Evangelical Conservatism* (New York, 2011), who see a direct line from McIntire to the religious right in the 1970s. Useful reading on McIntire's theology is John Fea, "Carl McIntire: From Fundamentalist Presbyterian to Presbyterian Fundamentalist,"

American Presbyterians (Winter 1994): 253–68. For material on McIntire's troubles with the Federal Communications Commission and his radio broadcasts, see Heather Hendershot, "God's Angriest Man: Carl McIntire, Cold War Fundamentalism, and Right Wing Broadcasting," *American Quarterly* (June 2007): 373–96.

22. Quoted in Erling Jorstad, *The Politics of Doomsday, Fundamentalist of the Far Right* (Abingdon, TN, 1970), 49.

23. Biographical material on Hargis is drawn from Arnold Forster and Benjamin R. Epstein, *Danger on the Right: The Attitudes, Personnel and Influence of the Radical Right and Extreme Conservatives* (New York, 1964), 68–86; Jorstad, *Politics of Doomsday*; and John Harold Redekop, *The American Far Right: A Case Study of Billy James Hargis and the Christian Crusade* (Grand Rapids, MI, 1968).

24. Forster and Epstein, *Danger on the Right*, 19.

25. Quoted in Redekop, *The American Far Right*, 17, 38, 51.

26. David A. Noebel, "Communism, Hypnotism, and the Beatles" (Tulsa, OK, 1965).

27. Quoted in Forster and Epstein, *Danger on the Right*, 75.

28. Donald T. Critchlow, *When Hollywood Was Right: How Movie Stars, Studio Moguls, and Big Business Remade American Politics* (New York, 2013), 141–42; and Kevin Kruse, *One Nation Under God: How Corporate America Invented Christian America* (New York, 2015).

29. Biographical material on Schwarz is found in Forster and Epstein, *Danger on the Right*, 47–68; Kruse, *One Nation Under God*, 148–61; and Donald T. Critchlow, *Phyllis Schlafly and Grassroots Conservatism: A Woman's Crusade* (Princeton, NJ, 2005), 71–75.

30. Forster and Epstein, *Danger on the Right*, 49.

31. Kruse, *One Nation Under God*, 152–53.

32. Forster and Epstein, *Danger on the Right*, 58.

33. Birch activities are examined in Milton A. Waldon, *Peddlers of Fear: The John Birch Society* (Newark, NJ, 1966); and for an inside account, see Gerald Schomp, *Birchism Was My Business* (London, 1970).

34. Robert Welch to Fred Schwarz, September 6, 1960; and Fred Schwarz to Robert Welch, September 19, 1960, Box 173, Herbert Philbrick Papers, Library of Congress.

35. George Racey Jordan, *From Major Jordan Diaries* (New York, 1952).

36. Alan Barth, "Report on the 'Rampageous Right,'" *New York Times Magazine*, November 26, 1961, 1–4; and George Harris, "The Rampant Right Invades the GOP," *Look*, July 16, 1963.

37. Quoted in Critchlow, *Phyllis Schlafly and Grassroots Conservatism*, 102–3.

38. Alvin Felzenberg, "The Inside Story of William F. Buckley Jr.'s Crusade Against the John Birch Society," *National Review*, June 20, 2017.

39. Fred Schwarz, *Beating the Unbeatable Foe* (Washington, DC, 1996), 250–73. Philbrick's career can be charted in his papers at the Library of Congress.

40. This transition in the John Birch Society from anti-communism to anti-globalism is explored in Charles J. Stewart, "The Master Conspiracy of the John Birch Society: From Communism to the New World Order," *Western Journal of Communication* (Fall 2002): 423–47.

41. A full discussion of conservatives and the Vietnam War and conservative divisions over war in general is needed, but extremely useful is Seth Offenbach, *The Conservative*

Movement and the Vietnam War: The Other Side of Vietnam (New York, 2018). This can be compared to Sandra Scanlon, *The Pro-War Movement: Domestic Support for the Vietnam War and the Making of Modern American Conservatism* (Amherst, MA, 2013).

42. Daniel K. Williams, "The GOP's Abortion Strategy: Why Pro-Choice Republicans Became Pro-Life in the 1970s," *Journal of Policy History* (Spring 2011): 513–39.

43. Daniel K. Williams, *Defenders of the Unborn: The Pro-Life Movement Before* Roe v. Wade (New York, 2016), provides new insights and research into the pro-life movement. Also extremely useful is Mary K. Ziegler, *After Roe: The Lost History of the Abortion Debate* (Cambridge, MA, 2015).

44. Quoted in Williams, *Defenders of the Unborn,* 89.

45. Williams, *Defenders of the Unborn,* 97–99.

46. A Harris poll is cited in Williams, *Defenders of the Unborn,* 131.

47. Useful in understanding pro-life feminism is Mary Joanne Herrold, *Catholic and Feminist: The Surprising History of the American Catholic Feminist Movement* (Chapel Hill, NC, 2008).

48. David T. Beito, *Taxpayers in Revolt: Tax Resistance During the Great Depression* (Chapel Hill, NC, 1989); Mark Leff, *The Limits of Symbolic Reform: The New Deal and Taxation, 1933–1939* (New York, 1984); and Marjorie E. Kornhauser, "Legitimacy and the Right of Revolution: The Role of Tax Protests and Anti-Tax Rhetoric in America," *Buffalo Law Review* (Fall 2002): 819–930.

49. An excellent summary of the politics of Proposition 13 is given in John M. Allswang, *The Initiative and Referendum in California, 1898–1998* (Palo Alto, CA, 2000), 102–48. See also Robert Kuttner, *Revolt of the Haves: Tax Rebellions and Hard Times* (New York, 1980); and Daniel A. Smith, *Tax Crusaders and the Politics of Direct Democracy* (New York, 1998).

50. Quoted in Kuttner, *Revolt of the Haves,* 72 and 92.

51. Anti-public employee attitudes were the predictive indicator of support for Proposition 13, as found in Max Neiman and Gerry Riposa, "Tax Rebels and Tax Rebellion," *Western Political Quarterly* (September 1986): 435–43. "Political alienation" and "political disaffection" were found to be a common thread among pro–Proposition 13 voters: see David Lowery and Lee Sigelman, "Understanding the Tax Revolt: Eight Explanations," *American Political Science Review* (December 1981): 963–74. Richard L. Lucier, in "Gauging the Strength and Meaning of the 1978 Tax Revolt," *Public Administration Review* (July–August 1979): 371–79 warned of large-scale voter discontent that could spread beyond California.

52. Clarence Lo, *Small Property Versus Big Government* (Berkeley, CA, 1990); and Jack Citrin, "The Legacy of Proposition 13," in *California and the American Tax Revolt,* ed. Terry Schwadron (Berkeley, CA, 1984).

53. Kuttner, *Revolt of the Haves,* 39, 42–44. For Jarvis, see his *Mad as Hell: The Exclusive Story of the Tax Revolt and Its Leader* (New York, 1979). Daniel Smith, "Howard Jarvis, Populist Entrepreneur: Reevaluation the Causes of Proposition 13," *Social Science History* (Summer 1999): 173–210.

54. Field Institute poll (May 1978), cited in Allswang, *Initiative and Referendum in California,* 109.

55. Allswang, *Initiative and Referendum in California*, 112–13.

56. Details of the movements are found in Kuttner, *Revolt of the Haves,* 275–316. Fears of a widespread tax revolt occurring at the time are found in Richard Boeth, "The Big Tax Revolt," *Newsweek,* June 19, 1978.

57. For example, see Smith, *Tax Crusaders,* 47–51.

58. This conclusion is reached by Kuttner, *Revolt of the Haves*, 1–28.

59. Williams, "GOP's Abortion Strategy."

60. Ronald Reagan, "Remarks to Administrative Officials on Domestic Policy," December 13, 1988, Ronald Reagan Library, https://www.reaganlibrary.gov/research /speechs/121388a.

Chapter 6

1. Limited insight into the rise of populism in Europe and the United States is found in John B. Judis, *The Populist Explosion: How the Great Recession Transformed American and European Politics* (New York, 2016). A more circumspect study is Benjamin Moffitt, *The Global Rise of Populism: Performance, Political Style, and Representation* (Palo Alto, CA, 2016); and see Fernando Lopez-Alvez and Diane E. Johnson, *Populist Nationalism in Europe and the Americas* (New York, 2018), which makes distinctions among European populist parties.

Michael Lind places the rise of populism in the United States as a response to the administrative state in his, *The New Class War: Saving Democracy from the Managerial Elite* (New York, 2020), which was published when *In Defense of Populism* was going to press. Both authors had simultaneous similarities in general conclusions.

2. Useful sources for understanding financial collapse are Carmen M. Reinhard and Kenneth S. Rogoff, *The Time Is Different: Eight Centuries of Financial Folly* (Princeton, NJ, 2009); and Andrew Ross Sorkin, *Too Big to Fail: The Inside Story of How Wall Street and Washington Fought to Save the Financial System* (New York, 2010).

3. This discussion of the Tea Party draws heavily on Theda Skocpol and Vanessa Williamson, *The Tea Party and the Remaking of Republican Conservatism* (New York, 2012, rev. ed., 2016).

4. "Santelli's Tea Party Moment," CNBC, February 19, 2009, https://www.cnbc.com /video/2009/02/19/santellis-tea-party-moment.html.

5. Skocpol and Williamson, *Tea Party*, 84.

6. Skocpol and Williamson, *Tea Party*, 23–24.

7. Daniel Schulman, *Sons of Wichita: How the Koch Brothers Became America's Most Powerful and Private Dynasty* (New York, 2014).

8. "Declaration of the Occupation of New York City," in Sarah von Gelder et al., *This Changes Everything* (San Francisco, 2011).

9. Quoted in "George Soros," discoverthenetworks.org, https://www.discoverthenet works.org/individuals/george-soros/.

10. George Soros, *Underwriting Democracy* (New York, 1991), 103.

11. Laura Blumenfeld, "Deep Pockets vs. Bush, Financier Contributes $5 Million More in Effort to Oust President," *Washington Post,* November 11, 2003; Jane Mayer, "The Money Man," *New Yorker,* October 18, 2004; and "George Soros."

12. For a full listing of organizations, see "George Soros"; and "Organizations Funded by George Soros and His Open Society Foundations," discoverthenetworks.org, http://archive.discoverthenetworks.org/viewSubCategory.asp?id=1237.

13. "America Is Under Attack by 187 Groups Funded by George Soros," humansarefree.com, humansarefree.com/2017/04/America-is-under attack.

14. Paige St. John and Abbie Vansickle, "Here's Why George Soros, Liberal Groups Are Spending Big to Help Decide Who's Your Next D.A.," *Los Angeles Times,* May 23, 2018.

15. Greg Moran, "D.A. Race: Stephan Easily Defeats Challenger Jones-Wright, Earns Full Term," *San Diego Union,* June 6, 2018.

16. For an overview of Black Lives Matter, see Keeanga-Yamahtta Taylor, *From #BlackLivesMatter to Black Liberation* (Chicago, 2016).

17. Lizette Alvarez, "U.S. Won't File Charges in Travyon Martin Killing," *New York Times,* February 24, 2015.

18. Alicia Garza, "Where the Leadership of Black Women Can Take Us," *Nation,* February 26, 2015.

19. Jessica Guynn, "Meet the Women Who Coined #BlackLivesMatter," *USA Today,* March 4, 2015.

20. "Opal Tometi," *Huffington Post,* retrieved August 21, 2008.

21. Kelly Riddell, "George Soros Funds Ferguson Protest, Hopes to Spur Civil Action," *Washington Times,* January 14, 2015.

22. "Mission and Vision," Borealis Philanthropy, https://borealisphilanthropy.org/about/mission-vision/.

23. Brook Kelly-Green and Luna Yasui, "Why Black Lives Matter to Philanthropy," July 16, 2016, https://www.fordfoundation.org/ideas/equals-change-blog/posts/why-black-lives-matter-to-philanthropy/.

24. Yale Law School, "Jackson's Bank Veto Message," Avalon Project, https://avalon.law.yale.edu/19th_century/ajveto01.asp.

25. Quoted in Matthew Dalleck, "The Conservative 1960s," *Atlantic* (December 1995), https://www.theatlantic.com/magazine/archive/1995/12/the-conservative-1960s/376506/.

26. David Goodhart, *The Road to Somewhere: The Populist Revolt and the Future of Politics* (London, 2017).

27. Adina-Elena Cincu, "Far Right Populist Challenge in Europe: Alternative for Germany and the National Front," *Europolity* (2017): 21–49.

28. Frank Decker, "The 'Alternative for Germany': Factors Behind Its Emergence and Profile of a New Right-Wing Populist Party," *German Politics and Society* (June 2016): 1–16. https://www.berghahnjournals.com/view/journals/gps/34/2/gps340201.xml.

29. Trump's nationalism invoked an outpouring of books, mostly hostile to Trump: Hall Garner, *World War Trump: The Risks of America's New Nationalism* (New York, 2018); Joshua Green, *Devil's Bargain: Steve Bannon, Donald Trump, and the Nationalist Uprising* (New York, 2017); John B. Judis, *The Nationalist Revival: Trade, Immigration, and the Revolt Against Globalization* (New York, 2018); Jill Lepore, *This America: The Case for the Nation* (New York, 2019); Rory McVeigh and Kevin Estep, *The Politics of Losing: Trump, the Klan and the Mainstreaming of America* (New York, 2019); and Roger Eatwell

and Matther J. Goodwing, *National Populism: The Revolt Against Liberal Democracy* (New York, 2018).

30. "Transcript of Donald Trump's Immigration Speech," *New York Times*, September 1, 2016. His America First foreign policy was articulated in a major speech in December 2017, "Trump Transcript: 'America First,' Security Speech," *Aljazeera,* December 18, 2017.

31. "Behind Trump's Victory: Divisions by Race, Gender, and Education," Pew Research Center, November 9, 2016; Robert D. Francis, "Him, Not Her: Why Working Class White Men Reluctant About Trump Still Made Him President of the United States," American Sociological Association (SOCIUS Report), Fall 2018. Especially insightful on the pro-Trump white working-class vote are Joan C. Williams's blogs on demographics: "What So Many People Don't Get About the U.S. Working Class," in *Harvard Business Review,* "Demographics," November 10, 2016; and "What So Many People Don't Get About the U.S. Working Class," November 18, 2016. Communications scholar Richard M. Perloff maintains that the white vote reflected "racial prejudice," among other things, in "The Blue-Collar Billionaire: Explaining the Trump Phenomenon," Centre for the Study of Journalism, Culture and Community, Bournemouth University, U.K., November 2016, http://www.electionanalysis2016.us/us-election-analysis-2016/section-4-diversity-and-division/the-blue-collar-billionaire-explaining-the-trump-phenomenon/.

32. For a quick summary of voter demographics, see Alec Tyson and Shiva Maniam, "Behind Trump's Victory: Divisions by Race, Gender, and Education," Pew Research, November 9, 2016, https://www.pewresearch.org/fact-tank/2016/11/09/behind-trumps-victory-divisions-by-race-gender-education/.

33. Salena Zito and Brad Todd, *The Great Revolt: Inside the Populist Coalition* (New York, 2018).

34. Isaiah 34:13.

Index

Acknowledgments

A brief written acknowledgment cannot fully express my gratitude to those who helped me in researching and writing this book.

First, I want to thank my research assistants Anthony Bonfiglio, Jake Sonnenberg, and Tanner Semple, who tracked down articles and books, undertook archival research, and shared ideas for the book as it developed. Anthony was especially useful in providing me with his research on populist authors; Jake buried himself in the Barry Goldwater papers; and Tanner flew to Washington, D.C., to spend a week looking at the Harold Ickes papers. Nathan Callahan and Nah Ohnsorg joined the project late to help with indexing and footnoting problems.

Next, my longtime friend since graduate school, Bill Rorabaugh, should be commended for reading three drafts of the manuscript before it went to press. His encyclopedic knowledge of American history, keen editorial eye, and general intelligence spared me many mistakes, although he should not be held responsible for any that remain.

My wife, Patricia Critchlow, read a number of chapters in draft. Her advice—"cut, cut, cut"—was heard but not always followed. Her sister, Rose Powers, also helped with research at the Minnesota Historical Society.

Roxane Barwick, my colleague at Arizona State University and some say supervisor, spent hours hearing me talk about the book, while we had many other projects that were of greater importance in the scheme of things—including undergraduate education. Her familiarity with the material facilitated the indexing of the book.

Three other faculty colleagues deserve mention because they are part of a team in the Program in Political History and Leadership, an undergraduate program at Arizona State University: Professor Jon Barth, Dr. Adrian Brettle, and Dr. Mark Power Smith. They make teaching at Arizona State University rewarding.

My editor at University of Pennsylvania Press, Robert Lockhart, is one of the finest editors I have worked with in my career. He is a model for other editors.

The David Katzin Family Trust provided the funds for this entire project. My appointment as Katzin Family Professor at Arizona State University was made possible by the good work of two development officers, Clay Tenquist and William Kavan. Since my appointment to this professorship, I have gotten to know David Katzin and his son Bob, both of whom have led me to conclude that we need more people like them in order to make a better world.

It should be added that none of the above should be held responsible for this book's interpretation of social protest and democratic renewal within the American political tradition.

CPSIA information can be obtained
at www.ICGtesting.com
Printed in the USA
LVHW030743240920
666832LV00001B/1/J

9 780812 252767